GUSTAVUS ADOLPHUS COLLEGE
ST. PETER, MINN.
LIBRARY

THE

(continued from front fla

S

cized charms of New York, the habits of American tourists, the richness of a Ravello landscape, and a thousand other topics. Sir Osbert's astounding knowledge of the byways of art, architecture and history dazzle and entertain the reader along his journey. Towns and countrysides are seen in their various and changing moods, so that a visit to them in Sir Osbert's company is as rewarding as it is unconventional.

This is the kind of book Sir Osbert's readers would expect of him: highly original and with a brilliance and richness of imagination that are unmatched today. For a real voyage or a literary one, no more fascinating traveling companion than he could be possible. *The Four Continents* will enchant his wide audience of friends and captivate many more into joining it.

LIST OF WORKS BY OSBERT SITWELL

PENNY FOOLISH. A Book of Tirades and Panegyrics
MRS. KIMBER. A Poem
THOSE WERE THE DAYS. Panorama with Figures
ESCAPE WITH ME! An Oriental Sketch-Book
TWO GENERATIONS. A Double Biography
OPEN THE DOOR! Short Stories
A PLACE OF ONE'S OWN. A Ghost Story
SING HIGH! SING LOW! A Book of Essays
LEFT HAND, RIGHT HAND! An Autobiography
  Volume I. LEFT HAND, RIGHT HAND!
  Volume II. THE SCARLET TREE
  Volume III. GREAT MORNING
  Volume IV. LAUGHTER IN THE NEXT ROOM
  Volume V. NOBLE ESSENCES OR COURTEOUS REVELATIONS
DEMOS THE EMPEROR. A Secular Oratorio
WRACK AT TIDESEND. A Book of Balnearics
DEATH OF A GOD. Short Stories
COLLECTED STORIES

Edited by Osbert Sitwell

A FREE HOUSE! Or, The Artist as Craftsman.
By Walter Richard Sickert

With Edith and Sacheverell Sitwell

TRIO. Dissertations on Some Aspects of National Genius

With R. J. Minney

GENTLE CAESAR. A Play in Three Acts

WHO KILLED COCK ROBIN? Reflections upon Modern Poetry
OUT OF THE FLAME. Poems
TRIPLE FUGUE. Short Stories
BEFORE THE BOMBARDMENT. A Satirical Novel
DISCURSIONS. An Illustrated Book of Travel
ENGLAND RECLAIMED. A Book of Eclogues
THE MAN WHO LOST HIMSELF. A Novel
MIRACLE ON SINAI. A Novel
WINTERS OF CONTENT. An Illustrated Book of Travel
COLLECTED SATIRES AND POEMS.
  (Ordinary Edition, and Limited Edition signed and numbered)
DUMB-ANIMAL. Short Stories
SELECTED POEMS, OLD AND NEW

With Sacheverell Sitwell

ALL AT SEA. A Social Tragedy in 3 Acts

With Margaret Barton

SOBER TRUTH. An Anthology of Strange Occurrences in the Victorian Era
VICTORIANA. An Anthology of Strange Sayings in the Victorian Era

With Nina Hamnett

THE PEOPLE'S ALBUM OF LONDON STATUES

The Four Continents

BEING

MORE DISCURSIONS
ON TRAVEL, ART
AND LIFE

BY

Osbert Sitwell

Drawings by Daniel Maloney

Harper & Brothers Publishers
New York

THE FOUR CONTINENTS

Printed in the United States of America

FOR
MINNIE FORSBURGH

ACKNOWLEDGMENTS

I should like to thank Mr. A. Everett Austin Jr. of the Ringling Museum for the help he has given me in several directions. I must also make my acknowledgments to the Editor of *Lilliput*, in whose pages "Making a Bolt For It" first appeared.

OSBERT SITWELL

CONTENTS

THE FOUR CONTINENTS

CHAPTER I

THE ORB OF THE MOON

My father used to complain of me that I always demanded last things first, expected the fruit of a career at the beginning; to be made a Field-Marshal the day I joined the Army, become Prime Minister the day I entered the House of Commons. And there may be something of truth in his criticism: since here I am, before a book is written, searching for a name for it. Yet equally I may urge in defence that it is difficult for an author to focus precisely the book he plans or to comprehend its full scope until he has found for it a title: the right lens through which to peer at the long prospect of work before him. As I lay on my bed at Amalfi, I reflected that soon I should be able to write a book *Round the World in Sixty Years*, the antithesis of Jules Verne's *Round the World in Eighty Days*, or again I thought of another adaptation, *Voyage Round the Inside of My Head*. Or I might christen the volume, as yet undefined, *Magnetic Meridian*, or *Where the Compass*

Points. . . . It was a delicate matter : because the title of a book — besides the inherent difficulty of finding it, and in addition to the fact that it can hold for the author some particular meaning — not seldom, when cast into the world, creates, like a stone thrown into a pool, ever widening circles that tend to obscure or distort its image. Thus the name of the last volume of my autobiography, *Noble Essences*, derived from a sentence of Sir Thomas Browne and designed to signify that it was concerned solely with the creative artists I had known in my life, yet to other more spiritual minds suggested other meanings, as will be seen from the letter below, which I lately received. The paper carried, stamped at the top of it, the sensible slogan, 'Be Kind to Animals by Not Eating Them, The Mandalay Vegetarian Society', and the letter ran —

We should feel grateful if you would be so kind as to consider donating a copy of your NOBLE ESSENCES to our Society's Free Reading Room as we are deeply interested in the sacred teachings of the NOBLE ESSENCES. Thank you.

With cordial good will to you,

Faithfully,

TAKI-QUA

P.S. We trust you will please mail the book per registered post as the Burma postal service is not going so smoothly at present. T. Q.

This last suggested to my mind that the postmen may now stop on the road to Mandalay to play with the flying fishes whom Kipling so prettily celebrated : however, since anything at all may drag up for an author the idea of a name for a book, I considered also

Be Kind to Animals as a possibility. But *Dumb Animal* seemed a better and somewhat similar title, and since I had made use of this for a book of short stories some years before, I abandoned that strain altogether and settled on a very different type and instance, of which I had previously thought, *The Four Continents*.

To begin a book is, in any case, to embark on a long and perilous voyage ; to begin, in particular, a volume of travel doubles the sense of starting on a journey. William Blake, when urging his countrymen to build Jerusalem anew, cried 'Bring me my bow of burning gold' : what words, in all humility, can I employ when about to try to build anew — for so the name of this book may suggest — the whole world, much of it already lost ? But though I do not aspire so high, yet *The Four Continents* is, as I see it, a proud and florid title, to me, at any rate, evocative, as I shall explain later, of elephants, turtles and camelopards in a formal but opulent countryside, and of stately figures wreathed in pearls and clad in, and crowned with, feathers. Moreover, because for nearly two centuries we have lived in a world of five, not four, continents, the ring of it is also perhaps a little old-fashioned — and this is exactly what the book itself is likely to become ; since the continents of which I propose to write, and in a manner less limited than its claim as a kind of guidebook could make it, notwithstanding would at their most flamboyant be terrestrial, whereas within a century books of travel will be concerned, not as mine is in the main, with an attempt at a new flexibility of writing, a new quickness of mind and rapidity of movement, so that we fly from Asia to Africa and back again in a few moments, nor, for the rest, with talk of the Middle Sea, the Middle West, and their climates, and with cottages and machines, and cabbages and kings and crocodiles — especially crocodiles — and one thing leading to another in a flight of arrows, or one thing delusively dovetailing into another, as the past does into the future — as I hope it does now while you read —, nor with the teeming past and dwindling future of this world, but with those other worlds besides our own that we now only see in night skies glittering or effulgent, and with their outlandish features. Within that period of time men will undoubtedly have mastered the difficulties of traversing interstellar space, and the books that I predict will describe the lunar landscape, the terrible leper whiteness of the ice-bound plains and great mountains, with their crags of snow and spectral mists, only now and then streaked by the still whiter play of its special Aurora Borealis, or tell of the vermilion vistas of Mars with its system of red plant life, in a world where the heart beats differently, and where scarlet, not green, is the symbol of life and growth, and these volumes will further be occupied, much occupied, with talk of the thinking beings who inhabit such spheres and of whom the author will certainly speak with alarm, and most probably with terror, disgust and loathing. (The animals or their equivalent, on the other hand, will be termed *quaint*, as, to the contemporaries of those who discovered them, once seemed the giraffe and crocodile.) But beings there will be — as others have indeed foretold before me, for James

Howell, in a letter on the subject dated the 2nd of November 1647 from the Fleet Prison, pronounces that whoever cries down the idea 'for a new neoterical Opinion' of 'a habitable world, and a Species of living Creatures in the Orb of the Moon', commits a gross error, for the opinion is 'as old as *Orpheus*, who sings of divers fair Cities and Castles within the Circle of the Moon', and states that among modern authors who would support it and 'plant Colonies in the Orb of the Moon, with the rest of the celestial Bodies', is *Gasper Galileo Galilei*, 'one who by artificial Prospectives hath brought us to a nearer commerce with Heaven': beings there will be, for the repeated assurances of the scientists that life cannot exist on other planets are the measure of man's abiding and indeed miraculous smugness and complacency; as though the universal and omnipotent power and purpose could not people at its will any star it wished, creating beings that could live like salamanders in the flames that surround a planet or within the glacier's green flow, dolphin-tailed! Or, if the moon be dead, then creatures will be found to exist in its ice-bound corruption, as they do here within a corpse: but life there will be, and man will find it. Surrounded already by the devastation caused by his inventions, and with infinitely more disturbing and intimidating prospects ahead of him, he continues unflinchingly on his path, the dangers concealed from him only by the mountainous shadows thrown round him by the sun of his self-esteem. Thus, who knows, one day we may reach better times again, though they will remain unexpected as will be the discovery of the new world itself: albeit there are so many inducements for man to go ahead with this kind of adventure that on occasion I have wondered whether the condition of misery from anxiety in which most of the world finds itself today may not be a conscious effort on the part of a Supreme Being to encourage him to dare more dangerous voyages, and in fact to lead him on, as the phrase goes, to 'try his luck' elsewhere. . . .

The politicians and the scientists have landed us (and notice the use of the word *land* in this connection) have landed us where we are — that is to say, where we each must live in perpetual dread of an outbreak of war more appalling than man or the devil has yet let loose upon us. It remains, therefore, for the same set of men to get us out of this terrestrial scrape. Men of forethought and imagination should be working day and night at the task of enabling us to reach Saturn, or Venus or Mars or the Moon — but let us for the moment fix on the Moon, alighting there, as most probably will the first man to reach it, because it is the nearest. Of course the possibility remains — though to me it seems unlikely — that when men arrive there, they may discover it to be inhabited by creatures of a ferocity similar to our own, but unless these strange natives were superior to us, not only in intelligence, but in the destructive uses to which they applied it, we should no doubt, all of our planet, soon proceed to help these beings to help their selenitic selves. We might even, to paraphrase Canning's famous aim, 'call in new worlds to redress the balance of the old', and train great armies of, in, and on the moon. But more probably a less vicious competition would arise, a new colonial phase, a new prosperity and a long era of peace, would ensue. . . . How should we labour to obtain this object?

Well, the chief deterrent today that prevents powers from fighting has often been said to be the fear of the expense that such a conflict would involve. To the contrary, the enormous cost of modern war makes an equal appeal both to the new race of paranoiac Mickey-Mouse-Men who govern us and to the committee of sabre-toothed tigers who direct our enemies. The scientists should obversely, then, labour rather to send the expense of the new rivalry rocketing beyond the cost of the new moon-rocket itself, to make it manifestly prohibitive; the struggle to be first in the moon field should, and must, be made to exhaust the world, statesmen and workmen alike, so that it plainly becomes impossible for any further war, except one waged with bows and arrows, to break out for a hundred years. By such restrictive means twentieth-century man might at last gain a breathing-space; while even if this argument be proved false and a war — the result, in the new cant phrase, of ideological rivalry — were to break out between the great powers, lunar oceans, plains and ranges would offer a far more tempting atomic battle-field to both sides than would any site on our planet, with its possibilities of explosive recurrence down to the earth's very core.

For these reasons among others, every time I read in the daily press of a man who intends or essays to despatch himself in a rocket to the moon, inwardly I cheer for his courage. I am as enthusiastic about these efforts as is any American school-boy — for in the United States the oddly named 'comic strips' revel in stories of interstellar adventures and enterprises. And in New York toy-shops you can buy packets of space-money, notes similar to dollar bills, but headed for use in Venus or Mars. And this growing interest of the young in space travel is in itself excellent and of good portent, because as soon as the first individual succeeds in being lost in the extra-terrestrial wastes, the effort of every country in the entire globe will be turned within a comparatively short time towards enabling its own nationals to follow his example, and the governments thus will be diverted from preparing for war, first toward schemes for reaching, and then for developing the latent wealth of the satellite body. The moon, snatched from the clutches of the despairing *fin-de-siècle* poet and freed at last from his wan rhapsodies, would be handed over to the eager, capable grasp of shopmen, business men and financiers: the whole of the pugnacious and competitive spirit of mankind would be absorbed, first by the showing-off involved in attempts to arrive there, and then in the sequent fascinating struggle for lunar power and prestige. The centre of interest would have shifted for ever: the most ambitious, the vainest, the most discontented, the bravest and the stupidest would colonise the moon: the effort should keep the busiest, and therefore the most mischievous (for the truly idle are concerned to accomplish little, either harm or good), busy, innocuously busy, for a long while. At the worst, were tremendous lunar rivalries and conflicts to follow, the enthusiasm of the

huge majority of mankind would still remain vicarious as that of the spectators at a Rugby football or boxing match, or of the red-eyed crowds that used to watch the goings and comings of units of the old professional Army: while, with good fortune attending, we might be spared even this; for when the first stage (that occupied by our attempts to land on the moon) finishes, there should follow a period of missionary enterprise and peaceful expansion, more prodigal, more exhausting, more profitable, more philanthropic — or philselenitic, should we write? —, than that consequent on the discovery and development of the great land mass of the Americas. A halcyon age of peace and happiness may be ahead of us if we follow in this direction. And not least of all for the writer of travel books. His prospect will be renewed and splendid. The planetary voyager in the far from distant future will be able to furnish us with accounts of macabre journeys along the great golden avenues of the nebulae and among the immense pallors of the lunar world, that dead world — but we must no longer moon on the moon but, after this glimpse of the future possibilities of literature, depart to the earth once more and confine ourselves for the purpose of this particular work of travel to a dead world of a different order, leaving others, as Thomas Urquhart has said, 'to search for land amongst the Selenits in the Moon, or turn Knights of the Sun'.

CHAPTER II

ALL ABOARD

IN 1748 a peasant in the neighbourhood of Torre Annunziata dug up in one of his rich fields or orchards a few stone statues and some pots and saucepans of bronze. This find caught the attention of the good King Charles III of Naples,[1] who greatly loved the arts, both ancient and modern. He caused further excavations to be made and thus disinterred Pompeii, which, as its full extent in the course of time began to be revealed, came by the very sight or sound of the syllables denoting it to represent to all educated men in England — and in England *an educated man* in those days signified only one who could quote freely from Greek and Latin poets and prose writers, and possessed an impregnable prejudice in favour of the classics — the most notable and complete antiquarian attraction in the world. Its chance discovery had come to them as an amazement and a delight. Year after year it disclosed its secrets, first to the Bourbon Kings of the Two Sicilies, for an interval

[1] 1716–1788, afterwards King Charles III of Spain.

to Joseph Bonaparte and his brother-in-law Joachim Murat, then to the Italian antiquaries, and, after them, to the rest of the civilised world. And with the coming of the mid-nineteenth century, when the religious and moral revival of the period reached its culmination, the name of the buried city began to add to its other fascinations a fortuitous moral. The place had been consumed, the Anglican paterfamilias concluded, because of its wickedness. Soon the word *Pompeii* contained to ordinary English ears the same infamous fleshly sound as Sodom and Gomorrah. The organs of sex, carved here and there on street pavements and inscribed with pagan indiscretion above the doors of certain houses, only emphasised the lesson; if you took exercise regularly, tempered with cold baths — or, as those addicted to them came to say, 'cold tubs' —, attended church once a week, and entered into hymn-singing with the correct pious unction, you would be free equally from the temptations that were the cause, and the catastrophes that were the result. It was the Roman laxity, the un-Christian luxury, that led to such a disaster as that which had destroyed the pleasure city, yet sometimes the visitor would wonder why this sole caution should have been so miraculously petrified in its abandon, and preserved for the artistic approbation but moral condemnation of future ages. Nevertheless, its marvels, so life-like in their death, continued not only to corrupt the artistic taste of Europe for about a century — which in truth they did —, but for more than that period to form the solid if exclamatory heart of many a travel book.

With the disinterment, however, of cities far older and more distant, yet now attainable, no less than with the disintegration of our own times, and with the almost total destruction of huge modern cities we have known well, the strength of the warning has waned, but not its necessity. The idea that a civilisation can perish, or be suddenly overwhelmed, no longer, alas, wears an air of novelty. We know now only too well that the plaster spectre of an incinerated terrier fighting against a storm of burning ashes is a portent we can surpass with a shadow stamped on a bridge at Hiroshima in Japan, that a modern bomb dropped into the crater of Vesuvius would wreak far wider and more permanent damage than the destruction of Pompeii or, indeed, than any mere volcano could by itself achieve. So today the ruined city may seem delusively to form for the reader but a trivial entrance from which to obtain a first view of what lies beyond, and through which to pass in order to reach the main body of the book. . . . In Naples the rain tattooed down on the pavements, the pale wind swinging it in strings like those of the beaded curtains that cover the door of so many *trattorie* in South Italy. It dripped remorselessly from all the eaves. But since this was our first visit to Southern Italy after the end of the 1939–45 war, we did not allow the weather to debar us from sightseeing, but proceeded with our plan to stay once more at Amalfi, and on the way there to walk again round the ruins of Pompeii. Usually one visits in fine weather that lost, dusty, stunted world of resurrected square stone pillars and of marble or bronze midgets : but in any case the tourist is before long so greatly exhausted by the miles of heavy walking, by the long explanations that are provided willingly, if not gratis, by the custodian, so utterly worn out by the insinuating persistence of the vendors of crude coral sex emblems and mascots, that he is ready before leaving the precincts to quarrel with his best friends. . . . Thus I recall that one fine October evening at the end of a strenuous day spent here some twenty years ago, I sat on one of the few remaining, or perhaps reconstructed, roofs in the dead city and became immediately engaged in a furious and almost tearful argument with my brother Sacheverell concerning the standards and merits of Greek painting in the classical age — a subject upon which I think each of us was as ignorant as the rest of the world (though it may, indeed, have provided the stimulus for us later to spend many mornings and afternoons in the Museo Nazionale at Naples studying the frescoes removed from Herculaneum and Pompeii ; from which hours we gained some knowledge and were able to remark how much and how singularly some of them resembled in texture, subject and feeling the works of Francesco Guardi).

That dispute was a long time ago, but I had visited Pompeii since. I had last seen it some fifteen years before, on a day in March, when magenta-coloured anemones sprinkled the ground of the amphitheatre with their tinsel stars — not the stout-petalled kind of anemone, with their rich and august tint of purple, but the delicate variety of wind-flower that opens and shuts with the sun's course and has a dark-eyed centre dusted with jet-black pollen. In a miraculous profusion this flower and many others surrounded the doors of every house in the empty city. The whole town, vacant except for guides and tourists, had yet seemed to be waiting for something : and indeed it had come, for war had engulfed it and a battle, we were told, had raged within its already broken walls for many hours — in years gone by one would have judged it an improbable event ; but we found it unchanged except that a few ruins were more ruined, and others, of a greater importance, had been newly excavated. . . . No, the rain today (for we had never before seen the suffocated pleasure-resort under these conditions) made a much greater difference to the look of the place than the passage of such crucial events and years had effected. The rain still swung its curtains — indeed they were thicker than ever —, but it seemed unexpectedly to impart to the streets an appearance of having a life of their own, to invest them with a new — or an old — reality. They exhaled now a sense of continuity. All towns tend to be empty of people when it rains, so that this void could be accounted for in terms of everyday life without the impress of disaster. Down the channels cut so long ago in the rain-coloured tufa the water ran gurgling as it had gurgled when the houses were inhabited, and even when one entered a low pavilion, reconstituted in the latest excavatorial fashion, the noise of the rain drumming on every stone surface in the open atrium encouraged the visitor to feel that little had altered since the first day of the discovery of Pompeii or, as for that, since the day of its interment.

. . . Yet outside, during the course of the last decade, the whole wide world, the condition of Europe, in particular, and the existence led within its cities, had changed more than in the previous two hundred years. For the Century of the Common Man lay dead before half its course had been run : though not all the outward symbols have gone. In consequence a glimpse of Pompeii is apposite in such times to the opening of a book of travel.

Today, it is true, most of the guides who cluster in the streets outside the most interesting of the houses, were as absent as the tourists : no doubt, wise men, they were sitting round a fire talking, and probably eating roasted chestnuts gathered in the woods on the slopes of the neighbouring mountains. But, in a restaurant not far from the ruins, both the food and the entertainment provided remained the same as I had remembered them for many years : the same long, non-negotiable strands of macaroni, dipped in the same professional poisoner's tomato-juice, the same sad beef, the same wine tasting a little of brimstone, as if out of a feeling for local colour and as a tribute to the sulphur-stricken city which was all the proprietor's livelihood. The same dancers of the same *tarantella*, whom I had first seen here some thirty-five years before, dressed in the same peasant costume of a hundred years ago, trod to the same jangling mandolin accompaniment. They had seemed, when last I saw them in 1936, to have grown very old : now, fifteen years later, they were plainly older, and their synthetic crows of joy and cries of merriment as they snapped their arthritic fingers and bumped and bounced energetically against each other, their jerky and crooked movements displayed upon the curtain of the rain, had now become a triumphant assertion of the will to live, and of a continued existence which in itself would have been unexpected when their figures were in repose. A fusty '*Funiculì, Funiculà!*' followed the *tarantella*. . . . Identical, too, was the hirsute old vendor with the white beard, who, from behind a beige barricade of smashed bits of terracotta lamps and other pottery, which overtly he was selling, conducted a brisker if furtive trade in more equivocal antiquities which indicated all too clearly the regrettable lusts and lapses of the old pagan world.

Fleeing from these lascivious embarrassments we moved on through the rain to see once more Santa Maria Maggiore, a baptismal church usually attributed to the seventh or eighth century. It may well belong, however, to an earlier date. It is situated in a position that eludes tourists, on the outskirts of one of those large slum-villages which seem a speciality of this valley: for the slums on the edge of Naples gradually dwindle and then become islands — slum-islands lost, as it were, in the rich land, and somehow a slum in an orange grove under the black dust of the tufa rocks offers a peculiar quality of horror that is lacking in a slum proper. The church of Santa Maria Maggiore stands attached to Nocera Superiore, only a few yards outside, but with no buildings in front of it. The slum-village behind it is situated to the west of Nocera de' Pagani: a bigger town between the mountains, and, in the eighteenth century, widely celebrated as the birthplace of the famous Neapolitan painter, Francesco Solimena.[1] (Incidentally, the definitive 'of the Pagans' enshrines the fact that the Emperor Frederick II, Stupor Mundi, settled some of his favourite Saracen subjects here in 1224.)

Santa Maria Maggiore, though placed so near the main road, is, as I have said, elusive, difficult to find if you approach it from the direction of Naples, and though my sense of direction is fairly reliable, I have on four or five occasions been obliged to make enquiries in order to reach it. Nor is this easy, since from that direction you approach the church through a flat countryside that looks poor and dirty for all its richness, for here there are no views, the prospect is broken up by high walls of adobe which enclose the road no less than the orange groves, and therefore preclude a view. After leaving Nocera de' Pagani, as a rule you pass few people on the road. Thus travelling on the day in question, we met only one man, a priest who bore, in addition to an appearance of extreme poverty, a strange air of holy remoteness. His soutane revealed the truth of a cliché — always a rare experience — since it was really 'green with age', the first black garment I have seen which could be correctly so termed, faded as it evidently was by many suns of Neapolitan summers. . . . Eventually, after a little wandering, we reached the round church, which has considerable dignity and plainly possesses an architectural importance. Though it lacks the fascinating mosaics of Santa Costanza in Rome — the black and white patterns which resemble

[1] 1657–1747.

those on batiks from the East Indies and those others, still more enchanting, in bright colours, which portray cupids at work at the time of the vintage, treading the grapes or collecting them in ox-wagons —, nevertheless, it is clearly related to that ancient church. Its flat spread dome belongs to an exceedingly primitive type, and is supported by sixteen pairs of columns, marble, granite and basalt. The capitals of these columns are also antique and most richly carved. Probably both columns and capitals were brought from Paestum which lies not far away and for many hundreds of years served as a quarry for the countryside. Nearly the whole of the interior of the main building is taken up by an elaborate font with eight granite columns. In the fashion of many other ancient buildings the whole edifice seems, through age and weight, to be sinking into the fertile and all-enticing ground. . . . From Santa Maria Maggiore we continued our journey to Amalfi, motoring through the pass that leads from Castellammare to Vietri. By this thoroughfare all the invaders from the north, Goths, Huns and French, had in their time made their way southwards. More peaceful now, its flatness is diversified by the numerous round stone towers, usually dating from the sixteenth or seventeenth century and erected on rocky outcrops for the purpose of trapping pigeons and quail in the migratory season. The method is to fasten a huge net between two towers and send up a decoy to lead the birds, who thus fly blindly into the trap and are caught. By what miracle the various species have managed to survive such wholesale treatment remains one of the avian mysteries ! . . .

. . . .

The next morning when I woke I suffered that sense of anonymous disorientation, following on dawn in a new place, which is the occasional bane of every traveller. It is true I had often been here before, but I had arrived the previous evening after so long a spell of absence that for a moment I wondered where I could be : then as the room brimmed with light from the window — it seemed from the whiteness of the walls like a white bowl over full, so full that it might spill out again — it became clear that, my surroundings being obviously pleasant, I need not worry. Besides, the place seemed familiar, but at some considerable distance in time. Plainly it was near the sea or a lake, for those disconnected wooden sounds, apparently of men hitting boats, that always accompany water-side life could be heard distinctly in the still air : but from my bed, in a recess beyond an arch, I could only perceive the play of light on the vaulted ceiling and the whitewashed walls, bright and rough as the lime-painted bark of a fruit-tree. The window was wide open on the sky, of which my room seemed part ; but now, every moment the light began to swell and unfold, as if the budding and flowering of a magnolia were to become sufficiently speedy to be visible in all its development ; then to lose its pallor and become at first nacreous, imbued with feathery tones of rose and lilac, then more shaggy and yellow until at last an explosion of gold within the room itself announced that the sun had risen outside — but that it was no ordinary sunrise. Now as I watched the rings of light that spangled the ceiling and the flights of golden discs that swept across it, a similarity of former experience enabled me suddenly to identify my surroundings and immediate prospects : the particular kind of display that I had witnessed was caused by a Mediterranean sun rising above mountains opposite but distant, its force then redoubled by a great space of transparent sea ; it must be, by the degree of intensity, a Neapolitan October. I understood : I was back again at Amalfi, in the hotel that had been a monastery, back again, for a meagre fortnight's stay, in my room in which in years past I had spent so many peaceful nights and arduous days of work : an environment so congenial to me, and so auspicious to my writing that, superstitiously inclined, I used always to write in notebooks bought in it. (Some amount of reason, however, may have underlain my folly, because Amalfi was the first place in Europe where paper was made, and though, as I am now finding out, the quality of it as manufactured to-day had deteriorated, it had, until the outbreak of the 1939–45 war, still retained something of its ancient style.) My eye, my mind, my memory and my imagination, seemed to work better here than elsewhere. In other climes, in other buildings, when to my misfortune my body is not here, even to recall the feeling of light and air within the bare white room — as I do now while I write at this desk — is a stimulus and source of energy. It was nearer forty years than thirty since first I stayed here, and nearer fifty than forty since first I beheld the Mediterranean ; which ever afterwards to me was, what its very name proclaimed, the centre of the earth, the magnetic meridian — just as to the Chinese China was the Middle Kingdom — and this was my favourite region in it. Back once again in Amalfi I felt the same easy cerebration, the same stirring of ideas within the head and emotions within the heart that I recollected as typical of the effect of this neighbourhood upon me. For a moment, a sense of life's rhythm, such as you only feel when you are idle, happily idle — that most rare sensation — inspired me : two decades had passed and a great war had stormed round the world, even involving these placid, if dramatic, shores — for the Allied invasion of the mainland of Italy had started just across the waters of the gulf, by Paestum, thence moving on to Salerno, over which city the sun had just risen.

I walked across to the window to take in the scene : the broken knife-blade profile of Mont' Alburno, and the great length of legendary mountains that ran from it southwards, but considerably below its serrated top, into the horizon that became the malarial coast of Calabria : then, spread between us, lay the great expanse of water, blue and wine-coloured in the main, but mosaicked with patches and tails of green, jade green and apple-green and lime-green, and streaked with stretches of tawny sand, while if you leant on the sill, you could see, far under in the foreground, beneath a sheer fall of rock, the quay. This jutting, slightly-curving stone platform from which the fishing-boats set out morning and evening had not itself changed or grown, but along the surface of the sheltering wall that ran down the middle of it were inscribed in gigantic white letters the old conflicting sentiments, but some of them new to me in form since my last visit. Moreover, since an indelible method, only lately invented, had been used equally by both warring factions, these notices can never, until such time as an opposite discovery is made, be erased as formerly by the authorities, but will confront the Day of Judgment itself with their prejudiced political purport. In the old days it had been all '*Viva Il Duce!*': now it was '*Viva Il Papa-Ré!*', '*Viva La Casa Savoia!*', '*Mort' al Ré*', '*Mort' alla Casa Savoia!*', '*Fini la Guerra!*' and '*Pace per sempre con la Russia!*'.

Overcome by the fatigue of the early morning, so luxurious a sensation when you can rest, I went back to bed and from that vantage point watched the changing scales of illumination. Arpeggios of light, rings and circles and stars, flickered over the ceiling and spattered the white walls, and through the open window, in the yet prevailing stillness of this young hour in a southern climate, the voices of the fishermen calling to each other while they prepared their boats were as distinct as, though smaller than, would be a voice speaking within the room itself. In the pleasant condition of lassitude produced by the light, the warmth, the feeling of air and sun, my mind wandered without will. . . . I marked how within the bare white walls the old Four Elements made themselves felt until it began to seem as if the space thus framed were formed of them, as during many centuries in a previous age the human body had been thought similarly to be composed of them. From where I lay in the recess, with my eyes in the shade,

and my body warm but in a pleasant freshness, I could note in what manner they asserted themselves. *Earth*, the soil, was represented by the cliffs of limestone whereto the former monastery was attached mid-way, as a snail to a rock, and of which it looked part ; by the remote mountains, and by the scents of lemon and orange blossom drifting even at this season in lazy gusts through the open window, and not least by the swallow-tail butterfly, that from its erratic flutterings and convolutions appeared to share the same delirium of light by which at the moment I was possessed : *Air* asserted its claim equally by the blue veils and the blue profundities of the sky, and by the indefinable prevailing fragrance, ever renewed, by the feeling of movement and the sparkle of the waves ruffled by a faint wind : *Water* by the continual soft murmur from below, and the perpetual dazzle of the light reflected on to the ceiling by the sea, while *Fire* held its own with the great raging globe of the sun itself. . . . Looking round, I claimed this as my chosen sanctuary. As I lay there, idly meditating, I began to try to think of a title for the book I wanted to write : *The Four Elements*, I wondered, or *The Four Continents* ? Or could some equation of the two be found ? Could Europe, with its long coast-line, extravagant for its size, be made to represent Water ; Asia, with its huge land mass, Earth ; Africa, with its great heart of flame, Fire ; America, with its countries born of freedom, Air ?

The Four Continents was certainly, where a book of travel was concerned, a title which possessed a certain majesty and space, a panache ; first I saw them, these vast land groups, in terms of architecture and painting, as immense arches of hewn stone, facing respectively Air, Earth, Fire and Water ; sky, garden, sun and sea. The first prospect was of clouds floating across the sky, a cloudscape built of every form, checkered, flecked, fleecy, mountainous, broken, or drifting in shapeless lumps ; the second, a gentle perspective of garden and woodland ; the third, a tangle of flames, like serpents, encircling a globe ; the fourth, a great storm, with waves battering against rocks. . . . Then memory obliterated these effects, and substituted permanently for them the four large panels of Brussels tapestry celebrating the same theme, the Four Continents, which hang in the drawing-room and in the ballroom at Renishaw : works of art designed by Leyniers and carried out by Louis de Vos some time in the middle of the reign of the Sun Monarch. These I have known and admired ever since my earliest years and I could see in my mind's eye, as I lay watching the southern Italian radiance expand continually within the small space of my room, these crowned, mysterious figures, in their formal attire, their features obscured by the passage of the years, descending flights of steps in a swirl of ostrich feathers, and I could summon up from the inside of my head the look of the prevailing rich and sumptuous darkness like velvet in which these beings had their existence, the bursts of light in the watery skies, the lions, the camels, the horses, the trophies, the pearls, the palm-trees outlined against the flashes between the clouds. Certainly these creations of the past belonged more to time than to space, more to the epoch in which they were made than to their subjects. At very first sight of them you would cry out 'French seventeenth-century!' rather than 'Asia!' or 'Africa!' and, indeed, *The Four Continents*, even as a title, manifested too antique a style, and I began to wonder whether the omission of the fifth continent would constitute an offence in the eyes of my Australian friends. If so, I would repeat to them the words, written in another context, of Thomas Traherne: 'People underneath, and fields and flowers, with yet another sun and another day, pleased me mightily: but more when I knew it was the same sun served them by night, that served us by day'. . . . At the same time I could not help surmising how the designer who had been responsible for these four Brussels panels would have visualised the fifth, had that great land in his time been discovered: Sydney Bridge, I am sure, and wallabies, and emus ruched with plumes strutting under the slashed trunks of gum-trees and among the feathery foliage of the wattles, and aboriginal Corydons, leaning on crooks, examining the fleeces of their flocks of outsize imported sheep, and a vista, no doubt, of the Great Barrier Reef depicting rocks covered with shells amazing in their multitudinous hue and variety.

Certainly the panel *America* — the latest discovered continent in the days in which this tapestry was made — shows it in an unusually romantic light: Netherlandish princesses of the time of Charles II are portrayed as squaws in the idealised idiom of the day; so that they can wear silk robes and carry on their heads springing clusters of blue and red feathers and be shown lolling under palm-trees, toying with open caskets of jewels, more fitting to Ormus or to Ind than to the lost forests and swamps of the Mississippi. In place of the wigwams constructed of reeds and skins, and decorated at intervals with dried human scalps, that we should have expected to find as the homes of Red Indian chieftains of that era, there towers up in the immediate background a sumptuous pleasure-dome, prophetic prototype of life in Newport: while as if Leyniers himself felt that he had been a little carried away by his enthusiasm, the balance of local colour is restored by the casual introduction in one corner of an alligator, and of several macaws in their extravagant liveries of sky-blue and scarlet. . . . *Europe* appropriately exhibits, in front of a palace, an enormous trophy, a stack of weapons, pikes, guns, lances, swords and drums, surmounted by an empty helmet — but with *Asia* my recollection had betrayed me, for I thought it portrayed an elephant hung with jewels plunging through a jungle, but I found on re-examination that there is no sign of that great beast, but, instead, a Hindu princess sits in the foreground wearing a head-dress reproducing the shape of an elephant's head, with tusks, and with the trunk thrown back. *Africa*, however, was just as I recalled it, a queenly figure poised on a flight of steps, and holding a sceptre, as if about to strike with it a kneeling camel just below her feet.

Nevertheless, the four continents when in actuality I viewed them and touched their ground, each defeated the notion I had formed of them in this confusing fashion: I happened, for example, to see many more elephants in America than in Asia, which as a child I had imagined to be a jungle of intertwined trunks — but then I have never visited the bare, burning fields of India, its clumps of tall palm-trees rattling dryly in a sudden wind, the dark, greasy rivers teeming with life — and with death — or the confused green intricacies of its jungles, nor have I seen in Burma the vast pastures of elephant-grass, out of which the backs of the vast beasts swell like grey mounds, as they peacefully munch, intent on their gigantic task of self-maintenance, though I have been fortunate enough to be allowed to talk at Pnom Penh to the sacred white elephant of the King of Cambodia — a beast in reality with an epidermis of an elegant, light flamingo-pink, and have been privileged to watch a herd of tame elephants trying to keep cool in the noon heat by plodding and splashing in the shallow waters, amid the clustered blue nenuphars of the moat which surrounds the vast ruined towers and temples of Angkor Vat. I have never, on the other hand, been granted an audience with the most interesting sacred white elephant of the Mandalay Palace (a kind of inverted Romulus or Remus, since, being a small calf when its mother died, it was suckled daily by twenty young Burmese women, and so reared[1]), but I have been able to wonder at and admire the stone elephants in the avenue of figures leading up to the Ming Tombs outside Peking — but of them I shall have more to say when the moment comes. The largest living elephantine congregation, however,

[1] See *Elephant Bill*, by Lieut.-Col. J. H. Williams. (Rupert Hart-Davis, 1950.)

that I ever beheld was gathered together beside the waters of the Gulf of Mexico near Sarasota, in Florida, at the winter headquarters of the Ringling-Barnum Circus ; in a sense an appropriate resting-place for them because during a long period, from the middle of the seventeenth century down to the beginning of the nineteenth, Florida with its gentle natives — like those of Chateaubriand's *Atala* —, with its pearl fisheries, its fantastically plumaged, almost fabulous birds, their feathers dyed apparently by the rainbow, with its placid waters of blue like a kingfisher's wing and its desperate alligator-haunted swamps, had captured the imagination of the peoples of Europe and had come almost to usurp the place held by India as a summary of exoticism a century and a half before.

Europe by the eighteenth century — as indeed by the twelfth — had become largely denuded of animal life : only herds of deer, a few but quite sufficient packs of wolves, some bears and the smaller mammals survived. And in proportion as a rich population of beasts grew more remote in time, the more fascinating it became as a conception. And the discovery of America had brought many ideas of animal and reptilian life that were new to European minds, not least of them the alligator. . . . You would have thought that centuries of awareness of the more terrifying crocodile of Africa would have prepared them for its American cousin, but no : it continued an exciting and disturbing idea. . . . To such a portent, to so outstanding a relic of other ages and reminder of other climes as the elephant, the European mind had gradually accustomed itself: albeit when first introduced into Italy by Hannibal as a means of warfare, it had ranked as the worst of Carthaginian atrocities, and had possessed for the Romans of the time something of the fabulous horror that in the modern consciousness attends the idea of the atom bomb. But a few centuries later the Emperor Charlemagne was always accompanied on his progresses by an elephant — the gift of a dusky opposite number —, and subsequently the Emperor Frederick II also displayed an elephant in his retinue — the memory of which perhaps lingered in the bas-reliefs of Malatesta's Temple at Rimini. So that by the eighteenth century the elephant, though it could always draw a crowd, had become an idea to which man was used. But the rhinoceros, that unicorn grown grossly material, or seen through the medium of a distorting mirror, had come to the three other continents as a shock, though a celebrated picture by Longhi shows us the armoured brute on exhibition in a Venetian eighteenth-century circus. As near our own day as September 1827, we find the Duke of Wellington complaining to Mrs. Arbuthnot that when he went to Windsor Castle to kiss hands on his appointment as Commander-in-Chief, King George IV would not mention public matters of any kind, and talked of 'nothing but a camel-leopard he has just got from Africa'; this animal was a giraffe, obviously then newly exhibited in England, though Purchas reports from one Fernández that Abyssinia contained '. . . Hares, Goats, Harts, Bores, Elephants, Camels, Buffals, Lions, Panthers, Tigres, Rhinocerotes, and other Creatures are there seene, and one so huge that a man sitting on Horse-backe, may passe upright under his belly : his shape is like a Camell, but his nature divers, feeding on leaves which he reacheth from the tops of Trees with his necke stretched forth', and on the margin of the book himself adds : 'This seemeth to be the Camelopardalis'. . . . But the impact of the crocodile and the alligator on the European consciousness in their respective epochs was far more severe. In ages when everything was believed to possess a divine purpose, the sight of them raised even in placid men's minds an unspoken question, and in the more enquiring despondency or terror.

As early as 1613 Purchas had concerned himself with crocodiles — but first, because of its virtue, I must begin with his account of a gigantic snake, which leads up to his description of them. '. . . Africa for monsters in this kinde hath been famous. . . . Attilius Regulus the Romane Consul in the first Punicke Warre, at the River Bagrada encountred with a huge Serpent, and planted his Engines and Artillerie against the same, whose skinne, sent to Rome for a Monument, was in length a hundred and twentie foot, as Gellius out of Tubero reporteth. The Scales armed it from all hurt by Darts or Arrowes, and with the breath it killed many, and had eaten many of the Souldiers, before they could with a stone out of an Engine destroy this destroyer. The Rivers of Niger, Nilus, Zaire, and others, have store of Crocodiles, whereof some are of an incredible bignesse, and greedie devourers, thirtie foot long, from an Egge lesse then a Goose-egge. Aristotle saith, that Crocodiles have no tongue, but I my selfe have seene both great and little dead and dryed, in all which I found a tongue, but very short, flat and large. Strange it is that they tell of the number of sixtie in this beast; the age sixtie yeres, the teeth, joynts, egges, and dayes of laying and hatching, being all numbred sixtie.

'The Crocodiles taile is as long as his body, his feet with clawes, his backe armed with scales almost impenitrable: hee moveth onely his upper jaw, and that so wide, that some of them are able to swallow an entire Heifer. They say also, that the Female layes her Egges where Nilus will make an end of his flowing that yeere, as if by secret Providence she divined how farre the River would rise. In ingendring she lyes on her backe, and through the shortnesse of her legs cannot turne her selfe on her belly, but by the Males helpe: from which being scarred by the clamours of some watching this opportunitie, she is easily taken: which they doe also by Pit-fals and other meanes. Foure moneths together in the Winter, they eate nothing: they are thicke-sighted by Land, and easier take their prey by water, which is done by their tayle. They are bold upon the fearefull, and fearefull upon the bold: yet a fearefull beast to encounter rising on his tayle, with such Hellish jawes and Devillish clawes over the assaylant, as require an undaunted spirit. . . . Authors tell of a little Bird, which as he lyes gaping, goes into his mouth, and picks his indented teeth, which he cannot devoure by reason of her sharp feathers raysed like bristles, when he offereth to shut his mouth on her: the Ichneumon or Rat of Nilus is said to gape for this occasion of his gaping, and then to runne into his belly and gnaw himselfe a passage out, therefore worshipped of the Egyptians.' . . . Purchas adds, among a few pieces of miscellaneous information, that *Dubb* 'is the name of a kind of great Lizard'.

Coleridge knew this book well; for he records that he had been reading it on the celebrated occasion when he fell asleep, and on waking proceeded at once to write out the poem he had dreamed — a process suddenly broken into, when there occurred the most infamous interruption in all literary history, and the poet was 'called out by a person on business from Porlock'. So was lost the thread of *Kubla Khan*. . . . Yet, though he knew this volume, he seems to have been more interested by Floridan alligators than by African crocodiles: for if we turn to his Notebook,[1] we find his condensation of an account of them given by William Bartram in his *Travels through North and South Carolina, Georgia, East and West Florida, the Cherokee Country, the Extensive Territories of the Muscogulges, or Creek Confederacy, and the Country of the Chactaws*; a book from which I extract the following passages. But first let us note by the way that Bartram seems to have been troubled as frequently by alligators and crocodiles — terms he uses indiscriminately to describe the American alligator — as nineteenth-century travellers in Eastern Europe and the Orient were persecuted by mosquitoes, fleas and the unmentionable bed-bug. Virtually, he found them waiting for him on his bed, or clinging to his mosquito-net. He saw them everywhere, and continually tried

[1] See *The Road to Xanadu*, by Professor John Livingston Lowes. Printed in U.S.A. (Constable & Company Ltd., 1927.)

to elude them without success. The passage I quote refers to a 'subtle, greedy alligator'.

'. . . Behold him', he writes, 'rushing forth from the flags and reeds. His enormous body swells. His plaited tail brandished high, floats upon the lake. The waters like a cataract descend from his opening jaws. Clouds of smoke issue from his dilated nostrils. The earth trembles with his thunder. When immediately from the opposite coast of the lagoon, emerges from the deep his rival champion. They suddenly dart upon each other. The boiling surface of the lake marks their rapid course, and a terrific conflict commences. They now sink to the bottom folded together in horrid wreaths. The water becomes thick and discoloured. Again they rise, their jaws clap together, re-echoing through the deep surrounding forests. Again they sink, when the contest ends at the muddy bottom of the lake, and the vanquished makes a hazardous escape, hiding himself in the muddy turbulent waters and sedge on a distant shore. The proud victor exulting returns to the place of action. The shores and forests resound his dreadful roar, together with the triumphing shouts of the plaited tribes around, witnesses of the horrid combat. . . .' And again, 'I . . . furnished myself with a club for my defence and went on board . . . but ere I had half-way reached the place, I was attacked on all sides, several endeavouring to overset the canoe. My situation now became precarious to the last degree: two very large ones attacked me closely, at the same instant, rushing up with their heads and part of their bodies above the water, roaring terribly and belching floods of water over me. They struck their jaws together so close to my ears, as almost to stun me, and I expected every moment to be dragged out of the boat and instantly devoured. But I applied my weapon so effectually about me, though at random, that I was so successful as to beat them off a little. . . . I . . . made good my entrance into the lagoon, though not without opposition from the alligators, who formed a line across the entrance, but did not pursue me into it, nor was I molested by any there, though there were some very large ones in a cove at the upper end. I soon caught more trout than I had present occasion for . . .' Bartram then goes on to relate how he was pursued by a daring old alligator about twelve foot in length, and he proceeds, '. . . and when I stepped on shore and turned about, in order to draw up my canoe, he rushed up near my feet, and lay there for some time, looking me in the face, his head and shoulders out of water. I resolved he should pay for his temerity, and having a heavy load in my fusee, I ran to my camp, and returning with my piece, found him with his foot on the gunwale of the boat, in search of fish. On my coming up he withdrew sullenly and slowly into the water, but soon returned and placed himself in his former position, looking at me, and seeming neither fearful nor any way disturbed. I soon despatched him by lodging the contents of my gun in his head, and then proceeded to cleanse and prepare my fish for supper . . . when, raising my head, I saw before me, through the clear water, the head and shoulders of a very large alligator, moving slowly towards me. I instantly stepped back, when, with a sweep of his tail, he brushed off several of my fish. It was certainly most providential that I looked up at that instant, as the monster would probably, in less than a minute, have seized and dragged me into the river. This incredible boldness of the animal disturbed me greatly, supposing there could now be no reasonable safety for me during the night, but by keeping continually on the watch. . . . It was by this time dusk, and the alligators had nearly ceased their roar, when I was again alarmed by a tumultuous noise that seemed to be in my harbour, and therefore engaged my immediate attention. Returning to my camp, I found it undisturbed, and then continued on to the extreme point of the promontory, where I saw a scene, new and surprising, which at first threw my senses into such a tumult, that it was some time before I could comprehend what was the matter. . . .

'How shall I express myself so as to convey an adequate idea of it to the reader, and at the same time avoid raising suspicions of my veracity? Should I say, that the river (in this place) from shore to shore, and perhaps near half a mile above and below me, appeared to be one solid bank of fish, of various kinds, pushing through this narrow pass of St. Juan's into the little lake, on their return down the river, and that the alligators were in such incredible numbers, and so close together from shore to shore, that it would have been easy to have walked across on their heads, had the animals been harmless? What expressions can sufficiently declare the shocking scene that for some minutes continued, whilst this mighty army of fish were forcing the pass ? During this attempt, thousands, I may say hundreds of thousands, of them were caught and swallowed by the devouring alligators. I have seen an alligator take up out of the water several great fish at a time, and just squeeze them betwixt his jaws, while the tails of the great trout flapped about his eyes and lips, ere he had swallowed them. The horrid noise of their closing jaws, their plunging amidst the broken banks of fish, and rising with their prey some feet upright above the water, the floods of water and blood rushing out of their mouths, and the clouds of vapour issuing from their wide nostrils, were truly frightful. This scene continued at intervals during the night, as the fish came to the pass.' The traveller is, for a change, frightened two pages later by two bears : a description I omit, though I cannot refrain from completing my extract with a further and final account of an alligator.

'. . . An old champion, who is perhaps absolute sovereign of a . . . lagoon (when fifty less than himself are obliged to content themselves with swelling and roaring in little coves round about), darts forth from the reedy coverts all at once, on the surface of the waters, in a right line ; at first seemingly as rapid as lightning, but gradually more slowly until he arrives at the centre of the lake, when he stops. He now swells himself by drawing in wind and water through his mouth, which causes a loud sonorous rattling in the throat for near a minute, but it is immediately forced out again through his mouth and nostrils, with a loud noise, brandishing his tail in the air, and the vapour ascending from his nostrils like smoke. At other times, when swollen to

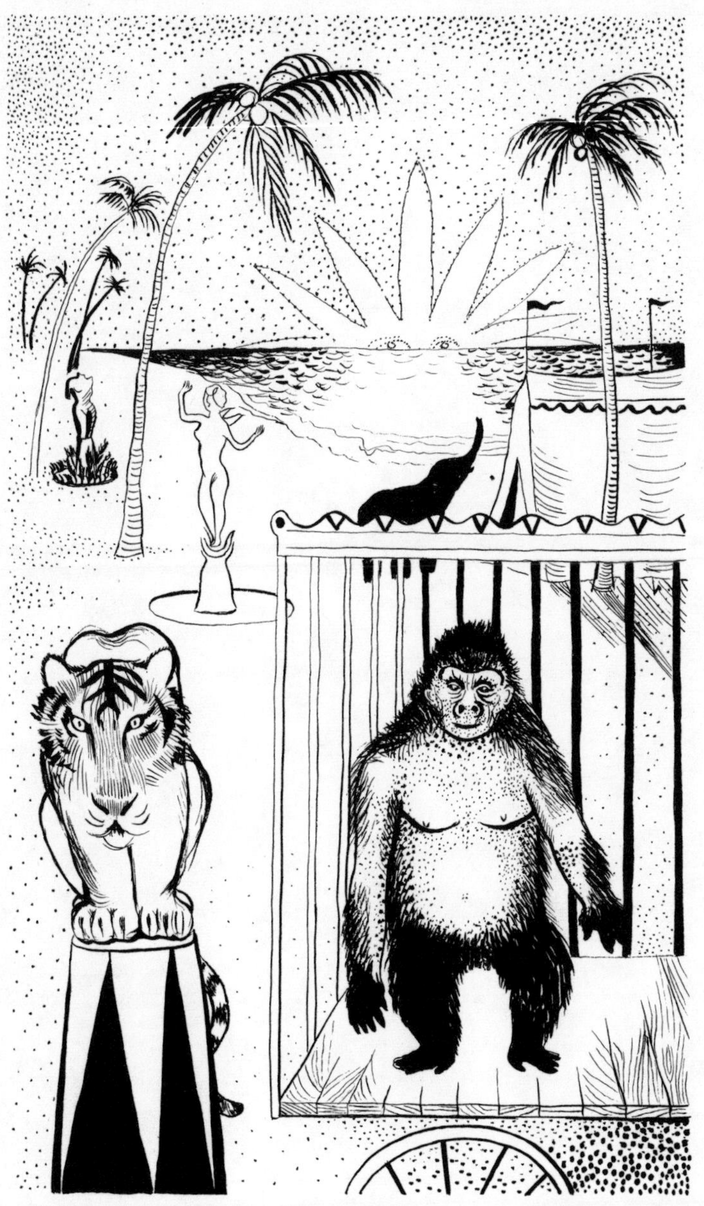

an extent ready to burst, his head and tail lifted up, he spins or twirls round on the surface of the water. He acts his part like an Indian chief when rehearsing his feats of war ; and then retiring, the exhibition is continued by others who dare to step forth, and strive to excel each other, to gain the attention of the favourite female.'

Before we take leave of these champion representatives of the Saurians, we may note that, even today, alligators, though less gigantic, exhibitionist and ferocious than were those of whom Bartram tells us, survive in the Everglades, the tangled forest core of Florida ; which district also retains still its untamed Indians, wild beasts and many kinds of water-birds of extreme beauty. . . . I, for one, can well understand the appeal of this flat land which depends for its effect on the look of sea and sky, in other words on the elements of this country, on Air and Water. . . . As if in offset to the wild beasts of the Everglades comes Sarasota and its great concourse of tame animals.

Sarasota is, in fact, one of the places I like best of those new regions which I have visited since the end of the 1939–45 war. The whole character of this region has been formed, or, as would now be said, 'conditioned', by the vicinity of the famous Ringling Circus, and by the genius and imagination of its master and founder, the late John Ringling, who was, in fact, responsible for the planning and planting of the entire district and for the erection of the museum which bears his name and that of his wife, The John and Mable Ringling Museum. Ringling had bought wide stretches of the country round, and showed a natural feeling and an unusual flair for how it should be developed. Besides being evidently a southern land, it was also flat country, and this lack of feature called for points of interest to be added, demanded that the stretches of sea which indented the coast should be emphasised, and that long umbrageous avenues should be planted, that gardens should be created and statues placed in them. Moreover, there must be not one or two statues, but scores, hundreds, even thousands — indeed, looking at the level environs, and computing what they required, it might have seemed that there were not enough statues in the world to furnish this landscape. But all the features I have named he provided, by placing the Lido on an island, reached by two long wooden causeways across the peacock-winged waters, by planting double lines of sub-tropical, and now lofty, pine-trees, and by raiding the antique dealers' yards in Spain and Italy in the early nineteen-hundreds, and there buying quantities of assorted single figures, or whole groups, in stone or marble. New and old, good and bad, these statues look well in their new surroundings under the clean trunks of tufted palm-trees, among the prickly pears, striking rival attitudes, among the aloes that seem shapes cut out of tin, and the bushes of hibiscus with their trumpet flowers of yellow, scarlet or salmon-pink. The enormous museum and picture gallery that Ringling built about two miles outside the town bears on its roof lines of statues that, aided by the lighting effects of the climate, by the large arcaded garden court with its orange-trees, and trellis over which coil great wreaths and whorls of *Bignonia grandiflora*, with their orange-coloured clusters of waxen flowers, somehow seem to look congruous and carry the visitor for the moment to an idealised Mediterranean, warmer in retrospect than in actuality. Near by, in the garden outside the Ringling Mansion — now also the property of the State —, legs and arms in stone and marble mingle in mossy, inextricable confusion with a tangle of vegetation : for here is still a batch of figures not yet placed. . . . Inside the Museum, behind the sheltering arcades, the pictures purchased, it may be, in a rather wholesale manner — for John Ringling had much to do and was short of time in which to do it —, none the less include many great and famous works : for example, the large Goya portrait of the Duchess of Alba, in a blue dress with a guitar, a fine El Greco *Christ on the Cross*, and the four large pictures by Rubens which belonged formerly to the Duke of Westminster and used to hang in the ballroom of the old Grosvenor House.

A museum such as this makes me ashamed to admit that I would as a rule much rather see an object or a picture in a private house than in a public collection. . . . Yet I am, I suppose, an amateur of museums by nature, and I only remember one occasion on which I was totally unhappy and disappointed. . . . I had been engaged to speak to a Society of Literary Ladies in the Isle of Man. I am a good sailor, but on the day in question the crossing from Liverpool was a tremendous experience : the boat was small, and rolled and rocked and reeled and pitched as if possessed, so that for the ensuing twenty-four hours I entertained a profound dislike of everything to do with the sea. . . . As the passengers landed, most of them in the same woebegone condition as myself, I saw waiting for me on the shore the kind lady who acted as Secretary of the Society I was to address. She shook hands warmly, and said at once,

'I know before you do anything else you'll want to see our famous collection of extinct seagulls. It's said to be unique.'

Now I have always hated seagulls, alive or dead : in life they are a greedy, predatory, bitter-billed bird tribe ; and in death they remain a damp or dusty, but always despondent sight. I was only longing for a rest and for a glass of some restorative, but I still felt too ill to argue, and in consequence allowed myself to be hauled round the museum to examine at some length stiff flights of moth-eaten wings. That museum — as I recall it, easily but always with some degree of repulsion — lacked personality, and it must be allowed that many public collections suffer from the same failing. . . . The John and Mable Ringling Museum of Art differs, however, from most others in this respect. Indeed it is probable that the chief reason for the liveliness and character which separate it so vividly from the ordinary run of musty, echoing buildings dedicated to the instruction of the public, is that the collection and the edifice which enshrines it were for long the aim, and finally the creation, of one man : a circus-master who became by his efforts, and through the good fortune that for many years attended them, a millionaire, and who was plainly a man of immense individuality, with his own ideas on many subjects. In addition, the Gallery is lucky enough to have, ensconced in this last pocket of the Baroque and Rococo, one of the most original-minded and imaginative of all museum directors, Mr. A. Everett Austin, Junior, who has created within the grounds the only museum of its sort in the world : a building disguised inside as a tent, and devoted to the old advertisements, dresses and painted display-cars of the Circus in all its developments.

If the generality of museums grow stuffy, and sterilise their own contents because they have no history, or are not infused by personal fire, yet I know of one other large collection that possesses as strange a story as that of the Ringling Museum at Sarasota : the Bowes Museum in County Durham, where, for a moment, and for purposes of comparison, we will alight. There, too, among the green hills and cool damp valleys of the North of England — a country so different in configuration from the flat sun-baked lands of Florida —, a vast collection was formed, and the building that houses it created, by the effort of one man and his wife.

Born on the 19th of June 1811, John Bowes was the illegitimate son of the 10th Earl of Strathmore and of Mary Milner. In 1820 Lord Strathmore married this lady in London at the fashionable church of St. George's, Hanover Square, and died the next day. John Bowes inherited from him great estates in England, in the neighbourhood of the museum he was to build. His career was unusual for one of his position in the era in which he lived. Though born out of wedlock, he nevertheless came into the world with a silver spoon in his mouth. He was educated at Eton and Cambridge, and at the age of twenty-one — after the passing of the Reform Bill — became a member of Parliament for South Durham : a seat he held for fifteen years. He must, too, have been a prominent figure in the English sporting life of the day, since on three occasions horses belonging to him won the Derby. In addition to having a house in London, he possessed another residence in Paris, and in that city he met Joséphine Benoîte, an actress known to the French public as Mademoiselle Delorme. Her energy found a further outlet in painting, and her work was proficient and banal enough to qualify her to show pictures in the Paris Salon. In 1854 this lady became Mrs. Bowes,[1] but she had also acquired at some time during her life, from the rulers of the miniature Republic of San Marino, the title of Countess of Montalbo. It is said that this honour was granted to her when she was a child : but what earned her the claim to it is never specified. Together for many years Bowes and his Countess planned — though he always maintained that the idea originated with his wife — to leave behind them a monument to their love, and to their interest in the arts. Mrs. Bowes laid the first stone on the 27th of November 1869, and it was opened — though alas neither of the founders lived to see the day — on the 10th of June 1892.

[1] The *Court Journal* for the 25th of April 1868 contains the following allusion to Mr. and Mrs. Bowes. 'Mr. Bowes who some time ago fell in love with the charming Mlle Delorme, then acting at the Variétés, and with characteristic pluck married the lady and bought the theatre, has just sold the latter back to M. Chabrier (who now has the Opéra-Comique) for 40,000 F.'

Mr. and Mrs. Bowes lived much in France — indeed, until the outbreak of the Franco-Prussian War, they had intended to place their museum at Calais, and had chosen to design it a French architect, Jules Pellechet, who was aided in his strange nostalgic effort by J. E. Watson of Newcastle-upon-Tyne. These two men, no doubt with the enthusiastic support of their employers, dumped down on a little hill a few miles outside the small town of Castle Barnard, in wooded country, typically English, this edifice, typically French. It dominates and dwarfs the landscape, and by its extrinsic and exotic quality enables us once more to measure the difference that exists between English and French taste. This enormous structure, with its massive rustication, and its attendant machinery of terraces and geometric garden, and its roof-line equipped with squat and lumpy towers, is imposing, if only by the sheer weight of stone emptied upon an innocent hillside. Though the style of it may be termed Posthumous Second Empire, yet through its conception and realisation sound echoes of the Louvre and the Tuileries, of Compiègne, of the *châteaux* on the Loire, and even of others in Belgium and Luxemburg, with a faint, the faintest possible, reverberation — perhaps this was Mr. Watson's — of the more Italianate Natural History Museum in South Kensington. Over the parterre hangs a similar dusty burden of memories (in no way lightened for me on the afternoon we visited it by a rehearsal for an open-air performance in the evening of Edward German's *Merrie England*). In the construction of the building, however, British materials have been substituted for French, so that the stone for the landings comes from Craigleith, Edinburgh, while the columns in the hall and the stairs of the grand flights of steps are of Aberdeen granite, very pink and sparkling, albeit they seem to present the same relation to marble that everlasting flowers bear to other, more transient blossoms.

The immense collection of pictures in this edifice — though it does not contain so many stars as the Ringling Museum at Sarasota — is amply rewarding to the visitor. Though there is naturally much of lesser quality, it possesses magnificent examples of the national schools of European painting, including, for instance, the splendid El Greco of St. Peter. Indeed the representation of the Spanish, Flemish and German masters is especially fine and unusual. . . . The many objects of art and industry shown in the lower storeys of the Bowes Museum were mostly gathered together — amassed, more perhaps than selected —, by the founders, but they have been added to from time to time, and the scope of the Museum seems to have slipped from the original desire to exhibit to the people of Northern England pictures by the great masters, and the most singular and luxurious products of European culture, to the more comprehensive aim of tracing the origin of mankind, and of displaying the arts and crafts of all races and epochs from the beginning down to the present day. Thus — let us consult the excellent catalogue — while in Room 10 there are pictures and ivory carvings and tapestry, and gilt candlesticks studded with precious stones, and English alabaster groups, the next-door Room 11, on the other hand, displays '*a collection of specimens from the main geological formations of Britain. These include examples of rock, a fossil tribolite, one of the earliest forms of organisms, fishes of the Permian period, and parts of trees, such as calamites, sigillaria and lepidodendron. Specimens of molluscs of all the principal geological periods are in the reserve drawers below. Above the case is a picture showing the geological periods in sequence, and their characteristic fauna and flora. . . .*' We note, too, that in another case are worked flints of '*Abbevillian, Acheulian, Mousterian and Aurignacian cultures*'. Room 15 is the Bowes Room, which exhibits portraits of Mr. Bowes and his wife, and pictures painted by her, as well as many pieces of elaborate mid-nineteenth-century furniture. Other rooms show in abundance French and German porcelain of the eighteenth century, and silver of the same period. There are also many associated items that would have rejoiced the heart of Horace Walpole, had he lived in later times. Thus in Room 19, in '*one of the floor cases is a silver swan mounted on glass rods. When it is in motion the glass rods give the impression of moving water and the swan bends its head to grab the fishes. The model was made in England in the eighteenth century by a man named Weekes and was sent to the Paris exhibition in 1867 where it was purchased by Napoleon III for the Prince Imperial. Mark Twain saw it there and mentions it in "Innocents Abroad" in 1869.*' In Room 9 we see '*a lacquer and ormolu commode . . . used by Lord Byron on his honeymoon at Halnaby Hall near Croft, in 1815*' : while in one of the four rooms on the ground floor devoted to *Teesdale Rural Life and*

Work, we can examine a cheese-kettle which was '*used as a porridge pot at Wm. Shaw's Academy, Bowes, the Dotheboys Hall of "Nicholas Nickleby"*'.

The Bowes Museum is vast, its exhibits are manifold. As we were preparing to leave it, and were creeping down the Aberdeen granite stairs in a battered and exhausted condition, we noticed on one of the lower floors a gallery that had somehow eluded us, labelled '*Ethnographical Section*'. . . . I was prepared to be defeated by it, but the determined friend who accompanied me urged on my flagging energies by saying, 'We can't leave here without seeing everything. You never know what you may miss.' So we dragged our feet along the corridor, to find ourselves in a lively enclave from the Pacific Ocean. It exhibited a number of superb carved and coloured fetishes from New Ireland and elsewhere, many tapa bowls and wooden figures inlaid with mother-of-pearl, but that which most fascinated me — and I have never come across such a thing elsewhere — was an assemblage of hats copied from those worn by European women in Polynesia and Melanesia. Judging from the elegance of these reflections, the originals must have been created in Paris, and their date one would presume to be between 1860 and 1890. No doubt the models had been brought to these remote atolls of coral by the wives of French merchants, and the women of the islands must have admired them so greatly that they had determined to imitate them. But their efforts were restricted by the fact that they had no ribbons or artificial flowers ; the only materials to hand were straw, and dried and dyed grasses. But with these they had been immensely successful, and the jaunty decoration had been most deftly adapted in this, their sole medium. Hanging above these hats was the rest of the clothing worn with them — scanty loin-cloths of dyed rushes — so that it was possible to reconstruct their appearance : the Gauguinesque figures, flat or robust in build, clad solely in these abbreviated, rustling tutus, but wearing on their heads at an angle that shadowed still further their dark eyes and upturned dusky noses, these enchanting hats. In this alien translation into other terms, with their straw flowers and ribbons stiff on the narrow brims, they exhaled an ineffable stylishness, and I most seriously recommend them to the notice of those who create fashions in hats, and who could undoubtedly derive inspiration from them for new modes.

To return to Florida from this glimpse of feminine vanity in the South Seas, this region has its own accretion of exoticism of another kind. . . . Who would expect to find beside the blue pellucid waters of the Mexique Bay representatives of the prim, neat, Puritan sects of the North-Eastern States?—but so it is. If you walk as far, in the reverberant heat, as the stone quay of this very southern-looking town, so new in its whiteness, you are sure to find there, waiting in their gigs by the archway which forms the gate to the small harbour, or walking up and down the quay itself, examining the boats massed at its side, one or two Mennonites [1] who have come to meet a friend arriving by steamer from one of the neighbouring islands, or,

[1] Followers of Menno Simons (1492–1559), a native of Friesland.

perhaps, to buy fish, red snapper, flying fish or pompano, for the frugal repasts that their creed imposes. They are plainly a farming community, but the men still wear black suits with crowned wide-brimmed black hats and sport a fringe of beard round their chins in the style that used to be termed in England a Newgate fringe : while the women are dressed heavily, despite the temperature, in wide black skirts with black bodices and old-fashioned bonnets frilled with a white edge, such as you have beheld above more buxom faces in the pictures of Frans Hals. They never use motor-cars, but ride in their gigs, driven by the men. All alike, both men and women, exhale the air of another century than this, and seen suddenly in these modern, rather flimsy and pleasantly gaudy surroundings, and among the gaily and lightly clad visitors, they a little resemble ghosts who have materialised at a fair. The majority of them came here from Pennsylvania and are descended from seventeenth-century emigrants from Holland and Germany. Certainly they seem to be strange neighbours for the white cranes stalking through the shallow lagoons and for the grey pelicans that flop down with such a fat thud on the blue waters.

In spite of the Mennonites, it is the contrasting atmosphere of the Circus that permeates Sarasota and its neighbourhood. . . . Thus the performance given each Saturday night in the crowded ballroom of the John Ringling Hotel is unique. There, within the space of a large room, which yet seems perilously small for such a display, you see a preview of a performance of the most dazzling and arduous feats of trapeze-walking and equipoise, and are privileged to watch the latest sprigs of the Circus dynasties, children of the fourth or fifth generation of performers, with the instinct for balance and showmanship running through their very veins, first try out in public the tricks which one day, near or far, will make them famous. . . . And for another instance of the atmosphere that pervades the locality, I will recount an incident that fell to the fortunate lot of an acquaintance of mine. He told me how on first arriving he had been obliged to take some shoes to be mended. As he entered the cobbler's shop he was astonished to see, lying in the window, a pair of shoes about size 28. This he would have condemned to himself as a brash and rather pointless kind of advertisement, had he not noticed that the soles of the shoes were worn through. This persuaded him to enquire of the proprietor their history, and he learned that they had just been thrown in there for repair by the Circus giant! An occurrence of this kind could only happen at Sarasota: because about three miles off, in a flat pleasance equipped with its own railway sidings, is drawn up on a track the white-painted railway train that each spring and summer carries the famous Circus, the largest and finest in the world, throughout the length and breadth of the United States, and here, on the ground, the artistes and animals rest or practise during the winter months from November till March.

Not far from the train is situated the square wooden stable which contains some fifty elephants; which though, as I have said, a very large elephantine congregation, does not compare with the multitude of elephants stated to have lived in Peking during the reign of the Emperor Kubla. These Marco Polo estimated at five thousand, but then the Venetian was given to exaggerating figures, as we can tell from his nickname, *Marco Milione*, and *five thousand* was a favourite description he employed to express the idea of a very great number. In addition, everything relating to the use of elephants in China is apt to be somewhat fabulous: the great beasts appealed by their size and reputation for age and wisdom, no less than by their strangeness, to the Chinese mind. If they are mentioned by a Chinese writer, some odd fact about them is sure to be related. Thus Tun Li-Ch'en, writing of the imperial elephants at the end of the nineteenth century, tells us that, 'If they were ill, oil would flow from their ears, and this was said to be the coming forth of their mountain natures'.

I called the collection of elephants at Sarasota a congregation, but it is more of an elephantine nunnery, for the inhabitants of the stable are now solely female. It was not ever thus, but on one occasion a few years ago, when the population had also included two or three male elephants, a bitter sex wrangle had broken out while these huge beasts were passing in procession through the main street of a mid-West city, thronged with spectators. The males had broken away and attempted a rape as vigorous, and now almost as celebrated in that region, as that of the Sabine Women once was in Rome. The band of shy grey nymphs stampeded in all directions through the crowds, trumpeting their alarm and virtue, still pursued by the males. Many of the people watching had been so much injured morally as well as physically in the course of this chase, that the male elephants had to be disposed of, and no others were bought to replace them, since elephants, being the proud but sensitive animals that they are, never breed in complete captivity: though if, as in Burma, they work for an eight-hour, Trades-Union day, and have the evening and night to themselves, they continue successfully to produce calves. (It is, perhaps, worth noticing in this connection that as soon as a mother-elephant is aware that she is pregnant, from that moment another female elephant or 'Auntie' comes to attend and wait on her during the remaining months.) . . . And before bringing these few notes on elephantine lore to a conclusion, let me add a further fact. Contrary to what, with the sound of their trumpeting still in our ears, some of us might expect, the musical taste of these beasts is extremely conventional: they know what they like, Delibes, Massenet and Gounod, and entertain a very deep aversion from modern works. Thus when the Circus proprietors, Messrs. Ringling North, commissioned Stravinsky, that true and amazing genius among contemporary composers, to write a march for the elephants, the great animals, directly they heard it, showed their opinion of the work by refusing to budge a single step. They indulged, in fact, in a sit-down strike.

The first afternoon, then, that I visited the stable, it contained only a peaceful group of sisters. The sun even in February possesses in this latitude an unexpected strength, so that these immense and noble giantesses with their primeval hides, reminding one of the earth when cracked and riven by the heat, were continually grasping and lifting up in their trunks great bundles of straw, Ophelia-like crowns which they placed as protection on their heads, keeping them there in uneasy balance till, after five minutes or so, they fell off and their wearers were forced to collect the straw all over again. . . . Even among this congregation, identical in personnel as it must appear to a newcomer, the crowd of circus-lovers possesses its favourites, of whom the chief is Ruth, an elephant of individual charm and intelligence. Imagine, therefore, how acute was the consternation among elephant amateurs, when, in the spring of 1950, as the Circus was about to set out from Madison Square Gardens in New York on its annual tour of the country, the proprietors announced the mysterious disappearance of Ruth. That an elephant could vanish so completely in such a city as New York seemed an odd happening, but no trace of her could be found, until at last, after forty-eight hours, detectives discovered the huge beast in the ballroom of a famous hotel ! The solution of the mystery proved to be that Ruth had been abducted by an enterprising publicity agent, who wanted by extraneous means to call the attention of press and public to a convention of business men for whom he was working that was being held in the hotel.

There, in the stable, the elephants stood today, wearing their improvised hats, quietly swaying their great bulk on their short round legs. They seemed not to notice the visitors, not even to see them, but only to pay attention to their own mahouts and grooms. . . .

To me they represented, as I have stated, Asia and not Africa, but all round us, in the same enclosure, Africa was most fully represented : indeed I saw here more beasts than ever I saw in that vast continent of jungles : where, it is true, I knew only the Mediterranean regions, not the dark interior, the spreading uplands or the gigantic lakes. Never yet have I been privileged to walk out at sunrise and find the impression of a lion's paw only recently stamped on the sand fresh from the night, or to see the branches of the jungle parted by the streaked body of a forest animal. Here, however, at Sarasota, I could for instance examine the famous gorilla, Gargantua, a mountain of black and hairy power, a roughly-hewn shape composed of tragic, pointless and mad rage, now happily defunct. Confronting Gargantua, but in a separate cage, sat Toto, his female counterpart, but amiable and coquettish. She squatted behind the bars and paid no attention to him, being much too busily occupied in practising each of her repertory of tricks, counting the fingers of one hand with those of the other, putting out her tongue or coyly trying on an inverted saucepan as if it were a new hat, and she at a milliner's. Often she aped — if I may use the word — shyness, and hid in her hands her black hairy face and had to be comforted or instructed, but always in Spanish, for she had been brought up in a villa outside Havana — where she had, I was told, led the usual life of a Cuban debutante —, and only understood that tongue.

This question of nationality, as it were, is important in every large circus. . . . As an example of what I mean, not long ago the Ringling-Barnum Circus bought a troupe of seals, known to give a very sleek and silky performance. When, however, the new artistes arrived, it was discovered that they fell into confusion unless told what to do, and no one could find the right language in which to address them. Since for similar reasons any circus is essentially polyglot, English, German, French, Spanish, Italian, Russian, Hungarian and Swiss Romansch, were each in turn tried on them, but they would not, could not, respond by the full display of their talents, until a Pole was brought in to harangue them in his own tongue. Immediately the polished, streamlined beasts began to exhibit their full programme and barked and sang their delight at finding a compatriot. They balanced, and then spun, brilliantly-quartered indiarubber balls upon the blunted tips of their pointed noses, slid and leapt, clown-like, through hoops and barrels and engaged in a hundred other diverting tricks. In the same manner, for Toto to do her best, it had been found necessary to recall from Cuba the footman who had formerly attended her and who could urge her on to further efforts when she became bored, and flatter and cajole her by references to former successes in Havana.

Very different from these two African gorillas, one frantic and distraught, a simian Lear sold into captivity, the other by disposition and upbringing a spoilt beauty, was the tribe of smaller apes now distributed in groups in communal cages. They chattered and gibbered or gazed out pathetically at the paraphernalia of their individual metamorphoses : for there on the wall, just beyond their reach, hung the equipment for their acts ; their clothes, ready for them to don and adorn themselves with in the spring, the red shirts, the blue trousers with stripes of scarlet braid, the small frogged sling jackets and hussar hats, the spangled coats, the wigs, the tarbooshes, while near them too stood against the same wall the necessary machinery, the bells they rang, the little bicycles they rode, the folding ladders, the tight-ropes, the cheque-books and pens, the miniature billiard tables and the balls and cues and cigars. Here, in their camp at Sarasota, they were at home, at their ease, in their carpet-slippers as it were ; and they swung from their bars as if they were branches, with a real or perhaps simulated *joie de vivre*, then stopped to peer at the spectators with a particular uneasy focus of their eyes, staring, as it seemed, through human beings into an impenetrable distance and darkness. But the antics of the monkey septs have detained us for too long, for there are also massive-headed lions and striped tigers and trefoiled leopards to visit, all of them with the rhythm of their long, lithe, jungle stride cruelly reduced by the size of their cages ; perhaps fortunately reduced. They glare at the spectators with an impatience born of their present impotence.

In the sunshine outside, in big airy compounds of wire, are two kinds of camel, Bactrian and African, and two kinds of giraffe, each wearing the bold design of its skin in a slightly different tone, lighter or darker, with a slightly different pattern, but each displaying it with an ineffable elegance, with a forest freshness and debonair shyness : (legendary beasts they looked, such as might be described in the future book of travel through the moon or Mars, so that I could quite well comprehend the stir their first arrival in London caused, and the content of King George IV at having seen them). But, next after Ruth and Toto, the most captivating of the captives was a female hippopotamus. . . . We approached the opaque, still waters of a pool, and my friend, Henry Ringling North — one of two brothers, nephews of the late John Ringling, who now own the Circus — called out in a tremendous voice, 'Lotos, where are you ? Lotos !' Immediately a commotion, as if a subaqueous bomb had exploded, ensued, transmitted from the muddy depths upwards, and after a moment's pause given up, no doubt, to who knows what feminine preparations, one of the ugliest heads in the world — one can only drop down to slang and call it a mug —, a long, mud-coloured face lined and tipped with a light tone of coral pink and full, apparently, of excrescent blemishes, and with a wide, enormous mouth, thrust itself with an air of conscious charm through the waters, gazing up ecstatically at her master. . . . Certainly the head was, as I have just written, one of the ugliest in the world and certainly no grace pertained, either, to the body, yet the sculptors of dynastic Egypt — and surely no artists more esthetically-minded could be found — admired these amphibious beasts because, it is said, of the beauty of the under-water courtship-dances in which they like to engage. The water must be crystalline clear in some patch of one of the great African rivers, and there you will see, far down, the male and female horses first face each other and then begin to prance and undulatingly to caracol and curvet. This may be mythical zoology — I suspect it, though I like the idea : but I feel sure that to me, rather than an Egyptian relief, they would recall inevitably from their appearance the dancing of two costermongers on Hampstead Heath on Bank Holiday. Nevertheless, it is possible that the whole form of these creatures may have been designed for under-water vision, for under-water admiration : perhaps they seem ugly only to us of a different element. . . . As we passed the seals, diving in and out, playing like porpoises, I thought of that same morning when from the beach of Sarasota a school of these mammals could be seen in the distance leaping in and out of the sea, and an American lady, about to bathe, had come up to me and enquired whether the creatures were sharks. When I said,

'No. They're porpoises. They do no harm', she replied,

'Well, they look kind-a mean to me!'

I emphasised my point. 'If you bathe, they'll only play round you.'

'Not round *me*!' she answered firmly.

CHAPTER III

THE MAN IN THE FRONT SEAT

We have, during the course of these last pages, examined — though only for a few miles — the sole continent of our four in which progress still seems to continue in the old nineteenth-century manner and even to have accelerated its pace. Perhaps only so long as you believe in progress can you obtain it, and the Americans just cannot imagine the possibility of not getting their own way (we English were like that, too, once). They have an entire, perfect and infectious self-confidence, never more genuine than when some real danger threatens them, though every now and then during peace the surface is broken by a series of nervous spasms and apprehensive shivers. The other three continents are now in the melting-pot, from which America has just triumphantly emerged as the grand nation of the Western World, and only countries that have already undergone a similar process, and are now cooling and settling, are likely to produce new shapes that are at once revolutionary and benevolent. Therefore I propose for a short space to consider the American national character as it has evolved.

In one important respect, America differs from all other historic nations. The most powerful of the free nations that remain free today has been fashioned before the eyes, at first inattentive, and then startled, of a few generations. To the Italians of the present era, Romulus and Remus and the she-wolf who suckled them must seem distant and rather lifeless symbols, a legend without dimensions, while equally to us of the British race, Boadicea must appear as a misty if sanguinary portent, roughly hewn, over life-size, resembling the figure-head of an eighteenth-century ship seen through the spray of waves. Hengist and Horsa, even the authentic William the Conqueror, are to Englishmen simplified types — but the fathers of the American Republic, Washington, Jefferson and their company, lived so short a time ago in terms of history that they are known in realistic detail of feature and character to every grateful American of whatever descent, or however recently derived from immigrant stock. For Washington was the father of the future melting-pot, no less than of the countrymen of his own time. The story of the axe and the cherry-tree may be an invention, but it should still be possible to find out, and since, if it be a legend, it is of so much more recent date, it must seem less dubious than that of King Alfred and his cakes. Of no other nation do we know so much about its founders, the opinions they held, the speeches they made, the lives they led, their tastes and outlook. All this makes the development of America into the chief world power of infinitely more poignant interest. Moreover, in a sense the American triumph constitutes the greatest and most typical example in history of biblical revenge, the final Christian or Jewish triumph of the poor and oppressed over the rich and powerful: because the grandchildren of many of the most wretched emigrants from Europe now hold in their grasp the destinies of the countries from which their grandfathers fled in destitution and despair.

Certainly the racial sources of the modern American are diverse: yet in spite of the various influences, what must strike an Englishman today is less the difference than the likeness of outlook between England and America. Though the blood-kinship has thinned, though storms may suddenly and mountainously arise between the two countries and then as suddenly subside, yet an Englishman in the United States, though conscious that he is not an American, can never consider himself as a foreigner, but feels that some new term should be invented to fit his status, just as, obversely, some new word should be minted to describe the footing of an American in Great Britain: for the American resembles the Englishman even in the very thing that has chiefly divided them during the last fifty years: the fact that both nations are of very mixed descent. And in this connection it must be recalled that for two thousand or so years Great Britain was the European melting-pot. Again, both countries breed a race of sailors, as you might expect from the length of their coast-line, and because, though our ancestry may vary, the forefathers of both English and Americans have had to cross perilous seas before they reached the land which they now people. The inhabitant of each country likes, too, to think of himself as standing always against the bully — though the bully varies, for American history books, the English reader must be warned, differ astonishingly from ours in the views they express. Thus King George III, our benevolent and beloved Farmer George, still ranks to Americans as a Prince of Darkness, and famous battles have been fought in America of which no Englishman of today remembers the existence. I was amazed to find, for example, that the city of Buffalo had once been burned by the British — but everyone in Buffalo knows it! And it must be remembered that the American War of Independence itself still looms more importantly in their shorter national history than in our longer one. Yet, whatever old quarrels may from time to time blaze for a moment out again, the most important fact remains that both systems of law come from the same stem, and that, above all, we are brought up on and conditioned by the same books: the Bible and Shakespeare are the foundation of American as of English literature. Indeed, our literature is still, and likely to remain, one. (If you buy a book, you do not ask, is it by an English or American author, but, simply, is it a good book?) So, it may be argued, and I argue, that writers have done much more for the solidarity of our countries than generals or politicians have accomplished, and that

Shakespeare has almost repaired the damage done to both America and England by the break in feeling that occurred in 1776.

To have visited recently, as I did, a country you have not seen for over twenty years, and to find that it has become more potent, its people more highly civilised in a political sense, constitutes for a man of my generation a wonderful experience. Since 1926 when I was last in the States — at the height no less of the Great Boom than of the Prohibition period when happy missionary bands of expatriates spread the gospel of the speak-easy through Paris, and indeed throughout Europe — the American people have grown up, and attained to a full sense of the world responsibilities that their position and still more their power imposes upon them. This new attitude they combine with their old and intrinsic warm-heartedness and hatred of oppression and injustice. Even if occasionally self-interest — always so much less dangerous in its effect on a nation than idealism — inspires their political wisdom, and the plans that ensue from it, there is always, in the colloquial phrase, 'more to it than that' : there also ever enter in the sometimes derided, but very genuine, factors of American benevolence and American generosity ; the result no less of history and background than of the size and nature of the country that has produced them. For these reasons, among others, I love America and Americans.

I woke up to my surroundings again, back in my room at Amalfi, so we have been half-way round the world without moving. . . . Walking to the window, I look at the ancient city below, pinched between the walls of the gorge. It had been forced to climb up the limestone cliffs by a sudden inundation of the sea, which, some six centuries before, had swept through the town, and had never more retreated : so that the fishermen claim that on a clear day they can still distinguish far below the calm surface on which they float, the streets, now crinkling with the waves, through which their ancestors walked daily, that they can perceive occasionally, far down, the antique figure of their patron saint, St. Andrew, on his cross, and that, moreover, when a dangerous storm is coming, a thousand-year-old bell, its tongue muffled by the water, gives them warning of it. Only the part of the city that stood in the crevice between the rocks has survived. Though atrociously modernised in the nineteenth century, the cathedral, with its jutting ceremonial flight of steps, dates literally from before the flood, having been built in 1206, and the crypt underneath it contains the body of St. Andrew, a most sacred relic which was conveyed here from Constantinople in the thirteenth century. . . .

Certainly, I thought, the city had changed little since I had first seen it, forty years before. It had remained beautiful and poor, very poor, unaltered under the tide of war that had flowed in here, and then out again, leaving behind it for a year or two an acquired and skin-thin sophistication. The sea below retained its old pavonine brilliance, that of a Limoges enamel. . . . It was time to bathe, before people were about, and I walked down the steps — not alas, running down them, two at a time, as was my habit twenty years before — down the steps to the foreshore, denuded at this hour. . . . Yes, the place had changed little : I was able from here to look back at the abrupt and mountainous grey background, where limestone cliffs and rocks swelled up to the sky like a fugue by Bach, yet somehow pagan, irrational, not rational and humane as is essentially the music of the great master. Nearly every crag showed a Christian church or chapel now falling to ruin, and filled with the columns, made of the very fabric, of the rustic pagan temple it had no doubt supplanted, so that the look of the landscape afforded a sense of continuity and seemed to affirm the existence of the supernatural : it would be easy, living here, to believe in nymphs and satyrs, in gods and devils. . . . At this moment my meditation was interrupted by a blare of voices, distractingly loud and unnatural, followed by the roar of a tune of almost unearthly vacuity. The roll of this tremendous but imbecile sound was redoubled by the backing of piled-up houses and of the honeycombed limestone rocks — it was caused, I now comprehended, by the nurses turning on the radio for the benefit of deaf and dumb children. That, at least, was an innovation : the macaroni factory that had stood empty and derelict for so many years on the promenade had become an asylum for these unfortunates. It seemed typical of the modern world that this music, which, even if some of them might have liked it, they could never hear, should be provided for them. . . . I continued on my way, round the cliff's edge. . . . The water still held in it the warmth of summer, and after bathing, I lay on the sand and thought of the future and what it might hold. Who could tell ? . . . Who would recognise good news now, if it came ?

The interior prospect certainly seemed depressing when compared with that which lay spread round. The coming winter in England did not allure me, yet despondency was a mistake, and I had for some years held the opinion that if only people would contract the length of their faces, and become, as the case might demand, a little less trivial or a little less serious, either abating their cries of dismay at someone else having cornered an extra half-pound of chocolates or an ounce of margarine, or curbing their talk of calamity and crisis, the position might begin to improve. But today, I apprehend, if a statesman were to attempt to announce some general piece of good fortune, he would not be able to make his voice heard above the sounds of mass grumbling and lamentation : because during the last two decades we have become so continually enured to bad news that we should scarcely know how to respond to good. Agreeable developments, which, owing to the genius of politicians in every country, are today almost outside the bounds of imagination, would, if they were in reality to occur, equally fill the newspaper with despondency and alarm. I tried to picture to myself what would be likely to happen if some event which by its nature should be equally pleasing to all the nations were to be made public — let us suppose the official intimation that the scientists had finally mastered, by means of nuclear or atomic energy, the material resources of the world, and that, in consequence, the governments of all the chief countries had in the course of the past few months arrived at a secret agreement to work together, to disband their national forces, to scrap their armaments, and to initiate a universal three-hour working day at full rates of pay. . . . How truly unexpected the results would be! Everyone would grow a longer, not a shorter, face. Free at last from the tyranny of the machine, man would be left staggering and gasping for breath, as though one team had suddenly let go in a tug-of-war. The menaces against which, the aims on behalf of which, multitudes had laboured and fought for so long would now be revealed as having no actuality: the individual, no less than societies and associations, would be at a loss for a cause to champion or a demon against whom to rage. As their opinions might incline them, many would refuse to believe the news, and would dismiss the whole matter as a Jewish or Roman Catholic plot, a Socialist or Tory conspiracy. Even in Russia, divergencies would become clear among the people, and bitter quarrels would manifest themselves. The press might for a day escape from governmental control, denounce the settlement as a triumph for anti-revolutionary jackals and hyenas, and demand measures of retaliation. The usual political purge, but bigger and therefore better, would ensue, and the cries of the victims as they were being liquidated, and the howls of the ravening crowd of onlookers, would be broadcast to the world. . . . In Wall Street an immense and catastrophic slump would follow the news of the agreement, and in Europe processions of demonstrators would parade the streets of the great cities, and there would be riots, with the mobs crying '*Give us back our Seven Hours!*' and '*We want our Armies and Navies!*'

The better the news became, the more violent the protests and outbreaks. Obversely, often the worse the news, the more enthusiastic the reception of it: for people, especially in Great Britain, have grown to love communal gestures of asceticism and suffering. Moreover, political values are so artificial and now change so rapidly that it is often difficult to tell good news from bad, or to remember who is the foe and who the friend. The enemy, the bogeyman, is always there, to frighten honest British children, but he now changes his name and identity with baffling ease and speed. A few years ago, for instance, the extinction of one man seemed to constitute an enormous benefit to the freedom-loving peoples: today his re-emergence might be made to appear in a similar light. . . . Let us pursue the matter for a few pages, since, after all, I have called this book a volume of *discursions*, and this description of it bestows on the author an added power of selecting and including, as well as a new mobility, while it gives him also leave to chase through a page or two any hare he happens to put up: so, abandoning sightseeing for a short while, you will rest on the beach and listen to my talk again. This time it will be concerned with the adventures of a journalist named Victor Curtis-Deane, who plays the part of *compère* in my tale — for this discursion will assume almost the form of a short story, though by its nature crippled in one respect. Perhaps, then, it is rather to be regarded as a satirical exercise: because I have, by the very essence of the theme that has chosen me to relate it — an author never chooses themes, they choose him as their vehicle —, been obliged to omit what would probably be the most pronounced feature of such a return from the dead as I shall attempt to describe for you : that is, the reaction everywhere, throughout the world, of the Jews. Their sufferings at the hands of the Nazis were too complete and abominable to permit in connection with them any trace of irony. Though it be true that in the actual world round us Herr Krupp has been awarded twenty-five — some say fifty — million pounds in compensation for his work, a similar development in a fictive world might be condemned by all the laws of taste. In consequence, I have kept the character flat and two-dimensional ; and the events imperfect. After this apology and explanation, I will proceed as well as I can. The action takes place in the immediate future, and the tale is named *The Man in the Front Seat.*

As the Chinese Communist troops drove further into Burma, Victor Curtis-Deane, a young British journalist, prepared to leave Rangoon by air : just as, two years before, he had been similarly compelled, together with other Europeans, to quit Lhasa. In spite of the nearness of the enemy and the danger of bombs, a rather pleasant sense of bustle, of people doing their duty and enjoying it, prevailed on the airfield. As he approached the machine he thought to himself, what a pity that I can't wait longer so that I could report the entry of the troops. But it was not at all certain that after their entry there would ever be another aircraft leaving for the West, since the Iron Curtain grew every day more voluminous and thicker, while to be left in a Communist Burma, without means of escape, was not an end to be desired. So Victor Curtis-Deane stepped up into the plane which was due to leave in a few minutes, and thus was already full of passengers, found his place and sat down. While he waited, he reflected that on this trip, so far he had not been really very lucky, because he had been away for many months, and neither here nor previously in Tibet had he found a real story for his paper. At that moment, his eye, scanning idly the passengers, lit on the face of a man with a neatly trimmed but rather long beard, who occupied a front seat. With him was a dumpy woman who had the look of a German *Hausfrau*. *Her* appearance made little impression on Victor, but the solid build and shape of her companion, the jutting nose, the rather red, coarse-grained skin, the line of the eyebrows, especially the eyes themselves — blue eyes which seemed to exert a considerable magnetic power — had something curiously familiar about them, held a front-page association which he could not place. He searched his memory for possible clues, but could not find a single one. However, he continued to scrutinise the man most carefully, and did, in fact, notice one or two small traits — such, for example, as the characteristic (it could mean anything or nothing) that whenever a passenger made a gesture in the direction of raising his right hand, the stranger would look self-conscious or guilty.

The engines had been throbbing, and the whole machine vibrating with them for some time, and it now soared into the air with a final blast of wind when the roof was shut. As the plane ascended, it was chased by Communist flyers, but fortunately its greater swiftness enabled it quickly to outdistance them. During these few moments of danger the passengers had grown very excited, all except the man in the front seat, who seemed scarcely to take in what was happening, and his companion who was occupied in regarding him steadily with eyes full of devotion and love. . . . The truth was that the stranger's mind was occupied with his memorable flight to Lhasa a few years before — an occasion he would never forget — when his remaining adherents (who could be numbered on the fingers of a hand) had smuggled him out of Berlin, its ruins blazing in the night like the Cities of the Plain. Never would he be able to forget the sight, the sound, the fury of those flames — all the consequence of his having been obliged, when his patience was at last exhausted, to offer resistance to the evil men on the other side. But he had no pity for the Germany which had deserted him, though he had been sorry to part with some individuals — the faithful Bormann, for instance, and the Goebbelses — however, they, at any rate, had also escaped from doomed Berlin. For himself and his companion no other course had been open save to leave the capital, to abandon all those fools, slaves and abject cowards, who had refused to fight for him any longer, though he had commanded them to continue the struggle, and had himself, infallible as he was, daily designed new plans for them to execute, whereby victory would have been surely snatched from the enemy. How bitterly he despised the German people, not only for their final refusal to obey him, but equally for their long years of subjugation to him, for their dull acquiescence, their brutish docility! How loudly he had raged at those who had earlier advised him to try to come to terms with the Allies, even if it involved his own temporary disappearance from the scene: for he had always known in his heart, with an inner conviction, that without his leadership Germany would perish — and look at her fate now, a great country split in half!

It had been rather difficult to hide in Rangoon. . . . Lhasa had been more to his taste, and had provided him with a safe refuge in a monastery (though Eva had felt the separation from him and had found life as a governess in a Tibetan family very trying, she had unhesitatingly accepted his decision). A cloistered life in Lhasa had always been his choice, ever since Rosenberg had told him how the lamas prophesied that the new spiritual force, the Buddha of our epoch, would come from the West to the East, and it had become gradually obvious to him that if, after all, he was not cast for the part of the world-conqueror, it must be that he was a great teacher, a Messiah. . . . How swift the end in Berlin had been: how easy he had found it to hoodwink the enemies, duped even on this final occasion! They had known quite well that he had employed two professional doubles, each of whom bore a sufficient resemblance to him to deceive the public and the newspaper representatives on any state occasion when he had reason to fear an attack on his life: yet it had never struck the enemy politicians and military idiots that the same system of physical duplication might apply to his subordinates and friends, to Goebbels, for example, and his wife and children, and to the faithful Eva Braun. Nor had it, apparently, occurred even to these democratic thinkers (and he sneered under his beard) that he could be ruthless enough — although they were always declaiming against his ruthlessness — to plot the bombing and incineration of these miserable tools, who served a purpose because of their accidental likeness to the great, but whose lives were only of use to the Fatherland when they died. A few charred corpses in the bombed Chancellery underground had completely taken in the Allied Governments and their posse of prying busybodies, poking about and trying to find out what had happened to him!

He stroked his beard for a while, following his own thoughts. . . . He had learned much in his retreats of the last few years, but, alas, he had been forced to leave Lhasa before his initiation had been complete: and now he had been compelled to emerge, since the Communist forces were almost at the gates of Rangoon, and it would not be in the interest of the world for him to face a trial by the Communists — that much at least was plain to him. Nevertheless, a terrible fate it was for such a man as he, whose least intention had for many years troubled every country on the globe, and who had for the space of a year or two governed almost the whole of Europe, to be a refugee and obliged to claim falsely a democratic nationality: but to such a pass had the poltroonery of the German people and the malice of his enemies brought him. What an indignity — and as he thought of his sorrows, great German tears formed in his eyes — a refugee, without home or support ! . . . Really he would have preferred to be arraigned. . . . He began to think of the Nuremberg Trials — he had followed the proceedings with impassioned interest — and of the ends which they had brought to so many of his companions and subordinates. Most of them, he thought, deserved what they had got. Only himself and, of course, the Goebbelses and Martin Bormann had been canny enough to escape. . . . Would the Allies now be sufficiently clever, he wondered, to catch him ?

. . . . . .

They were drawing near to their destination. During the journey Victor Curtis-Deane had spent much time in watching with close attention the man in the front seat. The stranger was not so lost in his dreams that he failed to observe it, and occasionally he would turn on the journalist the force of his eyes, with their singular, persistent and fanatical glazed blue glare. He had, Victor Curtis-Deane observed, an almost mystic air or consequence, of being of importance — at least to himself and plainly to his companion. . . . The machine began at last to circle downward, in order to land at London Airport. . . . At the gate, where passports were examined, Victor peered over the stranger's shoulder, and read the details inscribed on his passport. The name looked like *Adolf Schicklgruber*, American citizen, of St. Paul's, Minnesota, formerly by profession a house-painter. The entries, thus so modestly and even in part truthfully set out, now conveyed no hint of former notoriety either to Victor or to the officials : but outside the ground, a dark, taller, younger man was waiting to welcome the stranger. Greetings were exchanged in German, — suddenly Victor Curtis-Deane's mind and memory began to work : the aspect of the man in the front seat, the sound of his name, his profession, the look of the friend who had come to meet him, all slid into place and focussed. Of course, of course, the celebrated moustache had gone and the beard had been added — but it was Hitler ! So the rumour of his escape had been true ! HITLER ! he shouted to himself, HITLER ! accompanied by Eva Braun, and met by Martin Bormann, who was presumably living in London. Hitler ! HITLER ! It was the scoop of the century, Victor realised. He rushed to the telephone kiosk, slammed the door, and dialled the number of the great national newspaper for which he worked. When he obtained it, he demanded to speak with the Editor himself. His voice was shaking with excitement.

'It's Victor Curtis-Deane, sir. I've just flown in on the last plane from Rangoon — and I've seen *Hitler* with my own eyes. He was on board the same machine, and has escaped, I suppose, first from a monastery in Lhasa, and then from some refuge in Burma. Eva Braun was with him.'

Victor had expected a lively and delighted reply. Instead, the Editor's voice, always rather cold if polite, sounded now bored and incredulous.

'We've had that story before, Curtis-Deane,' he

said, 'and it proved untrue. All the papers turned it down, fortunately for them. It's old, cold news, and even if it were true you should have cabled it to us more than a year ago. I won't touch it at any price.'

From all the other editors to whom he applied, he received the same kind of reply. . . . Poor Victor went to bed dejected and angry. As he lay there, wakeful and restless, his mind reverted to the extraordinary events that had taken place at the end of the Second World War, and he reflected how singular it was that the fact of Hitler's death had been so quickly presumed and so easily accepted : because, after all, the whole world had recognised him as a tricky customer.

At last, after several days had passed, Victor succeeded in having his story printed in a paper in one of the Middle West cities of America, where a large portion of the population was of German descent. Once published, even if rather obscurely, the news took wings to itself and flew round the world, appearing, too, in the columns of the paper to whose editor Victor had first offered it — but, of course, it brought him no advantage. The news was free, and the press of every country revelled in it in its own way. . . . By that time Hitler was on his way by boat to Buenos Aires. On his arrival there the whole German colony had gone down to the docks to meet the Führer : the procession was headed by Goebbels and his wife and children (who, as soon as the news of Hitler's reappearance had reached them, emerged from hiding on their ranch in the Argentine and revealed their identity), and now, as their leader stepped on to the quay, all who were there welcomed him by breaking into the Horst Wessel Hymn. During a press conference at his hotel, Hitler told the newspaper men that he very clearly saw the errors of the past and had come back to save Germany and the world — but on this occasion he very wisely refrained from specifying the particular danger he had determined to vanquish. The papers reported that the Führer looked tired and depressed — and so he did, since after years of carefree liberty and contemplation, he expected to be arrested at once, to be placed immediately on trial, and hounded to death by both halves of the world, Communist and anti-Communist, united once again in their common detestation of him and his principles.

The competition engendered by the Cold War soon assured him, to the contrary, of a welcome from both sides. At first, it is true, the Allies and Russia made some weak, formal and face-saving attempts to obtain his extradition, in order to place him on trial for War Crimes ; but the President of the Argentine Republic refused to hand him over to justice, and denounced the whole proceeding as an international effort to infringe the Sovereignty of the State. Hitler made a generous gift to the late Madame Perón's charity funds. . . . The world in 1955 was merely an exaggeration of what it had been a few years before : the Cold War had grown colder, more icy. Germany was listless, still divided into halves, and therefore scarcely able as yet to exercise that mastery of blackmail with which her continual defeats in diplomacy and war had endowed her, and which she had learned to recognise as her greatest national asset. And though later, like a worm cut in half, the pieces would unite, at present each part retained the ideology imposed upon it, and pretended to wish to browbeat the other — but now the whole of Germany, a country prone to hysteria, seethed from end to end with joyous excitement, because it realised that with the return of Hitler the ability to make war again as one nation might soon be within its grasp.

Perceiving that with Germany in her present mood it would be dangerous to attempt to interfere with his liberty, the Allied politicians quickly abandoned their efforts to obtain Hitler ; instead of handing him over to justice, they competed for his help. The heads of the U.S.S.R. invited him to visit the Kremlin for a discussion of mutual aims : but Hitler declined their offer. They continued, however, in cordial communication with him and pressed him to come out as the champion of a Soviet Germany ; for they knew that Germans of all divisions, zones and parties, would flock to the standard of their old leader. The Western powers, also eager to make use of him, urged him to put himself forward as a recruit to Democracy, a convert — like the Emperor of Japan — to the American Way of Life. . . . The more sober English newspapers contented themselves with saying that towards the end of the Nazi regime Hitler had unfortunately been surrounded with lesser men, of evil counsel, who pursued their own paltry objects instead of an ideal. To them were due the cruelties of the system : whereas the Führer's private life with Eva Braun — that part of the official story was true : he had married her during the last two weeks in Berlin — offered the world an example of domestic virtue which, in these days of easy divorce, it would do well to follow. (This line appealed to moderate thought throughout the country, and Hitler received several flattering and generous offers from the B.B.C. to give a talk on the wireless to be entitled *Modern Marriage and What it Means*.) The more imaginative and flamboyant papers went further, and acclaimed Hitler as the Defender and Interpreter of the Great Democratic Ideal and the worthy pioneer of the Welfare State. . . . Soon both East and West were urging him to broadcast a message to the German people and to the world : (the negotiations between Hitler and the B.B.C. were carried on through the agency of Bormann, who had been working, it was now discovered, since 1946 on the German side of the B.B.C., under the name of Bormann).

A world-famous British statesman made an oration — speech is far too humble a word — in a large concert hall. To this every inhabitant of all the free countries was obliged to listen on the radio. He said that people sometimes falsely assumed that a great statesman was one who left his country happier and more prosperous than he had found it. With that timid and unworthy conception he would not agree. In his opinion a great statesman was one who could always surmount the crisis precipitated by his solution of the previous crisis. There were some who had even decried Britain's War Effort, but he thought it would now be evident to every man and woman in the entire globe that it had been triumphantly vindicated. Not only had we fought alone for years, never questioning the cause for which we fought, not only had we kept the struggle on and the sore open until the whole world was involved, when otherwise many countries might have remained sunk in the lethargy of peace, but now as a result of past quarrels — in spite, and because, of them —, in our new hour of need we had gained the friendship of this great man who stretched out his hand to us. It was for us to return that manly clasp, so freely given. To those of little faith, to those who quibbled and meandered, to those mean, weak souls who asked why, if the last war had been such an outstanding success, we found ourselves in this hour of need to which he had referred, he would only reply, with all the moderation at his command, that it might be that we were no longer a great power, except in a moral sense ; it might be that we had come out of our heroic struggle a poor country, instead of the rich land that we had been, a poor country divided as never before in our history ; it might be that in the course of it we had lost both the Empire and the enterprise which had built it up — but what did that count for, when we held in the other scale, the friendship of this true German, this good man — a man we had honourably defeated in the last war, and who had now returned, as if from the dead, to help us win the next ? Hitler — Herr Hitler alone and his immense influence — could enable us to build up that vast German army which was essential both to preventing war and to winning it when it came. A powerful German army was an integral part of — he would go further, and say a guarantee of — World

Peace. (Here occurred a cowardly interruption from the back of the hall from which the speech was relayed: it sounded something like 'Then why was it our object in the last one to destroy it?' After order had been restored, the great orator continued amid mounting applause.) 'Policy, I am glad to say, is guided by feeling, not by cold reason. True patriotism rests on no such selfish, feeble and petty foundation as intellect or commonsense. To put a question of the sort which the heckler, who has now been removed, put to me is unpatriotic in the highest degree — in war-time it is possible to deal with that kind of person — that is one of the advantages of war.' (Loud cheers and laughter.) Unfortunately, he went on, we could not employ those methods in times of peace, so he must content himself with saying that it was people like the man who had put that question, who had nearly brought Britain low. In the past, it might be that he and Adolf Hitler had had their differences (more laughter and cheers), but now he gave him Britain's hand of friendship. With him at our side, we could, in the war that was so surely coming — that terrible war, and he warned his countrymen that the enemy would use every trick, every cruelty, every devilish device at his command, to break our will and crush our resistance — and that we were already standing on a trapdoor, with a rope round our necks, and our heads protruding from the block of the guillotine, while at any time we might be stoned to death — but, he repeated, with that great German at our side to succour and support, we would fight as we had never fought before: we would fight on the beaches, in the bathing-pools, from the telegraph wires and the telephone booths, in the — at this point the audience grew so elated at the attractive prospect held out to it (for it had been taught during the past decade or two to confound suffering and stress with virtue) that the closing words of the speech were lost in a hurricane of cheering, which jarred the ears equally of lonely men on islands in the Pacific, and of mobs in the teeming cities.

The truth was, perhaps, that by now everyone was growing a little muddled in mind. Russia denounced Britain and America as Fascist powers with a brutal ideology. Britain and America denounced the new Fascism they saw arising in Russia. General Franco called for a statement of the Rights of Man. In the House of Lords, Lord Vansittart named Hitler as a Communist agent, and accused Victor Curtis-Deane of sheltering him and being the most dangerous of our enemies. He should, he added, either be deported to Russia or interned here without trial. The Comintern met in Sofia, and publicly welcomed the news that Hitler had reappeared : but he remained in the Argentine, and refused to take part in national or international politics. When he had given the world a chance to adopt him as its head, it had rejected him. . . . He saw now his mistake ; he had been intended as a great teacher, not as a statesman or general, so he preferred to remain henceforth immersed in formulating his doctrines, and to be a leader on the esoteric and hermetical plane.

Disputes raged and became still more numerous, and no-one at first knew upon whom to fasten the blame for this deterioration of feeling and the attending tumult — until suddenly Russia identified those who were responsible, and Malenkov ordered an immediate purge of all painters, musicians and writers : a development which America, Britain and the Western Powers emulated, convinced that out of it would ensue a general improvement in feeling and morale. It was agreed that in future only Hitler, Churchill and the President of the United States should be allowed to exhibit pictures in public. Thus in the end everyone except the artists — and Victor Curtis-Deane who, as a suspect Communist, could obtain no employment on any paper except the *Daily Worker* (for which he did not want to write) — was the better off for Hitler's return : because to win him to their cause, which neither side could ever achieve, and to prove how truly peace-loving they were, consumed much of the energy that would otherwise have been expended on preparations for war.

It is time now to leave the glittering beach where we were talking, and to climb the steps to the hotel : but as we mount, and the view becomes more extensive, it is difficult not to continue the story, along one line or another ; more difficult still not to wonder what similar impossibilities the future may not hold for us. Who can tell ; whom can we trust to prophesy ? Certainly not the politicians who turn by turn have led us down to where we are — perhaps the fortune-tellers, the magicians. . . . Let us survey a few of them.

CHAPTER IV

MAGICIANS

ONE drawback to living in a hotel is that, since, if it is to be well run, the proprietors are obliged to maintain a large permanent staff of workmen, there are often not enough necessary jobs for them, and in consequence, because employers always hate to pay for idle hands, work, unnecessary work, has to be found for them. Thus some repair, often totally redundant, is always in progress, with the accompanying sounds of hammering and shouting, or the men are made to paint a wall or ceiling, which otherwise would pass for years, and to waft round the whole building the concomitant smell. This very morning, upstairs — it is one of the peculiarities of the hotel in which I am staying that the monks who so many centuries ago erected it for their own use, designed it in such a way that you enter at the top floor, on a level with the terrace, and thence progress downwards into the heart of the rock of which it seems part — upstairs, I was saying, a gay band of painters and paper-hangers was at work in the wide, white corridor, and, as a result, the smell of paint and of size vanquished the competing fragrance borne in from the orange-trees outside, and would continue to hover in the air for many subsequent days. Visitors would complain as usual, and the hotel management would reply by practising their own magic, in which they doubtless did not themselves believe, but which it was hoped would calm the guests, a long straw in a pail full of cold water, or an onion cut in half and swinging on a string. But paper-hangers and painters care nothing for popularity ; and in Southern Europe they are by their very nature a gay, insouciant race of extroverts. Today, their olive-green Neapolitan faces wore the broadest and whitest of smiles, and their dress invested them with a certain functional dandyism : loose white clothes, further blanched with splashes of whitewash, and on their heads high hats or shakos made of pale, stiff paper, or of newspaper, but very stylish when tilted forward at the correct angle on the forehead. Some of the workmen, armed with a long brush fastened to a bamboo, were first daubing paste on large flat rectangular strips of paper, which they proceeded, when they had finished, to slap on to the walls, while others stood on trestles or swung in cradles hung aloft, and from this altitude attacked the cornice and ceiling, from time to time calling to one another, when not occupied in singing with melodious light voices snatches of local *canzonette*. They seemed bird-men of the upper air, thus clad and occupying these positions, or resembled so many Punchinellos, the traditional figures of a neighbourhood where even the brigands of the early nineteenth century had affected such masks and costume, except that in their general air the painters and paper-hangers are more lively, less heavily jocose and clumsily bawdy, and manifest an indefinable personal style. But then, as I have said, they are an elegant and happy tribe the world over.

In Peking, for example — I speak of 1934 —, they adopted a style apart and identifiable. Most of the workers in China wore blue clothes, but theirs were of a very light blue, worn with a round blue hat, and they seemed always to be laughing as they worked, even though in latter times their status must have fallen ; since, under the Ming Emperors, their trade was considered to be so important that they possessed their own quarter, Pasteboard Lane or Piao Pei Hutung. It was the custom then to paper the walls and ceilings of palaces and mansions with pictures of dragons and tigers, phoenixes, birds, lions, bears, flowers, leaves and insects. And, we are told, each creature or object depicted carried its appropriate complement, so that, for example, a dragon had to be matched with a phoenix, a crane had to be allied to a deer, a flower with a butterfly. Even historically so short a time ago as when I was in China, the paper-hangers in Peking had succeeded once more in widening the scope of their profession, and had become expert practitioners in a luxury trade that was in constant demand among the wealthy dead, as among their bereaved living.[1] They

[1] *In Search of Old Peking*, by L. C. Arlington and William Lewisohn. (Peking, 1935.)

cut out of paper, for instance, and coloured realistically the shapes of houses, boats, carriages, horses, pots containing flowering trees, the trunks gnarled and crooked in the Chinese convention, rare fruits and succulent dishes, thus imaging in turn all the symbols of the life of rich people who loved pleasure. These decorations were then carried in the funeral procession, and later ceremonially burned, so that the departed spirits would be able to lead in the next world the same hedonistic existence to which they were accustomed in this : (no doubt by now the revolutionary government has changed all this, and decreed fair shares for all, after death as well as during life). But we must now halt no longer by the wayside, but continue the rather circuitous, not to say circumlocutory, route along which I am leading the reader, by way of Amalfi and then of the paper-hangers' lane, to the Peking Observatory near by, and so to the magic of which I wrote in the last chapter, and which was both the chief origin and business of this office.

I visited the Observatory during one of my last days in Peking, on a hot noon in late May 1934. Throughout the whole vast region of North China, and perhaps especially in the Great City itself, winter turns almost in a day to flaming summer. Trees break their leaves and fruit-trees blossom impulsively and without stint over every wall, and the mauve and odorous torches of the lilac glow within every courtyard, its entrance guarded by a dragon-screen. The rose already blossoms, and as Tun Li Ch'en writes, the shouts of the vendors of this flower come now loudly, now softly.

It is, in fact, summer, high summer, and not spring. The city seems to have become lost in a forest, or transmuted to a vast encampment of green tents pitched for protection against the Gobi Desert, which even at this season, and indeed throughout the year, is apt to send on the speed of its winds detachments of tall, whirling dust-devils, to gyrate in columns and spirals and dance like dervishes in every open space, in the calm cloistered garden of a temple, in the great courts of the Forbidden City, and among the litter and rags of meaner places. Now today, above the tree-tops in which no leaf stirs, you can only perceive the painted eaves and orange or blue glazed tiles of a temple, or the stout towers and magnificent roofs of the Forbidden City : all else, the whole mud-coloured one-storey metropolis, appears to be woodland, and the shards, the fragments of discarded clothing and nameless relics of squalor are hidden by green shadows, just as effectually as they were in another earlier part of the year, when the old houses of brown-grey brick were opposed to the general flashing whiteness, which gave every twig, black and cold as iron, a new value, and when figures in padded clothes plodded along in a strange perspective against the gleaming nullity of the snow. Yet even today, when Peking looks its best, it would be difficult at first glance to estimate the importance of this building on the city wall, or to gauge its place in world history — as difficult as, equally, to comprehend that the sad and dusty quarter in which it stands was formerly no less famous for its man-made gardens than for its natural beauty, that the dry ditch you pass on the way was once the celebrated P'ao Tzu Ho or Bubbling Stream, and the course of its clear water, which sprang from the Jade Fountain in the Western Hills, was carefully and elegantly planted, and continued a favourite place for picnics, both in summer and winter, in the long, golden days of the Ming Emperors. Among these pleasances stood several temples, but of these nothing now survives. The Observatory alone has outlived all the features of the district to which it belongs, and this fact by itself might be sufficient to afford a stimulus to the imagination: but there are other reasons for it as well, since here, Science, as so often, was born of Superstition: in more than one sense, for, as I have pointed out,[1] when Kubla Khan created Kanbalu, or the modern city of Peking, the position of every building in the Forbidden City was first most carefully calculated by geomancy. How much more industriously must the sorcerers have employed these methods before choosing the site of a building erected under the next dynasty for the purpose of observing the heavenly bodies, and among other purposes, therefore, for casting horoscopes for the Emperor and members of the Imperial Family. Many of the ancient instruments have disappeared, but others still stand. The two armillary spheres in bronze, constructed by the great Chinese astrologer Kuo Shen-Ching, were temporarily not to be seen. Their history in recent years had been chequered: they were seized by the Germans after the Boxer outbreak, then returned to Peking under the Treaty of Versailles; removed from Peking by Chiang

[1] See *Escape With Me!*

Kai-Shek's Government to Nanking, and subsequently once more given back to the Observatory, in, I think, 1935, the year after my visit. I do not know their fate under the Communist Government, but probably model tractors have been substituted. . . . The two small copper cisterns that are set up in the little east garden are the vestigial relics of the famous water-clock which was made under the orders of an Emperor of the Ming Dynasty, and which Edkins [1] mentions as still being in perfect condition in his day. Most of the instruments which are yet standing belong to a later epoch, having been fashioned in the 1670s by the renowned Jesuit priest and astronomer Father Ferdinand Verbiest at the command of the Emperor K'ang Hsi.

Those that remain are to be found on a terrace level with the top of the city wall, and from this spot to-day, when no wind stirred the green leaves, no sound was borne up to one : unless it was the gentle, regular beating of a gong, which at times I thought I could just distinguish. This gleaming trail of sound would denote the passage of a blind fortune-teller, making his way along a distant alley, and pausing no doubt, every now and then, to lean on his long staff, while he beats the gong which he carries in his right hand. And this faint music, whether substantive or imagined, combined with the scientific instruments, caused one to revert, and to reflect once more how, in every part of the world, but particularly here in Peking, science had been born, almost accidentally, of superstition, and each, because of the shame felt at the close connection,

[1] J. Edkins, *Description of Peking* (1898).

was fated to persecute and destroy the other in succeeding ages. In the city of Kanbalu, the city of the Great Khan, as it was then called, Marco Polo tells us that among 'Christians, Saracens and Cathayans there were about five thousand astrologers and soothsayers'. They possessed their own astrolabes, and Kubla provided for them so that they could spend their time in the exercise of their art. It must indeed have seemed a paradise to them, and the spiritualist of today must long for a similar leniency and patronage.

In Europe, too, the Philosopher's Stone was the superstitious matrix from which ungrateful science was cut, and as late as the reign of Queen Elizabeth both science and magic were practised together. For instance, the eminent Doctor Dee, who was Queen Elizabeth's physician, and invented the pocket-watch, was highly interested in magic and practised rudimentary spiritualism. That he had in earlier years dabbled in conjuring tricks and sleight of hand had long surrounded his name with an aroma of charlatanism ; but there was more in it than that : I possess at Renishaw an object which claims to be a magic speculum used by him. It consists of a flat black oval pronounced by a geologist to whom I submitted it to be 'an *Artificial Lead Glass*, whose main components are lead oxide, soda or potash, and silica'. Such glasses, he added, had been made from very early times and were quite distinct from obsidian. In fact it is a mirror of dark glass, and in its depths the Doctor and his medium, Kelly, the sinister Irishman, who always wore a black skull-cap crammed down on his head so as to hide the fact that his ears had been cropped for felony, may have gazed in order to call up spirits who would foretell the future.

With this and other magic implements the two men made the round of the European courts, telling the fortunes of the reigning dynasts, the Emperor Rudolf and the King of France, for example. What can they have seen as the future of those strange beings, so splendid yet so sombre in ruff and doublet or in armour that they seemed to match some other element than air? Nothing, I think, for the Doctor was deceived and Kelly was inventive. I have myself often peered into this same glass, wondering what might be revealed, but I have seen nothing but an infinite perspective of polished darkness and muted reflections. . . . Nevertheless, all writers contain within them some native and inevitable sense of, and skill in, reading the future: thus at the beginning of this book, written some six months ago, I was concerned with coming efforts to reach the moon or Mars, — and today I read that a conference has been called in London, where, as I was sure would be the case, ex-enemy and Allied scientists 'collaborated in the most cordial spirit', in order to take the first step towards space-travel: and after this announcement of their meetings, the news followed that the conveners received more than five thousand offers from men and women anxious to shake off the shackles of the earth, and to be among the first to essay such a voyage. Yet nothing of this had occurred when that first chapter was written. . . . But I must return, to finish for the reader the unedifying story of Doctor Dee and Kelly. For many years their collaboration continued until at last Kelly revealed that the spirits had decreed that he and the Doctor should for a time exchange wives : but this pronouncement so infuriated the good Mrs. Dee, who had for long suffered from the friendship between the two men, that she turned Kelly out of the house, and he was banished for ever. . . . In more recent years Hitler was known to have an astrological forecast of influences and impending events executed for him, and handed to him every morning by his pet magician, so that he could act in accordance with its revelation, and take advantage of the chances and equally avoid the dangers it revealed. And it has been said, too, that Sir Winston Churchill, knowing Hitler's weakness in this respect, and wishing to benefit from it, had a horoscope of each day similarly prepared for himself, according to identical principles, and laid on his desk every morning, so that he could gauge Hitler's mood, and follow as far as possible the involved and intricate workings of the German War Leader's mind and the probable direction of his actions. . . . But today in general, the two streams have parted ; the atom and hydrogen bombs have become man's adult responsibility and are not to be attributed to the Devil of his infancy. Fortune-tellers are no longer — or very seldom — supported by the state : though I read that in Burma the day chosen for the Declaration of National Independence had been selected by astrologers in their state liveries, and that when the morning came, the newly acquired status was proclaimed by magicians clad in scarlet robes blowing upon rams' horns. . . . But for the most part, as I was saying, Science and Superstition, now mortal enemies, but once combined in a single form — as the Greeks held that men and women had in the beginning been one shape split in two —, have parted company for ever. Or so it seems. But the truth is, perhaps, that though the scales in which they are weighed differ in every age, yet you cannot kill either Superstition or Science, and one will continue to be confused with the other, and to be extracted from the other : so that some belief, such as the very old tenet that plants, if they grow with the waxing moon, prosper particularly, will in time be explained on a rational level of moon-rays and the like.

No doubt, however, even today in Peking under Communist rule, Superstition only lies hidden in the cocoon of fear from which it ever and again emerges. Or it may be more open : the blind man may still sound his obscure way through the back lanes, to tell the future of his clients by feeling the lines incised on the hand ; the soothsayer at the fair held in the courtyard of a vast, deserted monastery, now nationalised or become a labour exchange, may still pour sand on the ground, to predict the future by the way its grains fall, or he may throw down a handful of beans or nuts for the same purpose of divination. But the oldest of all methods, and said to be the most precise as well as the most difficult, is that of reading the lines of the face.

I have never known in my life any experience more embarrassing, even intimidating, than to be the object of the bland golden stare, so unyieldingly impersonal, of a face-diviner intent on his science. . . . The magician was brought into the courtyard of my house in the

Tartar City: he at once sat down, cross-legged, and at a lower level than where I was sitting. With eyes that never wandered and never blinked, he peered up at me, beginning at the chin, and working very slowly to the top of the forehead, reading the face as if it were a map, tallying every line in the face with another, so that after he had finished the upward reading, his eyes would then flicker from a line near the mouth to one by the ear, so as to test the connection or solve the contradiction that he thought he saw between them. After a time he began to talk, and my friend, C. M. Macdonald, then the *Times* Correspondent in Peking and my landlord, stood by us to translate for me. In a year's time, the diviner said, I should 'grow a moustache' (this phrase in Chinese, I was told, signified that I should become Prime Minister or Leader of the Government). He also prophesied the birth of several sons in the coming years. They would, he declared, eventually attain distinction, though at first inclined 'to go to the east when I told them to go to the west': in other words, they would be headstrong and wayward. . . . And one thing he predicted truly: that in the space of a few years I should be involved in a celebrated lawsuit which I should win. (In 1941 I was obliged to bring, in conjunction with my brother and sister, a libel action, in which we were victorious, against *Reynolds News*.) The art of deducing the future of an individual from the lines of his face is perhaps not very far removed from phrenology, if it is applied to future events instead of being employed solely for the delineation of character.

Phrenology was in the latter part of the nineteenth

century a popular and accepted form of fortune-telling; the truth being, perhaps, that any system of scanning the future is as good as another, always providing that a genuine gift inspires it: and remembering always that you are more likely to predict the future, if you try to predict it, than if you do not so attempt: out of dust, sand, tea-leaves, coffee-grounds, falling nuts, the flight of birds, sciomancy, crystal-gazing, astrology and the lines of hand and face, the true psychic may be able to reveal something true: the false prophets will never extract anything but falsehood from whatever technical medium they use. The truth is, alas, that fashion prevails in fortune-telling, as in all else, religion included. Phrenology was the psychic mode at one time. And I recollect that I came across the end of this fashion, as of so many others, at Scarborough. There a phrenologist plied his trade all the year in a room that looked like a tent, in one of the more derelict streets of the old town. He had obtained some reputation. All the summer his booth would receive one visitor after another, and he would feel the bumps on their heads and prophesy. But in the winter, when the waves flapped their threatening seagulls' wings over the quays, and their spray filled the air and penetrated to the streets of the town, and the scream of sea-birds filled the ears, then he would sit for long hours, waiting. And so one day, taking advantage of the knowledge, my sister, at the age of sixteen, visited the magician. She found a middle-aged man, whose face was of a melancholy cast, and of a considerable, almost feminine refinement. His hands were delicate, with long and sensitive fingers, very clearly articulated, while his cranium, baldly swelling out of a fringe of greying hair, seemed to offer him a perfect field for his own practice. He examined her head carefully, and at the end told her that she would one day be a famous poet : though at that time she had as yet written no single verse, and he, I would take it, must have been unused to feeling the heads of members of so rare a sept.

Soothsayers like to work in seaside towns, to which flock foolish visitors in good mood, who only, many of them, come for the day, so that the magician has never seen them before, and will, he thanks his stars, never see them again, to be told of the failure of his predictions. To balance the success I have described, I must now record how lately, in an attempt to recover from a bout of influenza, I stayed for a few days in a seaside resort, and there consulted a professional diviner of the future. . . . I was sitting on the pier, sheltered by a glass screen, on which the dried spray had left elusive patterns, and was reading a novel in a desultory, post-influenzal way, when suddenly I saw a man unlock the door of a fortune-teller's den — I had previously examined the window which detailed his accomplishments — and on impulse I followed him. He was small and dark as a gypsy, and regarded me in a business-like manner. He proceeded to offer me his various lines, hand-reading for ten shillings, cards fifteen, crystal-gazing a pound : or a special combination for thirty shillings. I decided on a simple hand-reading. After a scrutiny of both hands, he looked fixedly at me and said, 'You are very well known ! You have carved out a career for yourself and are famous. . . . You are on the boards. You are a music-hall star!'

I was rather disappointed, but after all, he was a professional fortune-teller, not a magician. . . . Only twice have I met convinced and self-styled magicians, one, an unhappy man whose magic made him happy; a consumptive who, as his hold on the physical world round him grew weaker, became ever more convinced that it grew stronger in a world to which very few, and very favoured, possessed the key. This was, of course, one of the delusions induced by his decline; but it rendered him both excited and contented. In that absolute dominion of his, he comprehended secrets, he told me, incommunicable to others: though he was privileged to correspond with the illuminated few, who, like himself, had been chosen. The esoteric knowledge of which he was the master had been derived, he alleged, from very ancient manuscripts discovered a few years previously in Constantinople — and my mind reverted to him, though long dead, when I met my second Wise Man, by accident, singularly enough, in that very city, in the Grand Bazaar. . . .

It was a May afternoon, and I recall the look of it. The dome of the sky was very blue, the sun flashed out with all the ardour of the latitude, gilding the city, turning even its many dusty and deserted places to gold, yet the wind still swept down, as it had for a whole month, from the steppes and tundras. It was cold, very cold, and, in spite of the sky, the waters of the Bosphorus were grey and ruffled. Only the innumerable judas-trees of the city spoke of the spring: for they were in their full flower, small clusters of magenta blossoms resembling the flower of the vetch loading down the end of each branch, and in their exuberance even outlining the leafless arms. . . . Inside the Grand Bazaar it was warm, with a stuffy, airless, mid-Victorian heat, and an unpleasant lingering smell. In its long round-roofed corridors that resemble cement railway tunnels, a hot nineteenth-century gloom still prevailed, and even the multitudinous goods displayed with such ability by the vendors, who called your attention to them as you passed, even the representatives of so many different races who throng here, even the colours of the silks, the shapes of the furniture, the thousand attractions that were offered, did not prevent the scene from being depressing : the very atmosphere proclaimed that you were in an obsolete place of business in a defunctive city, the buildings of which by themselves emphasised that every earthly glory comes to an end, and that all is vanity except the ever-glowing core of truth. Nevertheless from this sentiment the passing moment drew a special clarity and light. And the spectacle in the Bazaar offered its own interest and beauty. Best of all was the part devoted to jewellery. This tunnel differed from the others : it was larger, and behind the stalls long stone seats mounted, as in a Roman or Greek theatre, though here not towards a cerulean sky, but to a dark and dusty roof. The surrounding dinginess, withal, perhaps enhanced the sparkle of the jewels, scintillating under the artificial light : branches of flowers in precious stones or paste, stars and decorations awarded by the Sultans in their day, brooches and uncut gems, all competed with one another in hue and radiance. I noticed at one stall, hanging from hooks on screens that stood above the display on the counter, several eighteenth-century watches, apparently made in France for the harem market : for they were plainly of French workmanship though the faces carried Arabic numerals. These watches showed a wide variety of taste : their shells were often not only magnificent, but mechanically elaborate, so as to help the idle spend the time before they read it ; but that which I liked best was contained in an outer shell of bloodstone. I looked at it attentively, and noticed that the price of it was marked plainly in ink on a label attached to it : in itself an unusual circumstance. All the same I expected to have to bargain for it, for this was the prevalent practice in all oriental cities : moreover, I was accustomed to it, having lived much in Italy, where, however, the competition did not so much resemble a battle for life or death between adversaries — it did here — as an exercise of skill, founded on a knowledge of real values and greatly enjoyed both by winner and loser. . . . I enquired of a vigorous-looking man who stood by the stall, without a hat, but with a shock of black hair standing upright, which added greatly to his natural piratical appearance, what the price might be. He must, I concluded, be the shopman, though he had made no effort to sell me anything, and now that I addressed him returned no answer. In spite of the want of interest he evinced, I went on talking, making offers, until a figure sitting behind and above the stall, at the level of the proprietor's head, on one of the stone tiers I have mentioned, rose to his feet and spoke to me. In the obscurity I had not noticed him, but now I beheld a most impressive apparition, a very tall man, with a handsome aquiline face, and with dark eyes, melancholy but yet burning with a fire of their own. His long beard was black and glossy, with a touch of Bluebeard's blue in it, and he wore a flowing black cloak and a wide-brimmed black hat. It was impossible to tell to what race he belonged. He might have been a Syrian, a Turk, a Spaniard or a Sicilian. In a voice without accent, yet by its intonation plainly foreign, he said, pointing to the stall-keeper,

'It is of no use trying to bargain with him. He is the one man here who never varies his prices.'

Startled by this interposition, I enquired, 'Who are you?'

To my question, I received the proud and unusual answer, 'I am a magician!'

The stranger, however, though I pressed him, would divulge no more about himself: but it was a reply in some fashion appropriate to the background, and to the city in which it had been given.

. . . . . .

Of communal or co-operative magic I have seen, no doubt in company with many other travellers, an instance in North Africa. Whilst staying at Kairouan, I visited the Zaouias of Aissaouia; a Mohammedan sect the members of which indulge in special customs and inherit strange traditions. After you have once seen a gathering of them, subsequently you can always tell one who belongs to this group by the peculiar air of pointless ferocity he will affect, and by his eyes which will reflect a fearful emptiness of thought and feeling; a vacant dullness, induced, it is said — or, if natural to the subject, still further emphasised — by a perpetual state of semi-intoxication that results from drinking the juice distilled from one particular cactus. . . . The Hall of the Zaouias is not far from the famous Grand Mosque of Kairouan, and offers a comment, as it were, on those parabolas of marble pillars, resurrected from Roman soil, and compelled to support so barbarously a Moslem roof, like the Cathedral of Córdoba, which has a similar origin. Yet it is of supreme interest, in the quality of beauty it offers. The very clustering of the pillars, the sheer number of them, the wasteful but singular manner in which they have been treated, all go to make a memorable impression: the traveller, who comes into the building not knowing what to expect, finds himself lost in a petrified forest, where each dead tree that obscures the view is of a different kind. Though the men who erected it were in several directions most civilised, the mosque remains, nevertheless, the sort of edifice which would have been constructed to the order of the Moor in *Petrouchka*. The underlying barbarism has survived the disappearance of the race of Arabs who built this great place of worship, and is to be felt strongly — much more strongly, and for reasons that soon become obvious — in the Hall of the Zaouias.

I approached it at night, alighting in a courtyard full of palm-trees, and entered a rather darkly lit and lofty apartment. There I watched a line of men, younger and older — some still boys, some ancient, all of them naked above the waist, — linked together, with arms round each other's neck and shoulders, dance in a line, with a strongly stressed broken rhythm, continuing for about an hour, meanwhile chanting jumbled choruses, until they had reached some further state of incoherence and mumbo-jumbo stupidity. They rolled their eyes as if scarcely conscious, and their heads nodded and jerked. There prevailed soon a genuine sense of evil, if dark, dull evil, that was unmistakable ; as though some spirit, not wholly developed and remaining in its essence brutal, controlled them communally : but as the evening proceeded, you felt too, and in contradiction of this, that some fraud was being practised — though I do not know in what it consisted. After they had by chant — it cannot be called a song — and by the rhythm of their movements attained to an even further state of absolute trance-like fatuousness, that yet was combined with a certain insane state of excitement, the older men, the adepts, unlinked their arms and let the younger ones continue their dance separately. They then took from a table the leaves of a prickly pear — not the fruit, but the flat, disc-like leaves covered with bristles hard as steel needles —, and offered them to the neophytes to eat. The youths stopped their whirlings and with an overwhelming eagerness began to munch and gobble this substance, a more fitting food for the leather jaws of dinosaur or pterodactyl. After this — as it subsequently proved, only the first part of an unusual meal — was over, they began again to dance separately, lolling their heads and rolling their dull round eyes all the time, as they spun in loutish ecstasy. When these gyrations became less frantic, they were served with the next and last course, each of the boys being given several large portions of jagged, broken glass. This, too, they consumed with every outward sign of enjoyment, savouring it, as it were, and then noisily champing it.

As I watched them, I wondered how far this unusual diet was a trick, and how nearly it might be related to a performance I had often seen in London many years before, at the fair that used to be held behind the Mile End Road. There, before it had been burnt down, had stood Wonderland, and gradually the open space had accumulated other uses : a Jewish music-hall had come into being there, at the back, and the rest of it was taken up — I speak of the years immediately preceding 1914 — with tents and booths. In one of them, the inside lining of which, I remember, was composed of Union Jacks, sat the impressive female who had won the title of *The Fattest Woman in the World.* She wore an exiguous bathing-dress and the whole of the exposed portions of her vast anatomy was covered with designs in tattoo. Over the great sweeping canvas of what should have been the small of her back, rolled an English landscape, with cows coming home past a windmill and by water-meadows to the Manor Farm : each thigh, the pillar of some temple, was a Medusa-like writhing of red and blue serpents, while her shoulders revealed a sacred subject, conventionally treated, and her arms were coyly encircled with a neat design of blue convolvulus and pink roses. . . . But, next door to her, I was intending to say, in a booth devoid of patriotic decoration, lived a giant, more gently tattooed, but, for all that, a titanic confusion of serpents and anchors and hands clasped in a friendly grip, and with a list of names stretching successively from shoulder to wrist, recording, without apparent regret, the order in which one fair rival had supplanted another : Molly, Mary, Daisy, Ethel, Doris, Mildred, Popsy, Rose, another Doris, Ada, Alice, Violet, indicated that all men, even giants, are fickle. First he allowed the spectator, who had paid the required fee of 2d., to admire him as he flexed his biceps, that were like the mountains in a contour map, then he lifted weights with a ponderous rather shaky mien. After this — for he was versatile — he breathed flames out of his mouth like a human dragon, and then he set to and enjoyed his evening meal of broken glass. During this repast, consumed with a certain ostentation, his eyes revealed the same emptiness, as of a room garnished but about to be invaded by devils, that I now noticed in the lack-lustre orbs of the dance team that was performing for me here at Aissaouia, once more rolling and nodding their heads and jerking their bodies : for they had begun to dance again and to grow more agitated, while my mind wandered. They whirled, moaned and hit their trunks. Then suddenly they stopped, and the older men, taking wooden mallets, hammered wooden pegs through the thin flesh above the shoulders of the neophytes. The repetitive noise of the blows blunted the cries of pleasure. Plainly they did not suffer at all but gloried in their affliction.

Magic, even of so low an order, is rare today, though

the rumour of it existed in South, and especially South-Eastern, Europe until the war. . . . I remember, for example, that in Greece, the proprietor of a hotel situated among the ruins of a famous holy place, now remote and lonely, had won more than a local celebrity as a werewolf. Superstitious people would relate how he had been seen and heard howling round the precincts at the time of the full moon, and that on one occasion a guest in the hotel, his ears catching this noise, looked out, and seeing what appeared to be a large wolf just beneath his window, had hurled a soap-dish at the brute and had cut its head open. At this there was a tremendous ululation, and the animal raced away. But the next morning and for several days subsequently, the proprietor was seen to be wearing a bandage round his head : a story which, though very absurd, gained wide credence. . . . Howbeit, when I was staying in the hotel with a party of friends in 1933, I recollect that one of them, Berners, who knew this tale, was determined to take no risks, and believed in the efficacy of shock tactics, on distinguishing the proprietor's footsteps soon after midnight approaching his room, threw the door open and there revealed himself clad in blue pyjamas, on all fours on the floor, wildly barking. . . . The proprietor, werewolf or no werewolf, had, Berners told me, seemed in no whit disconcerted ; he had not howled back in reply, but had said most politely, as he passed by, and as if noticing nothing unusual, 'Good morning, m'lord'.

In Italy I have seen more than one reputed witch. And in Sicily, when out for a walk, I have watched a magician of a simple kind. We heard a blast on a trumpet, and made our way towards the sound. After a moment we found ourselves in an open space between grey rocks, and there, surrounded by staccato vegetation, by prickly pears, striking their strange, static attitudes, and agaves like ocean weeds — the haunt, they might be, of octopuses — stood a youth with a tangle of black curls and a conical black felt hat, like those worn by peasants in Pinelli's drawings of a hundred and thirty years ago, or now sometimes affected on the screen by Chico Marx. His face was olive-skinned and bore an expression of faunal wildness : he might in other days have posed to an Italian master for a portrait of St. John the Baptist. He could not have been in his pitch long, for no-one had arrived yet to consult him, so he took up his short wooden trumpet, which, like a huntsman, he carried slung round him, and blew another call — this time a fanfare, cacophonous yet lively, that made the rocks tremble. . . . Soon we heard footsteps, and some peasants hurriedly arrived to have their fortunes told for the sum of ten centesimi. The youth would firmly press his thumb on the rubber stopper of a glass bottle about a foot high, and full of clear water, that surmounted the small brass-studded casket that stood by him on the ground. At this pressure a small devil, made of red glass, would drop down from his hiding-place at the top of the bottle, and sink to its depths : simultaneously, a small drawer in the casket shot open, and presented the client with a printed programme of his future, couched in terms designed to appeal to Sicilian peasants:

the orange crop would prove to be tremendous, he would inherit a painted cart from Great-Uncle Pancrazio ; the favourite cow would get well and next year safely produce a female calf. . . . From the South of France, where pagan traditions run deep, in the land between Marseilles and Spain, cases are occasionally reported in the press in which black magic is involved, or witchcraft. And in Ravello, above where I am writing, there was a famous story of black magic about a century and a half ago. . . . But now there is no feeling of it in the air. All is limpid and full of heart. Snatches of Neapolitan *canzonette* still float down to my room from where the painters and paper-hangers, the white bird-men, float on their trestles. The smell of paint lingers and prospers. Everything is practical with an Italian practicality. The only magic that persists is the magic of the light on wall and tree and tower.

CHAPTER V

TOWERS

In Southern Italy each golden day of October is a separate summer, self-contained and with the cool rind of a ripe fruit. This morning it was the element of light again, of fire, rather than the sea, in spite of the expanse of it and its continual murmur, that dominated the scene. As I threw back the shutters and looked out, the great flame kindled on the mountains had spread as far as the hill opposite and had caught the broken top of the round stone tower that crowned it, the Castello di Puntone. And this was appropriate and of good augury, for today I propose to praise towers, to acclaim their beauties and oddities, and those of the cities, ancient and modern, which are composed of them.

When I was a child, the hopeful construction and the tragic fall of the Tower of Babel was my favourite pictorial theme, and I can see it now, with the happy and industrious ants building it so busily, and its spiral roadway that was planned to lead to the sky, though it still had far to go when the Tower fell. This was the doomed idealism of towers, akin in tragedy to that of the walls that never yet stopped invaders, the Great Wall of China, the Maginot Line, our own Roman Wall, the walls of many cities such as Troy. Always the fable of the Tower of Babel emphasises the dangers of planning and of illusion, and the proverbial fall of pride which brings such warm comfort to the hearts of the humble. Its fall was as fatal to man as that of Adam and Eve, and the collapse of the League of Nations was a kind of anniversary celebration of it, while the plain faults of the successor to that body perhaps herald another. The Tower of Babel, however, one could examine only in pictures, though to a child they seemed tremendously convincing, but I will write shortly of towers I have seen and their history. So let me now sweep the harp-strings with my hand and sing in honour of them.

Of towers I sing: of towers, steeples, minarets, spires, turrets, cupolas, *campanili*, belfries, pagodas, pyramids and skyscrapers — this last a fine exaggerative term worthy of its significance. I have passed on their mountain of rock the ruined towers of Acro-Corinth, situated above the city of sweet grapes and acanthus leaves carved in stone: I have seen the Giralda, that tower that rears itself so elegantly above the narrow streets of Seville, with their wine-shops full of enormous tuns of amontillado and manzanilla, and its patios and orange gardens, and beds of the largest violets in the world, and I have seen the Giralda's counterpart in

Kairouan, of which I have just written, still unconverted from the Moslem faith, pointing towards the dull, hot sky of Africa. I have lived in the Tower of London, — my bedroom looked out on the back of the White Tower, once known as Julius Caesar's Tower — and know well the frosty splendour of its autumn mornings, the foggy darkness of its nights, and the shadows that linger hauntingly under its gates and portcullises. I have raised up my eyes with delight to the tall tree — though because of the height at which it grows, it looks from the ground but a weed or a bush — that decorates the top of one of Lucca's marble towers, turned golden by the accumulated lichen of many hundreds of years. By the most prosaic grey light of a dull morning, I have walked under the bulging minarets of Constantinople, built at the order of some turbaned Bluebeard of a Sultan out of the remnants of Byzantine churches, and I have seen the Palace of the Popes at Avignon by moonlight, first coming across it in the darkness of an alley at its very side, so that when I happened to glance up at the sky, my eye following the perpendicular run of the line towards the great splendour of the moon, was quite unprepared for the leaping loftiness that it encountered. In the country outside Peking I have wandered along the desolate paths of winter, past deserted pagodas, when under the eaves of each tapering storey the bells that hung from them, rippled by a sudden clout of wind, have seemed to play a song of spring, fragile and shrill as the first buds on a tree. I have noted how the shell-like spires of Wren's churches in the Strand bear themselves so proudly against the smoky red sky of a London sunset in October, and have climbed to the upper chambers of the towers of the Alhambra at Granada, built in a brick the colour of a rather tawny rose (though many have celebrated the delicate majesty of its courtyards and gardens, few writers have praised the magnificence of its stout walls and towers) ; as a boy I beheld a lunar rainbow between the two great towers of Bologna, surely the tallest of all ancient buildings and a fit home for magicians and astrologers, and I have gazed up at the helmeted towers of Carcassonne, so full of wonder, whether their quality be due to Viollet-le-Duc or to some earlier architect ; I have looked with amazement at the fortress towers of Bodiam, and I have been able to examine at my leisure the domed cupolas of Angkor Vat, where bats in their segmented flight squeak in the corridors along the walls of which dancers dead these many hundreds of years perform in stone with living grace and vigour, and I have looked closely at the four sacred visages that smile so mysteriously from each of the fifty and more towers of the Temple of Bayon. I have watched the golden towers of Santiago de Compostela change their aspect as they are captured by the sweet Galician rains, and I have drawn near, across sandy plains dotted with agave and prickly pear, to the twin towers of Mexican churches and cathedrals, to Tenochtitlan, and to the Church of the Rosario in Puebla, with their reverberations from distant quarters, from Moorish Granada, from Churriguera and from the Aztecs, all joined together within mouldings that resemble worm-casts in pink stone or gold. I have looked with delight on many steeples and belfries in northern Europe, and have equally admired the lofty and intricate ruined towers of the city of Antigua in Guatemala, where the roofs of some churches now afford pasturage for grazing sheep, while large owls nest underneath them, above the pillars of the naves, and I have been astonished by the nautical architecture of the Tower of Belém outside Lisbon, from which Prince Henry the Navigator used to watch for the return of his ships after their expeditions of discovery. I have often watched the great *campanile* of Venice growing at many heights from the ground to its full stature, during the years it was being erected after its thousand years of existence had collapsed in a single instant in a cloud of dust. I have seen the tower of Westminster Cathedral lifting itself into the opalescent upper air of London, adding its own note to the sky-line, and, in the clear winter of Peking, I have visited the Bell Tower, the haunted Fox Tower, and the Drum Tower, refashioned half a millennium ago by the Emperor Yung Lo out of the materials of Kubla Khan's building of the same name — the Drum Tower in which stood for so long the famous water-clock known as *The Brass Thirsty Bird* —, and I have with joy watched the building of many new skyscrapers in New York, the greatest tower-city in the world.

As I was looking out of my window, I was saying, the sun just caught the top of the tower on the hill opposite and crowned it with gold — or was the whole building, rather, an illusion, a creation of the sun's ? — for one could not exist without the other, and, indeed, sometimes I have thought that the light of a country, the illumination of air and sea peculiar to it, may in fact have evoked its system of architecture. Certainly in Greece the sun has ever and again summoned up for me on rocks above the blue waters, varied by stretches of inlaid wine-purple and lime-green, the columns of temples that have their existence only for the moment that they appear to me. Similarly I have seen instantaneous gothic towers and tall pointed arches assemble themselves out of the misty twilight of northern Europe in winter, while in the arid and burning sands of Mediterranean Africa, cool, whitewashed Saracenic cloisters materialise in mirages as often as do pools and palm-trees. Even the crooked spire of Chesterfield church near my home, a landmark which is said to have derived its terrifying corkscrew twist from the Devil having wound his tail round it, might be a creation of the atmosphere, of the prevalent fogs and rains of the district, and the darkness which broods alike on its native coal-mines and moors, and might be an epitome of them. But this spire, the first unsuspecting glance at which has given so many persons a shock, almost of horror, is admired locally, I apprehend, not for its beauty — albeit the interior of the church is fine and contains the remarkable sequence of Foljambe tombs, now pushed away behind a new and hideous High Anglican altar — but on account of its tortuousness, since men of the north, by their very natures open and humble, like to be astonished, and therefore love the grotesque and the intricate (that is why they so admirably and lovingly built gothic cathedrals), the topiary garden cut and trained and cramped into endless reprehensible patterns and variations, while a tower that is out of plumb, is crooked or inclines more than it should, exercises in countries both northern and southern an irresistible fascination over the minds of the uneducated ; because the nature of its fault or deviation is factual, and therefore easily to be comprehended by those to whom esthetic qualities signify nothing. Twice two is four, but beauty is but a wayward thing. Thus the simple tourist will willingly visit the Leaning Tower of Pisa, and even climb up to the top of it, while to the same person the exquisite colour and fabulous delicacy of its arcading, and the whole marvel of that group of honey-gold buildings planted down in their flat green meadow — surely after the Piazza San Marco in Venice the most exquisite grouping and setting of any buildings in Italy — carry no message of amazement. He will not even, it may be, notice the leaden roofs, light yet solemn and dry in tone as the hide of an elephant, nor the gigantic stone lion that peers down, for no apparent reason, as if ready to spring, from a green thicket growing at the top of the robust walls of brick and stone that enclose the whole space.

Moreover, the Leaning Tower is scarcely tall enough for its position. In flat lands, Holland or Lincolnshire, towers must be very lofty to make an effect, or be set upon a hill, as are the towers of Lincoln and Durham cathedrals : but those of a smaller sort should only stand on crags, point an eminence, or crown the highest levels of terraced slopes. Here at Amalfi they seem only to be man's extensions of the natural limestone formation or framework of the landscape, suited to it as are the flowers to the soil they grow out of. Sometimes, even, turrets and cliffs seem to be the work of the same great architect. The round towers, higher on the hills, were mostly those that the nobles built for a refuge in troubled times, then there are the open-storeyed *campanili* of the churches, lighter constructions of three storeys, bearing a cupola at the top, and, lower down, the square, squat, battlemented towers built on rocks jutting out into the flat expanse of sea : but these, too, had their own purpose, and were — the majority of them having been erected in 1569 to 1570 by Master Pignoloso Cafaro of Cava — intended to carry sentries, who would watch the coast for Algerian or Turkish pirates, and give the inhabitants warning of the appearance of any strange vessel. Such for the most part are the towers of the whole neighbourhood, of Amalfi, Atrani and Ravello, that mountain city in miniature, which, when you reach it, opens up to show, disposed upon the hills round it, its own green system of life, of stone walls, vines and chestnut woods, poised aerially above the seagirt cities below. The tower of the cathedral at Ravello is beautiful, but still more so was the *campanile* of Amalfi, which, with its Romanesque and obvious Saracenic affiliations, with its green-tiled cupola and elegant eighteenth-century coat of plaster, painted in pink and white sugar-stick stripes, seemed to unite these warring influences into one warm and fragrant blossom. Alas, the purists, those new puritans, have at last succeeded in stripping it, to show the correct period brickwork underneath : but even today, though it has lost the quality, light and incommunicable as an aroma, that came from the friendly mingling of many centuries united in one faith, it yet exhales its own loveliness, and yet retains, as part of the polychrome decoration of the upper storey and cupola, the Saracenic tiles and Persian bowls that, inset like jewels, impart to the whole building an exotic air.

Among the towers that crown every rock here is one that tradition alleges to have been an outer tower of the Duchess of Amalfi's palace. It stands above the Val del Dragone on the road up to Ravello from Atrani, and though a deep chasm separates you from it, you can still nevertheless distinguish the green floors round it, edged with the foundations of their green walls, which were once palace rooms, poised precipitously above a sheer wall of rock, and now only to be reached by goats who crop the fragrant leaves of thyme and rosemary and other herbs. There, it may be, were enacted in real life the scenes that go to make up Webster's great play, *The Duchess of Malfi*. Now all physical splendour has departed, only the skeleton remains ; everything has gone except the echo. Echoes, like houses with windows for every day in the year, and like catacombs and leaning towers, are beloved of the packs and herds of innocent tourists of today. Therefore is an old man stationed at the side of the road nearest the rock across the valley, who, in the hope of financial benefit to himself, shouts over the chasm in the direction of the tower. You would think the unearthly grandeur of the landscape would deter him : but no ! He cups his hands and shouts, and the sound comes back instantly, magnified and transmuted.

> *Delio.* . . . This fortification
> Grew from the ruins of an ancient abbey ;
> And to yond side o' the river lies a wall,
> Piece of a cloister, which in my opinion
> Gives the best echo that you ever heard,
> So hollow and so dismal, and withal
> So plain in the distinction of our words,
> That many have supposed it is a spirit
> That answers.

Did Webster, I wonder, know of this so far-away echo, of which he made such memorable and sinister poetry, or was its appearance in his play coincidental ? . . . The second alternative would hardly seem possible. And the point to be emphasised is that the echo that comes back from the rocks is in keeping with the play : laughter, shouts, ribald cries, return at once, but with their tone altered, turned grave, sombre, sullen. The voice that flies back at you is that of an *alter ego*, recognisable but hollow in tone, laden with some burden of woe : every call suffers a change, undergoes a tragic twist of sound, if not of sense as in the play : but that, too, would not be difficult to imagine if you listened long enough and were alone.

> *Antonio.* . . . but all things have their end :
> Churches and cities, which have diseases like to men,
> Must have like death that we have.
> *Echo.* 'Like death that we have.'

Delio. Now the echo hath caught you.
Antonio. It groaned, methought, and gave
  A very deadly accent.
Echo. 'Deadly accent.'
Delio. I told you 'twas a pretty one : you may make it
  A huntsman, or a falconer, a musician,
  Or a thing of sorrow.
Echo. 'A thing of sorrow.'
Antonio. Ay, sure, that suits it best.
Echo. 'That suits it best.'
Antonio. 'Tis very like my wife's voice.
Echo. 'Ay, wife's voice.'
Delio. Come, let us walk further from't.
  I would not have you go to the cardinal's tonight :
  Do not.
Echo. 'Do not.'
Delio. Wisdom doth not more moderate wasting sorrow
  Than time : take time for't ; be mindful of thy safety.
Echo. 'Be mindful of thy safety.'
Antonio. Necessity compels me :
  Make scrutiny throughout the passages
  Of your own life, you'll find it impossible
  To fly your fate.
Echo. 'O, fly your fate.'
Delio. Hark! the dead stones seem to have pity on you,
  And give you good counsel.
Antonio. Echo, I will not talk with thee,
  For thou art a dead thing.
Echo. 'Thou art a dead thing.'
Antonio. My duchess is asleep now,
  And her little ones, I hope sweetly : O Heaven,
  Shall I never see her more ?
Echo. 'Never see her more.'

No sound, the scientists allege, is ever lost, no least murmur but is numbered like the hairs of the head : somewhere the cries of the Roman mob still reverberate, somewhere the dying speech of Cleopatra yet lingers, somewhere if a drama took place among these walls and towers, the words spoken, the words and their echo, still survive, and may one day, by means of some instrument as yet uninvented, be captured and recorded. . . . Other towers have other histories, almost as ghostly, and at Scala, nearly on a level along the hillside with the tower of which I have been speaking, is a gaunt medieval palace, part tower, part prison, part slum, in which popular belief asserts that Lenin lived during some years of his exile from Russia.

Towers are everywhere an expression, perhaps, of defiance, or of men being under the necessity of seeking a refuge. As such, a tragic quality often pertains to them ; but the towers of Northern Italy in general, and of Tuscany in particular, possess a beauty of their own, different from that of towers in the south. They are taller, simpler in line, but larger at the top, bursting into open platforms under pointed arches, as the stalk of a flower bursts into blossom. Indeed they have some resemblance in shape to the Florentine lily. . . . My Italian home, Montegufoni, stands at the very centre of this country of towers, and from time to time I climb up the steep stairs of my own tower there, in the morning or at night, to allow the feeling of the country round to permeate my consciousness. In April or May after dark, the sheer volume of sound is scarcely to be believed until you hear it : a great symphony, swelling from the ground, from what water there is, and pouring from the trees, and only occasionally blasted by the loud, ribald dissonance of some trumpet, a large-mouthed brazen serpent, blown by a member of the local band, the *Società Filarmonica di Montegufoni* : for on a fine night the peasants who compose that body like to tootle and bombinate in solitude, each man sitting on a wooden chair outside his own house. The incessant love songs or hunting cries of the birds, the chafing legs and wings of insects resembling the sand-paper and skull music of Cuba, the myriad voices of the pool, among which some are individual enough to be recognised, provide a background of sound for nocturnal life, for the dances and flashings of the fireflies who light their way above the flower-beds, round the lemon tubs, and down the ribbed avenues of the cornfields. . . . Or in the daytime you can watch the milk-white oxen treading their slow coupled path across the chequer of green and brown fields, shot with a yellow sheen from the sun, and look down at the great terracotta and orange-lichened roofscape below, its different contours seeming to show like those of a map in relief. . . . My father used, with a large air, to remark sometimes when it rained, and he would pace up and down one of his long rooms, 'Everyone should have a gallery to walk in, in wet weather'. Similarly, perhaps, everyone should have a tower in which to spend an hour or two above the worries of the world in a cool and airy seclusion.

From the tower of the castle you can perceive how almost every hill culminates in a tower — and so it is if you travel through the country itself, passing the walls and towers of Castel Fiorentino, or of Certaldo, where Boccaccio was born, and where now the women sit knitting in front of their doors, on chairs placed on the herring-bone brick paving that survives here, such as you see in the pictures of the primitive masters, (they wait for some event, but none occurs, except, perhaps, for the arrival of a new stray cat from the modern town below) — and so it is until at last you reach, some thirty-five miles south-west, that unique whole city of towers, San Gimignano. In the distance, as you approach it, you behold such a collection of towers on the skyline as only New York can offer in the modern world. A cluster of slender, lofty towers of varying heights lift their heads into the pure, clear air with a singular grace and strangeness. These, it is true, are less tall, less robust than the towers of New York, but their proportion to the buildings lower than themselves is the same, and the clarity of their outline. San Gimignano, in short, constitutes a prophecy of New York. But when you enter the ancient city, you find that, though nearly every street ends high in the air, in a burst of Tuscan countryside, shrill greens, rich warm reds and browns, it is a city of a few dusty and wind-blown piazzas and of many narrow and gloomy ways — though I must admit that when I visited it in the autumn of 1947 the atmosphere had for a few weeks become quite otherwise, frenetically sportive : for Fox Films, like a conquering army, had occupied it and taken over, and were, it was said, paying almost the whole population — for Italy, a people rather dour and severe — to dress up and dance and sing. . . . And how the citizens revelled in the job, all the more perhaps because it was scarcely in their natures ! It cheered even the most melancholy, and those of happier temperament — and they existed even here — felt that the occasion had been worth waiting for all their lives hitherto, now that they were to be paid regularly for enjoying themselves. . . . No householder was allowed to look out of a window, if it faced the Piazza del Duomo, without first waving, and then clasping, a quasi-medieval bouquet (also supplied by Fox Films), and no stranger was permitted to cross the Piazza to La Collegiata, unless he enveloped his form beforehand in a cloak or domino, since a Carnival scene was being portrayed, though the whole set was more true to Nice in 1903 or 1904 than to San Gimignano in the time of Cesare Borgia : with which period, though you might not have guessed it, the film in the course of making was concerned. Enormous heads made of papier mâché and coarsely painted, like the vastly enlarged heads of ventriloquists' dummies, were carried along at a run by bands of boys and girls pranked out in some film dream of dress in the Middle Ages, covered with fluttering ribbons, and clutching what I am sure were termed nosegays. As they ran, they laughed and sang, now in a self-conscious manner, because, though at first genuinely excited by the money they were earning, when they had, by their singing and dancing, given true expression to the feelings within them, the producers had told them they were not doing it in the way in which young Italians would be expected to sing and dance by farmers in the Middle West, and had obliged them to give a correct impression of excitement in terms of the film. So it had become a highly stylised manifestation of joy : similar in spirit to the shop signs painted for the benefit of those who cannot read or write. . . . But, indeed, the entire film possessed a verisimilitude all its own, since, for one thing, it was devoted to the life of Cesare Borgia, Duke of Valentinois, and the action placed in San Gimignano, almost the sole town in Italy which that great and energetic leader had never visited. I remember, too, that the chief star, a famous and delightful man, told me that it had been hoped to shoot a scene in the gardens of Caserta, with their mid-eighteenth-century formality and perfection, but that unfortunately this background had not at the time proved available. . . . Meanwhile the people of San Gimignano, under the delicate but austere shadow of their towers, danced to order and sang the frolicsome Edwardian ditties composed for them.

In corners of the town the old, quiet life went on. For the most part those too old to sing and dance were not compelled to do so, and were, of course with certain reservations, allowed to lead their own lives. . . . Thus, from the cloister of Sant' Agostino, the little old monk, Fra Gregorio, with his tortoise-like neck thrust out of his ancient body enclosed in its brown habit, and with his kind, good face corrugated with wrinkles in a fashion that would have held a Flemish painter entranced, still emerged to show tourists the frescoes by Benozzo Gozzoli, in the choir, that depict the life of the saint. The old man would point out the salient features with a long bamboo cane like the fishing-rod of a Chinaman in an eighteenth-century decorative panel, but at the age of ninety-two he had not full mastery of the erratic movements of his pointer, and the eyes of various of the visitors suffered the narrowest of escapes. Invariably Fra Gregorio would end up by indicating the likeness of a strapping and personable young man of about twenty years of age, and enquiring of the visitors if the painting did not remind them of someone ! He would then put down his bamboo cane, cross his hands in front of him, and drawing up his frail old body and bent neck as straight as he was able, stand directly beneath this figure, and stare fixedly in front of him. The visitors, nonplussed, would usually make no reply, and Fra Gregorio, with an air of disappointment that conveyed, too, a suggestion that he found the visitors today rather dense, would then explain that as a rule the whole world recognised how much it resembled himself : often people could hardly tell the counterfeit from the real person. It was evident that for him in his innocence the seventy years that divided him from the figure on the wall above did not exist. . . . About him there was a holy simplicity that is to be found sometimes in the Italian character, usually so realistic. His life, which had not altered for half a century and more, fitted into an ancient and ascetic pattern. He slept in a cell giving on to the cloister of Sant' Agostino. He rose at 4.30 every morning, prayed in the church, then swept the floor with a broom made by himself out of fresh green branches.

At eleven he ate a little watery vegetable soup and showed visitors round the church until it was dark, when he retired to bed for the night. He lived on the fifty to sixty lire a day that he was paid : but, withal, he was perfectly content, the first really contented man I had met for a long while. Besides his alleged resemblance to the young man painted by Benozzo Gozzoli, he had other small vanities, and was immensely proud of the fact that he had been chosen to show Queen Victoria over this church on some long-forgotten visit. . . . With all his perfections and imperfections, Fra Gregorio seemed, more than did the by now well-practised professional revellers in the Piazza, to belong to this world of towers on the hill.

Let us turn from it, and from its dead and desiccated dreams, to the other city of towers. In a book of travel written some thirty years ago, I first suggested that a comparison might be drawn between San Gimignano and New York, and the subsequent development of the huge American city has only seemed to emphasise the similarity. New York, with all its evident faults, is yet the greatest and most moving of modern cities. If the nobles of San Gimignano erected their towers for their own defence, those in New York were built for another purpose, it is true, but to defend an abstract idea, a vision. It must be remembered that New York, the material capital of the world, is not only the gateway to a continent, such as during its long reign was Constantinople, but that also resembling that same city in this further trait, and similarly akin to Venice, it is a new Rome built by refugees to shelter and protect their dreams on alien soil. Who can laud enough its unique glories or adequately inveigh against its equally unmatched squalors, who can sufficiently praise its beauty, its towers that are not to be believed, its air of gaiety and of bustle, its museums, noble or fantastic, and its places of learning, its varnished acres of plate glass, or denounce its great white fields of floating paper lifted up by the dark wind in the waste spaces of Harlem ; who can raise for your eyes the violent vagaries of its climate, the long reign of golden days in the autumn that culminate in diurnal mountains of snow, its rabid heats and sudden rages ; what pen can summon up for the reader the sound of the horns of a thousand motor-cars barking in united and exacerbated protest against being held up in a traffic block far down under the enormous rock-like buildings, or, for example, the other-worldly exhilaration of lunching in the club on the Chrysler Building's seventieth storey, so that you look down on a strange prospect composed of clouds and the tops of other skyscrapers ; who can picture for you, reader, the rows of polyglot holiday-makers resting on benches in the sunshine of Central Park, or paint for you the ingenuity of that designed landscape, with its lakes and tunnels and flights of steps ; who can describe for you the strangeness of arrival in this city either by boat or train, of the first sight of its lilied skyline from the water, or from the railway, of the passing glimpse of the ranks of the dingy squat houses of Harlem, with sable young noses pressed palely against the panes of the windows so that flashing eyes can watch the trains go by ? . . . But at least, difficult task as it may prove, I can attempt to sketch certain sides of it for you, try to explain to you certain things about it and spread out for your inspection certain of my personal opinions concerning it: such as that, though, as I have said, the way by rail or water is in its kind without rival, nevertheless the great city should be approached by road in preference to either, because its massive marble stations, full of moving staircases, and containing halls echoing with conversations and formerly a-clatter with broadcast dance-music, and so lofty that the proportion of the dark-faced redcap who slouches through them is that of a fly crawling at the bottom of a window-pane, can to a stranger prove somewhat intimidating, while, too, to arrive at the docks is a sombre anticlimax to the voyage up the river; whereas first seen from Long Island across one of its several superb bridges New York truly presents its real appearance of an island-city, its high towers facing you in clumps across the water and seeming to grow rooted there like some gigantic plantation of trees.

New York is, in fact, a prodigy of paradox. In the daytime its proud edifices express material riches so overwhelming as to transcend materialism and to represent a will for prosperity of such strength as almost to rank as a spiritual aim. Its aspiring buildings have been drawn out of the living rock of Manhattan by the magnetic force of gold in the same way as flowers or trees are forced up towards the sky by the attraction of the sun's gold rays: they have been forced to this vertical development, too, by an unparalleled concentration at their base of human beings within the narrow borders of a small island. Thus set within a limited space these high clusters of roofs, these pyramids, pagodas and steeples, these cupolas and belfries, so unpredictable and so monstrous in their beauty, have been obliged through their very constriction to expand upward, compelled to mount in this fashion towards the heaven through the characteristic clear sparkle of the New York air. They constitute equally a spiritual expression of good fortune and a supreme material expression of the will to succeed. But though in the daytime the crowds, the displays in the windows of the shops, the thousands of motor-cars (so numerous that they have to be left outside in the parking-places throughout the day and the night) are all a translating into other mediums of this determination, yet when at the precise early moment of the evening that every light in every building is switched on at the same instant till gold pours down from the windows into the tender dusk as if honeycombs were not waxy but transparent, and the illumined oblongs spill their streams and torrents of gold into the deepening darkness with a refulgence that is yellow and green-white with still the gleam of honey in it, then the city becomes visionary and improbable, a city devoted to dreams and born of them. For that is what it is, a metropolis of dreams realised and unrealised — an assumption supported no less by the vivid riches of the shops than by the extravagant beauty of its museums —, a metropolis of dreams of every age and intensity. And this is to be felt all the more strongly at night when the clamour is stilled, and it is dark, and the people who live packed in the compartments of the great boxes and honeycombs, or lie piled up in the layers of its towers, stir in their deep slumber : for New York, as well as being the solid realisation in concrete, brick and marble, of the visions of its inhabitants, is also the expression of dreams still unaccomplished, and perhaps never to be achieved, because this thronged city is the capital of nostalgia, and the ache of it will never be assuaged. In the people of its streets is represented every race in the whole world, and each skyscraper is a Tower of Babel, full of foreign tongues, and just as in the daytime you can examine quarters entirely given up to a resident racial sept, so at night, when these whole enclaves have surrendered their waking consciousness into the dark hands of unknown powers, the dreams of the men and women who together in their numbers and by their acts go to make up this splendid cosmopolis of a city are to be felt weighing heavily upon the air.

What is it that they dream ? Dreams national and dreams individual. A whole nervous city of Italians — nervous of outbreaks of violence and of arrest — builds in its sleep piazzas clean and well-ordered, where ice-cream can be consumed in peace, but piazzas full of a southern warmth of affection and founded on those they knew of old, laid across the tufa of Naples or pressing down on the rich soil of Tuscany, and neighbouring grey groves of olive, or glossy fragrant woods of lemon- and orange-trees. Adjoining the Latins, the Chinese have in actuality established a city where no disturbances are allowed, supremely disciplined at night as in the daytime, but in this civilised district, above the lighted lanterns of many colours and the street signs that crackle in light up the front of a house like rockets made permanent, their dreams, tinged perhaps with the magic of opium, are of flowering trees and goldfish and of tame birds carried in cages into gardens where rare flowers blossom, in the heart of a country where the laws protect you and a man can build up his fortune without fear. Near by, the septs of Ireland, in their dreams now at last admired and powerful, toss and heave in their sleep, fighting for their personal ideal of freedom — the freedom to fight. Then, not far off, the Slavs create in their own terms their visions of paradise, while, across a broad avenue, the Spaniards conjure up for their own comfort crusades and civil wars in which every man conducts himself as should a true *caballero*. The adjacent colony of Scandinavians dream of everlasting and omnipresent cleanliness and of a summer which is one long, intellectual winter. The Jews, spread throughout all these communities, indulge their ancient vision of milk and honey, but in terms of a new city, whereas in compressed quarters a rival body of Armenians dream of winning bargains over the Israelites, and of worshipping Christ without fear. To the north, segregated in their dusty blocks and musty apartment-houses, the sable African armies of the sun dream of Rolls-Royces and of television sets, or of Sunday Schools and white aprons, and deep voices melodiously praising God, while under the shelter of their tin petrol-can roofs the dark-faced inhabitants of the Puerto-Rican enclave dream of cool, clean cities where without labouring the colonial man rules and the white man is subservient to him.

In the daytime in New York, the black man may be a porter or a labourer, at night in his dreams he is a swarthy prince, a millionaire set in a jewelled surround; the Italian may be a boot-black or a cook or a waiter, but in the small hours he is *sindaco* of his native town which has been mysteriously transposed to the States: at noon the Czech may be a maker of furniture, but by the light of the moon he is a national hero, the centre of some folk-dance captivating in its rhythmic stresses: awake, it may be that the Armenian sells carpets, but asleep he eludes the Pasha's sword and leads with ancient Christian cries a rebellion against a forgotten Sultan whose turban, shaped like some vast cottage loaf, falls down on the blood-stained ground as his head is severed. And all these acronychal dreams and countless others, all this amorphous weight of nostalgia, all these longings so evident in the syncopated popular music of the epoch, made concrete in Tin Pan Alley, are in the silent night most plainly to be felt. Then the air is loaded with sorrow and ambition, with regrets forlorn and white as the bones of dead men and with hopes bright as their youth: and all these are as apparent to the nocturnal antennae of the senses as in the daytime are the names written over the doors of shops, and indicate race in the same way that the goods sold in the stores, or the food in the restaurants, the *spaghetti*, the *smörgåsbord*, the German sausage, similarly declare the various nationalities of the tradesmen and their customers and indicate their aims. Thus the city, when its streets are empty and, even under the brilliance of its lighting, darkness can be seen to flow through them like a cleansing tide and the vacant spaces take on an appearance of depth and grandeur, has an especial quality, to be found of an equal strength nowhere else in the world, and this dead leaden burden of dreams is as much at night its individual attribute as is the sharp-eyed bustle of New York's sunlit hours, when the city carries with a natural swagger all the elegance and splendour created or left in the modern world. Darkness lies with a particular weight on the deserted cliffs of Wall Street and with a particular sadness on the wide windswept pavements of the Bowery, where a few down-and-outs have obversely crowned their dreams with sleep — alcoholic dreams, at which they have been working all day long, so that now they lie stretched soddenly unconscious and, through this means, at last again innocent, on the pavements, and whether the stones are damp or dusty, to them it is the same. . . . So when in the small hours you open the window, and the cool darkness flows into the heated room, it is on a beautiful and improbable city of dreams that you look, some tragic, some naïve, but many of them practicable and to be achieved in the future, near or distant, by the labour of these same dreamers when awake during the working day. Thus in the main the dreams will be fulfilled, and the hopes that prevail over the fears are justified.

CHAPTER VI

THE ELEMENT, AIR

It was hardly light yet. The rhythm of muffled steps — no doubt from feet wearing the rope-soled shoes of the region — sounded from the long, white monastic passage; and the aroma of coffee and the smell of food cooking also offered the slothful another luxurious reminder that some visitors felt they must, or indeed were obliged to, get up early. But I lay in bed still, waiting for day to start, and pondered — as the fragrance reached my nostrils — on food and its effect upon human beings. Perhaps, I argued, no nation with good food was ever heroic, while, on the other hand, none with bad food ever produced great art: (indeed, in support of this second generalisation you will notice that in the houses of painters the fare provided is nearly always enticing, original and stimulating; which suggests in turn that cooking is nearly related to esthetics). To schoolmasters, of British private and public schools, bad food is a pleasure born of pain, and usually they like, still more, to supply it to the boys under their care, as a substitute perhaps for flogging, of late years rather discouraged : but to politicians alone, I hold, — though it may be true that personally in their own houses they may offer their guests a good meal —, is the widespread consumption of long and ill preserved food originally of bad quality desirable, and even essential ; for war greatly magnifies the position of every politician, who, for its duration, will rank as a statesman and a spokesman of his country. And such a diet as he permits the public to have prevents those on whom it is inflicted from using their common-sense and renders them continually hysterical. They become heroic and intransigent, and wallow and welter in the sentimentality of over-life-size phrases. So that it can be seen that the provision of adulterated and contaminated food may be the result of an intentional policy, rather than of accident and ill-fortune, because only a general madness on the part of the voters would keep in power some of the governments we have lately suffered, and the best way of inducing first the necessary debility, and the sequent amnesia and insanity, is by a mild but perpetual and universal process of food-poisoning. . . . As opposed to democracy, tyranny flourishes rather on absolute lack of food, for tameness in man, as in horses, depends on an insufficient supply of oats. But as I lay there meditating on these lines, the sky outside all at once asserted itself, not least within the bounds of the room, became of more importance than the earth or things earthy, and even the haunting fragrance of coffee departed suddenly, for today air was evidently the governing element.

Sometimes throughout the light hours the land and sea wore a close-fitting cap of blue: but today clouds had already taken possession of the long range of mountains, superb in line and colour, running as far as the eye could follow them into the sea, and had converted them into still higher and more delusive shapes. And in its turn the rising sun seized on this new combination, and turned both mountains and clouds into monstrous heaps of peony-heads or roses. On top of the nearer and lower hills, fragments of cloud hung like wool torn from a sheep's coat by a briar, clinging there with a damp persistence, but the great airs coming from over the sea would soon dislodge them, sweeping them back to dissolve into the sky. From far below on the shore, desultory cries and sounds of human activity reached one, and the fishermen reclining against the stone wall that separates the two levels of the quay had already begun the unending task of patching their great lengths of slimy fish-net, its brown mesh spread out on the rough, wet slabs of the pavement, and in the small harbour, over the ancient drowned city, a brig was preparing to sail back once more right round the foot of Italy to its home port on the Adriatic coast — but no sooner did it start than it returned again, for the sea proved rough and the whole race of Mediterranean fishermen very reasonably regards rough weather as weather in which to remain at home.

The sky was certainly all-important today: and if you stared into it, you could watch the formations continually arranging themselves in fresh patterns, as, similarly, in a child's kaleidoscope ; except that in this case they are of lighter, softer colour, and opaque instead of being translucent. The clouds aggregated and were again lost, then reassembled in a new composition — but in a style with which, though here intensified, we are familiar : it is still the fleecy European sky, albeit modified by the light-giving Mediterranean with its colours of wine and flowers — for each continent has its own sky, cloudy or crystalline. Africa presents its effects of atmosphere, torrid, turbid, so burning in their intensity that often they seem to smoulder without light in a general consuming of air and cloud — under such skies as these was Othello born ; like the enormous lands under them, they offer grandeur, strangeness and strength, but lack grace, too large for the human race — it seems as if only some god, or some vast extinct animal, forgotten by the rest of the world, could match their proportions. Asia has in the south its red and purple skies, fringed with mist by great heats, and in the north its sparkling blue dome, full of whirling particles from the Gobi Desert. But though you must admit that the skies of Europe, like its soil, are those most clearly intended for man, yet if you wish for clouds, or equally for cloudless skies, you must go to America — the United States, or to Canada : for, as I have written earlier, nowhere else will you find such wide skies, so much air or freedom, except when snow dwarfs and suffocates every prospect. But there, too, there can be a white and scintillating splendour not to be found elsewhere. Thus, one day, arriving at a station, I struggled out into snow which would, I was sure, bury me, and must extend, minute after minute, day after day, mile after mile, as far as, and indeed further than, the North Pole — and just at that moment of blinded, blundering exasperation, for an instant the flakes stopped falling, the light of the sky came through so that the city of Ottawa was revealed, as though it were the Heavenly City itself, glittering in its heights and depths of snow, a collection of top-heavy, dark stone buildings, the weight of them and their high, enormous roofs eased for the instant by the snow, the public monuments, models of commonsense, converted temporarily into snowmen that would melt away at the sun's caress. This fabulous stronghold of the snow, as it seemed, offered the perfect example of *sharawaggi* ; (a term used in the eighteenth century, and purporting to be a Chinese word, but really invented by Horace Walpole and his group of friends, to denote the quality of beauty to be found in an unintentionally picturesque arrangement of apparently irreconcilable features). It was the very leaden weight, and the robustness, sharp and clear, of the lines of these clusters of Victorian edifices now smothered in snow, that created this vision from another world, of a Polar metropolis, sprinkled with diamonds, and with no movement, no inhabitants except the motionless snowmen. This sky was darker than the earth, and for once small — for usually these new lands seem as a right to be crowned with the largest skies, just as they possess, too, the longest and broadest rivers, the oldest and tallest trees, the most stupendous of waterfalls, the most splendid of all bridges.

Sometimes in Europe you will hear Americans denounced for bringing to the attention of foreigners in conversation with them such phenomena as I have just cited — in short, for boasting. It seems to me natural enough, however, that when they communicate to you interesting information about their country, they should expect you in return to be interested, and it would certainly be stupid of them to deny the prodigiousness of the features of their continent, whether natural or created by man in sympathy on the same scale, or to attempt in any way to palliate or excuse the facts. Nothing, no amount of effort or training, could ever squeeze the vast eruptions and gigantic cataclysms, the enormous joys and sorrows of the North American territories into any but a heroic mould. The lands of America are lively to the point of exaggeration, they are hot or cold, but never tepid. There is a natural rhetoric in the American soul to match that in the American soil: which is precisely why Hermann Melville and Walt Whitman are such prophets and interpreters of their country. Walt Whitman's poems in especial, if broadcast regularly, would make more friends for the citizens of the United States than would any amount of lectures on the American Way of Life and the gadgets attached to it. By listening to them the people of foreign nations would be able to seize more surely than they would through any kind of propaganda the particular character and qualities of the Americans, and of American democracy, and appraise more gratefully the spontaneous generosity of it.

Look up then into the sky above America, gaze into

its lost and limitless vistas! In these boundless and vast dominions of the sky, clouds build up more quickly than elsewhere and are as swiftly dispersed. No man would be a slave, no man would barter his freedom under such a canopy. Indeed it may be the air of freedom they here inhale that persuades so many visiting foreigners — among them some from my own country — to register with a, for them, unusual speed and precision the adverse views they have formed in so short a time of the strange and hospitable country in which they are staying, for freedom can stir up some people to be disagreeable and rude as easily as it will encourage others to be more amiable and kindly. But it might render them less critical if, when the first vituperative fever had worn off, they left the enormous cities and went to the country of the Middle West. The stranger in these immense tracts will feel lonely and abandoned: he will soon wish to find a neighbour, and if he meets one, to speak to him in a friendly fashion. American friendliness arose perhaps from the scale of man to the landscape, and of the general population to the country, and so, it may be, did the feeling of neighbourliness. This last attribute pervades the people of the great cities no less than the rural communities, and is evinced in many directions: thus I recall, as an instance of what I mean, the taxicab driver who, on depositing my sister at the door of her hotel in New York, said to her, 'I enjoyed our talk so much I should like to continue it another day. I'll ring you first, to tell you when I'll arrive, if you'll give me your name.' Even the expression 'You're welcome!' which you so seldom hear in England ('Thank you', 'You're welcome!' or, better still, 'You're sure welcome!') is a sign of American friendliness no less than of American politeness.

Thus the sense of loneliness gives birth to that of the brotherhood of man: the people are in consequence kindly; but they are proud, equally, of their technical achievements, unmatched elsewhere. And this pride inspires in them idealism and ambition — the ambition to emulate nature in their country, to build houses, bridges and dams to tally with the proportions of the world they know. But though the American may build so high in the air that the edge of a cloud may catch on the top of a skyscraper, and lie tethered there as yonder on the summit of Monte dell' Avvocata, it will nevertheless be impossible for him thoroughly to achieve his aim. He could build and live in the highest tower in the world, but Babel would look only a toy fort in this luminous immensity. And of these particular qualities of the American character or soul, New York — though often the people of the United States protest that the city in no way typifies America — is the pattern and quintessence. When the gigantic airs of the American autumn break the spell of summer, independence and freedom can be felt in the atmosphere and almost perceived in the sky. And one year, just when the autumn had turned to deep winter, I heard a mutinous tornado smash like a riotous mob the smooth and glittering windows of the New York shops, and the next morning I was able to see the waters of the East River climbing over the walls down town into the streets so that motor-cars and taxicabs were drowned up to the middle of them. Thus I know — or rather can imagine a little — what sea and sky could do further.

America then, as I was saying, can be too hot or too cold, but never dull: and the excitement it offers seems to have a physical basis. A certain liveliness, an air of bustle and stir seems to rise from the earth itself and to animate the general public, even in the sleepy southern cities, while the skyscrapers of New York pouring out their whole armies of business men and workers carry this sparkle to its highest degree. These buildings, born of the strength of the Manhattan rock and the limitations of its island site, resemble little else in the world. For the prototypes of them at their best — I do not refer to the narrow towers of New York, for I have just discussed thoroughly their starry emulation, but to the broader, more robust edifices — we have perhaps to turn to the Escorial, the royal palace and mausoleum built by King Philip II some fifty miles from Madrid, or journey to Pienza. There Pope Pius II built the strange and beautiful Piccolomini Palace to celebrate the fact that Pienza was his home town, and we may note that its construction was supervised for him by his Secretary, Cardinal Borgia, afterwards to become known as Pope Alexander VI. The restrained and refined palace that resulted dwarfs all else, even the impressive cathedral at its side. Yet it does not essentially pertain to the city it dominates, in the way that the Escorial belongs to the stony tableland out of which it has grown. No, intensely, immensely alone, the Palazzo Piccolomini rises out of the little crabbed and bitter city on the stained walls of which the Communists have written their slogans, as usual calling for death and liquidation : whereas the enormous, sad bulk of the Escorial, an example and prediction, though it, too, can be seen from many miles away, always remains intrinsic, a flower of its own country with nothing contradictory, nothing extraneous or imposed, although it combines magnificence with severity. Such an edifice is it as only the most unselfish architect could design and the most austere prince could accept, a fine but dour body for a soul, and suited as a shell to the purpose it was built to serve. The Piccolomini Palace at Pienza, on the other hand, though in its line equally simple, is a monument dictated or prescribed, raised on its hill so that the traveller may see it from a great distance and wonder what it may be, what tragic drama it celebrates. It stands as a monument of pride, and the city in which it was built had to be named after Pope Pius as Stalingrad had to be named after Stalin. One link in common, however, these two ancient palaces manifest : they are both far more akin to buildings in the New World than in the Old, nearer to skyscrapers than are the flat imitations of such edifices in Paris or London. Moreover, both the Escorial and the Piccolomini Palace are the fruit of dreams, though of a different order from those out of which New York was reared — lifelong dreams of personal or spiritual splendour.

New York, withal, is not only a city of dreams but a collection of surprises, and two of these — the house of Mrs. Nadelman and the Cloisters Museum — I now disclose, and shall proceed briefly to describe. . . .

We Europeans are not surprised to find a great artist living in Paris, London or Rome and it may be a rancid vestige of European superciliousness to be astonished at finding that a great artist flourishes in a suburb of New York, but such is — or rather was — the case, for Nadelman had died a year or two before I was privileged, by the kindness of his widow, and the good offices of my friend Lincoln Kirstein, to see the house as the sculptor left it. Situated in Riverdale, an old and umbrageous suburb of New York, the house itself, under the spreading shadow of a superb old tree, is plainly full of atmosphere : but in addition it is full of the personality of one man. . . . I do not want here to embark on a discussion of Nadelman's work, but merely to describe his house, its ambience, essence and contents — first, however, a few words must necessarily be said about his career.

Nadelman, a Pole, was born in 1862, and brought up in Warsaw, where his father was a goldsmith. Mr. Kirstein, in his recent book *Elie Nadelman Drawings*, has reproduced certain drawings by the young artist, then a boy of fourteen, which, as the author indicates, clearly predict the adult sculptor's attitude towards the use of volume and in fact constitute a prophecy of the introduction of cubism into the art he practised. After living in Munich, where, as a boy of twenty-one, he went to study, he moved to Paris to work. There he achieved a certain fame—indeed, Lincoln Kirstein in his preface tells us that Matisse had a notice fastened up on his studio wall : *Défense de parler de Nadelman ici.*

In London, where in 1911 he held a one-man show

at Patterson's Gallery in Bond Street, he enjoyed what may be termed a one-customer success, for Madame Helena Rubinstein (now Princess Gourielli-Tchkonia) purchased the entire contents of his exhibition outright.

In 1914 Nadelman went to settle in the States, where he married an American lady. In 1915 he held his first American exhibition, and in the preface to the catalogue and in the book *Vers la beauté plastique* published in 1921 he incorporated passages from his former *Pensées*, some of which had appeared in various catalogues in Paris. In these he asserted, as he had always maintained in private, that he was the inventor of the whole Modern Movement ; a claim which his work goes some way to support. But whatever the basis of it, there can be no doubt that he was as a sculptor not only imbued with great originality and equipped with superb technique, but endowed with genius. After the hostile reception of his exhibition and of his preface, he never again exhibited in New York, so that there as elsewhere he was quickly forgotten, except by painters and a few patrons—so utterly forgotten that when I met my old friend Aldous Huxley in the Museum of Modern Art, and we climbed upstairs together to see the Nadelman Memorial Exhibition, he was able to say to me,

'How is it that you and I, who have haunted studios and exhibitions all our lives, have never before heard of this great artist ?'

Nadelman, though he never again showed his sculptures in public, continued to work steadily in his studio at Riverdale, substantiating one after another of his dreams : for in his final as in his first period he was still devoted to experiment. In his last phase he was concerned to bring sculpture back into the lives of the people and to place it for the first time in the modern world within reach of the purse of the ordinary man. With this purpose in view, he began to make hundreds of little figures in clay or cast plaster. Though it is true that the sculptor intended to make use of them on the grand scale as well, nevertheless he was successful in bestowing upon them the strange dramatic qualities of the doll, while he infused them, too, with the grandeur and muffled perfection of Tanagra statuettes. Indeed, many arts and civilisations had contributed to their creation. Kirstein indicates, for example, their affinity to Byzantine Madonnas, once described in a memorable phrase by Frederick Rolfe as those 'unruffleable wan dolls in indigo on gold'. This derivation — first pointed out to Kirstein by Pavel Tchelitchew, the painter of *Hide-and-Seek* — is natural in an artist who came from Poland. And since Nadelman seldom sold his work and was not concerned to do so, his house grew full of the riches he created.

When the door was opened, it was as though one had entered a forest of sculpture, of every possible size and material, but always inspired by some personal vision. Figures sprouted in every direction, with something of the dry drive and vigour of cactuses. A billiard-table was entirely covered by small-scale figures, with innumerable minute variations of expression and material, so that as you looked at them you might equally, by some transposition of the senses, be listening to a fugue by a great composer. The modulations, ever shaped anew, yet bore a kinship one to another, so that the experience of seeing them was also like walking into a whole new world in the course of being created, an unknown world of significant puppets and progenitive midgets. Every room was full of the dead sculptor's work, which lived with an intense flame, full of the marble trunks and heads and figures of his neo-classical period, of wooden figures, and of those in papier mâché and terra-cotta. Though all these fruits of several periods were beautiful and interesting, to me the most moving were the carved wooden groups or single figures, such as the Tango Dancer or the Woman Playing the Piano. They show an ironic or satirical appreciation of form, and of the world, which is intensely personal, and the pervading flavour of genius no doubt affronts those who like ready-made opinions, and are always from fifty to seventy years behind the times, regarding the buying, even now, of a Manet or Renoir as a great adventure. Moreover, these carved figures in another medium seem to manifest something of the same quality that is to be found in the paintings and drawings of Seurat: the same creation of light and shape out of darkness — so that I was not surprised to learn from Lincoln Kirstein that Nadelman had been much influenced by them. (And here in noting the persistence of Seurat's influence, we may also record the fact that it is nearly always good, and that though his theories have often been derided, it is curious to observe that the more nearly those painters he influenced followed them, the better were the results; thus Camille Pissarro, Sisley and others are only to be accounted great artists when in their work it is possible to perceive the influence of this painter.) Nadelman, however, did not need this creative influence to show his genius, which is apparent in all he did. . . . Essentially, this Pole from Munich and Paris became an American artist, offering in the creation of his last years a new human scale to the immensities of the enormous landscape. Indeed he became as American as another expatriate, Greco, became Spanish. . . . And the United States should now fulfil its destiny: to become the chief nation in the world to produce art and to cherish the artist — for, though it is in contradistinction to its past, and though few people have yet realised the change that has taken place, America is at present the only country rich enough to finance leisure — the very soil of art.

Not far from the Nadelman house is the Cloisters Museum, where members of the Rockefeller family have turned their dreams, too, into an amazing reality and anchored them to the city. This vision has indeed materialised without any of the tinge of the nightmare that might have been expected, since to remove from Southern France several Romanesque cloisters, however beautiful they may be in themselves, and dump them down in a suburb of New York, there to be shown by artificial daylight while, in addition, herbs, flowers and fruit-trees brought from the borders of the Mediterranean are compelled to flourish under glass in the courts, would seem to be a proceeding fraught with artistic dangers. The outside of the building is unobtrusive and homogeneous, while the cobblestones that once formed the surface of the streets of old New

York have been used most successfully for the paving of the approach, and of courts and terraces ; and the whole scheme fits well into the hill on which it has been placed. Moreover, every imaginative method of displaying the treasures housed in the halls and chapels of which they are part has been brought into play. The richness of the contents is overwhelming. Room after room is filled with matchless examples of French and Burgundian sculpture, and two of the world's greatest sets of tapestry are here displayed in the most perfect manner : the famous Unicorn set, and another, a little earlier in date, which was found in recent years in an outhouse of a country mansion in Ireland and was said to have been used recently as sacking for potatoes. This Museum serves as a magic carpet to carry you back to medieval Europe. When you leave the precincts, you walk out of the Old World into the New. Though I think that in America all museums should face the future rather than the past, the Cloisters Museum admirably does both, and it must be admitted that the site for it was selected as if by inspiration : the tourist is once more in a little kingdom of his own. The view is splendid: you look across the broad, sparkling waters of the Hudson to wooded heights — a stretch of country also bought, in order permanently to secure and stabilise the prospect, and given to the state by the Rockefellers. From the terrace, autumn — that American autumn with all its false promises such as only spring makes elsewhere — could be seen flaming through the woods, while the sun left fiery dragons of cloud to float in the enormous sky.

CHAPTER VII

SOUND AND SILENCE

THIS morning when I threw back the shutters against the white walls and opened the windows wide, though the sky had caught fire and the sun, coming up behind the mountains, seemed to hover and then rise like a phoenix taking flight, nevertheless a sense rather than an element was plainly in charge of the day and, in defiance of the splendour of the light, a sense other than that transmitted by the eyes. One lived in sound rather than air, and breathed it. The illumination that seized on the room, as fire catches a bundle of twigs and sticks, threw ripples and rings and quiverings on every surface, splashed and sparkled in every corner, showed everywhere the dazzle of sea and sun : yet scarcely did one notice this commotion of light, so overwhelming was the volume of sound that entered at the same time, for today was a Saint's Day, and the bells of the various churches had started their competition — friendly, though it sounded hostile — which was to last, with short intervals, until darkness fell, and to resemble the clash of armour in a medieval charge. So, for a short while let us voyage round the dominion of sound, that vast territory of fulmination and echo, and explore also its complement and reverse, the umbral empire of silence, the dark companion to this glittering planet: for, after the manner of night and day, these two are joined to each other, yet opposed. Reverberation from the towering limestone cliffs behind, hollow and overhanging, doubled the jangle and clamour, which for a time would remain steady, and then suffer all at once a whole series of convulsions, so that it was only possible to wonder what emotion or, more probable, what variant of epilepsy had seized the ringers.

The surprise was all the more vehement because I am used to bells, to the smug peals of Anglican seaside churches, calling their respectable but always diminishing flocks to worship, and the angry mutter of the bells of the Catholics, calling sinners to repentance. I have even enjoyed from a room high up, near by, the carillons of the New York spires, gaily gurgling some familiar hymn-tune on Sunday morning, and repeating with unction the jingling refrain. At Montegufoni, the bell of the church, situated just below the garden terraces, on certain occasions starts to ring at five in the morning, continues intermittently all day, and seems almost to let loose its clamour within my bedroom. Fortunately, the modulations of its voice, holy but menacing, please me. The sound of bells can be angry, solemn or warlike, it can proclaim the peace of God or summon the faithful to fight His enemies, it can, to

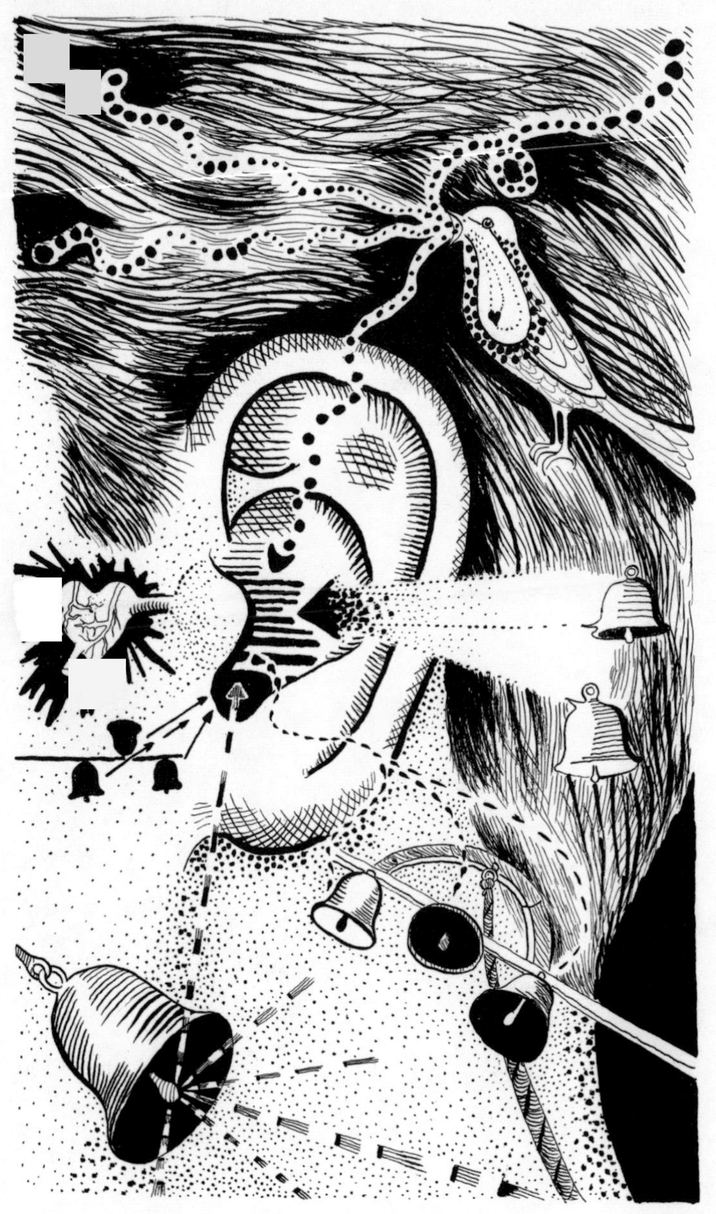

my mind, alarm and intimidate more than it can cause us to rejoice, but almost all bells, whether their music is prosaic or discordant and strange, can insinuate an air of sanctity — and Tuscan bells particularly. They are often frenzied, they rattle and clack and clank and cry, they submit to every form of syncopation, but their voice is undoubtedly holy, asserting the will of God in a pagan, fruitful and opulent countryside. They induce, withal, an exciting consciousness that there is a shadow to the magnificence of the seen world, the shadow of death. They impose the spectral image of the Cross over the ever recurrent glimpses of Ceres and the Fertility Goddess, over the corn and the grapes, the gourds and figs and olives. Moreover, Tuscan bells are never afraid. They make as much noise as they want. They bear witness to the existence of God with a note almost of threatening, and even with their lightest tintinnabulation, so far from timid, they blot out completely for the moment the liquid songs of the nightingale — in this region to be heard all through the day as well as all through the hours of darkness — and of thrush, the earthy croaks and scrapings of frog and cicada, and the aery sounds, the buzzings and flutterings and bumblings of a warm day in this garden. Then, at times, much more rarely indeed, the bell of the Castle, that hangs high above the door of the Great Court, near the Chapel, is rung, a little cracked and discordant, and bellicose, too, as it should be, since it was cast, its inscription tells us, from the metal of guns taken at the Battle of Manfredonia, and when it rings, the ancient din of battle seems to sound far down, under its sacred calling, as if through the prayers of a priest you were suddenly to detect the words of command of a former officer. All day long the bells of the church below will be subject to unexpected and inexplicable explosions of sound, and on not infrequent occasions their frenzy is joined to that apparently of every bell from every church and chapel and oratory of grey-green stone or rosy brick on every hill-top in Tuscany — for even the smallest collection of houses will have its place of worship, which will probably be found to contain a first-rate work of art, even today. . . . But we are comparing sounds and not discussing churches.

The bells of Tuscany, I was saying, are often holy in their sound, but those to which we are listening in Amalfi are louder, older, fiercer and still more minatory. There is about them a Moorish or Saracenic percussion. They contain for the corolla of their music the echo of African drums, even though the calyx seems Christian, and they are nearer always to fanatical ecstasy. Or is their sound in reality older and more pagan, a relic of the classical world ? Just as the framework of one of the smaller temples of Paestum remains as the core of the present cathedral of Pesto — ostensibly an elegant and pretty rococo edifice of the eighteenth century, the whole skeleton having been reclothed, as it were, in this alien, inappropriate but warm flesh—, just as every pillar in every church or palace in the region was pillaged from the classical city, so, perhaps, the bronze for the doors of the cathedrals of Ravello, Amalfi, Atrani and Salerno, though fashioned in distant Constantinople or at Trani or Melfi on the oriental coast of

Italy, and the bronze for the bells of the churches, may owe a similar derivation to the great doors of the famous temples at Paestum, and thus the sound of the rejected and abandoned cults may yet linger within the peals that summon to Christian worship. Howbeit, in their sound is never now to be detected any pagan joy-in-life : the ringing and its alarms are plainly connected with the soul — your soul —, the corruptions of life and death, with the truths of Heaven and the truth of Hell. Though the setting, the crags and torrents and green, oases-like gardens poised on sheer precipices of rock that is the very storehouse of the sun's energy, the pure line of the far mountains, the blue sea, patched with green and purple and gold, no less than the intimate features of the place, the jonquils' gold cups starred round with white, that spring, apparently without soil, from every crevice in the limestone, the diverse display of grey, green and brown gold in the general foliage, the narrow clefts of the valleys filled with lemon-trees, all are beautiful, supremely beautiful, yet with these the bells are not concerned : indeed, it is as if they tried to accentuate differently the loveliness of the landscape, and thereby to blot it out. They do not wish a man, as he watches the blue, pagan smoke from his bonfire ascend, brown against the grey of the rock, past the towering crags, up into the unflecked dome of azure, to reflect in what a pleasant and what a marvellous place he lives : no, to the contrary, mounting to a climax, the bells impose the spirit upon the flesh, so that nothing else can be heard except this voice nagging you to go to Heaven in its own way, not the genial murmur of the sea, not the hammering or shouting of the fishermen, nor the sounds of them beating the sides of their boats, to entice the fish into their nets, nor any of the lonely mountain cries floating down from above. All these the bells smother in their bronze embrace and carry up to Heaven. The landscape is honeycombed at the level of the sea with grottoes, and at all other altitudes with caverns, that look a fitting refuge for an anchorite — think, then, what the sound must be when the bells enter, the volume thereby multiplied and adding to itself a muffled but booming edge: think, too, of that transmuting echo of which I wrote in a previous chapter; with what a hollow and unearthly significance would it invest this concatenation of brazen tongues and clanking chains. . . . And who, you might well ask, can be found to ring the bells in some remote fortress church, riding a cliff and surrounded with broken roofs and ruined houses, what special race of angelic or diabolic ringers attends on them? Nor do they seem, these rustic peals in forgotten villages that were once large towns, to have much connection with the religion which they serve and proclaim. Yet, I suppose, to a stranger of a different faith — let us say to a Mohammedan from one of the cities of North Africa, — who came on a visit to the Latin countries, it would be the continual clamour of church bells that might linger in his memory afterwards, and that would for him impart even to the rather secular populations of the large Mediterranean cities a certain air of holiness, just as, obversely, it was the sounds of the Mohammedan world of Africa which impressed on my mind the piety of the people. . . .

All day long, we had been motoring towards Fez, and as we drew nearer to it, but at a distance still of some thirty or forty miles, we began to feel the emanation of a great and ancient city, in the same way that you have the identical experience when approaching the environs of Rome or Paris or London or Peking, some essence, indefinable but not to be confounded with any other, asserting itself in the atmosphere. Unlike a European city, Fez has no outer suburbs, and is enclosed by its own walls : but even the brown-faced, brown-legged, shaven-headed peasants, who in their dazzling white clothes worked in the sepia-coloured fields — hardly so much *fields* as wide territories —, seemed to carry some unidentifiable echo or tradition, perhaps of Pharaoh's Egypt. It was not until darkness had enveloped them that we arrived before the majestic crenellated walls of the city, and outside the gates the strings of camels, the story-tellers and snake-charmers and lank ebony minstrels, hung with cowrie-shells, from the dark interior of the continent, and the jostling, wondering crowds that surround them by daylight, had taken their departure. Yet, though we were to see some of these marvels the next day, and during the week that followed, no impression was to prove stronger than that of the first night. It was the early spring, an April that resembled a cold March, but the sky blossomed with stars, and these same days happened that year to fall within Ramadan, and each night was tinctured with its particular character. The fast of the day was over as we entered the gates, and figures hurried eagerly down the narrow, twisted streets. And during all the hours of darkness, voices sounded from old palaces and houses, challenging the unbelievers. You would wake in the stillness and blackness, to listen to these deep tones, such surely as at times the Crusaders must have heard, and to strange wild cries and songs that testified to Allah or denounced the infidel. However many times you woke, you would still hear these loud snarls and roarings. . . . It would have been impossible, you would have said, for any sound to have been more impressive. Nevertheless, more pregnant yet, and in spite of its superficial and obvious impiety, in some curious way the most religious sound I have ever heard, was the tumult and uproar created continuously by the Tibetan monks who alleged that they were praying for universal and everlasting peace within the precincts of the Lama Temple in Peking. In the vast but dilapidated Hall of the Wheel of the Law was collected a rough mob of monks in murrey-coloured robes. Some merely watched and jostled, others only joined in the proceedings to the extent of uttering short, sharp yells at regular intervals, while those actually responsible for the prayers squatted on the floor, turned the prayer-wheel and howled without ceasing like hungry wolves. Notwithstanding, it must be admitted that this outlandish clamour held within it some undeniable primitive force; something pertained to it of other worlds than this, something of antique, lost religions, and something of Hell as revealed in dreams. . . . But more startling than any sound can be a silence.

We have not yet attempted, as we have said we would, to explore the enormous empire of silence: now we must do so, endeavouring to assess its extent and dimensions, what it means and can mean; for example, the sudden benediction after noise of silence, which appears actually to increase the scale of what you see, so that entering an empty hall with no sound in it, it seems both loftier and larger than it would at other times. (So, though other writers have seen it as Pandemonium, to me Domdaniel, the hall of the sorcerer beneath the sea, must be vast and silent beyond imagination, an oceanic enclave of gigantic mutes.) The stupid fear silence as they shun solitude. When men, individually or in crowds, are moved by some surpassing emotion, by surprise, terror or some supreme beauty of the spirit or the flesh, silence falls on them. Silence is the tribute of wonder and the attribute of holiness. In the dream existence which is half our life, but shattered at once by any sound, no noise enters, no voice, I think, speaks: in it we play a muted drama, and those who communicate with us do so soundlessly. But though the reiterant rattle of a dog barking, or of its equivalent in the mechanical world, an engine running, can dwarf any scale or situation, can shrink the mask of tragedy itself, yet many beasts have agreeable voices, warm and furry, or clownish as the seal's. In what domain, though, of sound do animals dwell? Their range is limited. And if, as it is often alleged, and might indeed be deduced from the focussing of their eyes, their sight is different from that of men, so may be their hearing: they can identify a sound, perhaps, at a greater distance, but that which is identified has always a more personal appeal, signifies the approach of food or a danger; never, I apprehend, carries a hint of Heaven or a threat of Hell. But though we may not know for certain how animals hear, we can be sure that birds hear much, very much, as we do: albeit we can never tell if they are conscious of the beauty they create. Several kinds of birds have been endowed with mimetic gifts, and judging from the imitations given by parrot, minah and jackdaw, and since they can present, as they do, with such accuracy — even though they may inject into their rendering of them the unflattering caricatural quality that seems inseparable from birds' speech — the sounds we make, they must hear them as we do. (No dissection of a living bird's brain by a scientist is necessary to prove this point.) But though men may not altogether enjoy the imitations of their voices that birds offer them, the wise and the sensitive have always liked the song of birds, and that I believe is because it calls attention to the background of silence, and emphasises the peace of woodland or garden. (Most of all does this apply to a nightingale, who enhances silence as a fire embellishes a cold night.) So that when a man thrusts a singing bird into a cage, and keeps it there, he is not deliberately being cruel, but in his stupidity is trying to bring into his house part of an idyllic scene, to imprison in it the aromatic air, and sunshine, and blue sky, and early morning and evening among trees and flowers, and every sort of freshness and many kinds of silence — for with these things he associates the song of birds. Silence is of infinite variety : there is the silence of mountain-tops, the silence of Macbeth leaving the death-chamber, the hush after the birds have ceased their vespers, the silence of expectation — no moment in the theatre is so exciting as when the chatter of voices and the clatter of tea-cups dies down, and the curtain rises on a new act —, the silence of peace active, and the silence of peace passive, which is the silence of the tomb.

Who that has ever experienced — I nearly wrote *heard*, so definite and compact is it — the silence of Agamemnon's Tomb can ever forget it ? . . . Similarly majestic in its stillness is that of the approach to the Ming Tombs. . . . The road from Peking, after you have passed Ch'ing L'ung, was in those days — I write of the spring of 1934 — a matter of belief rather than of fact; only the eye of faith could discern it. After travelling some thirty miles from Peking, you discover the first sign of the famous tombs where thirteen of the sixteen Emperors who constituted one of the noblest and most powerful of Chinese dynasties, and ruled their huge Empire from the middle of the fourteenth century A.D. to the beginning of the seventeenth, lie buried : a *p'ai-lou* or triumphal arch of great magnitude and reputed to be the most beautiful in the whole vast territory of China. Formerly, you then proceeded down avenues of trees, but these have for the most part long ago been used for firewood, though one or two isolated specimens survive : you pass through a few lesser archways, and after the last, there, facing you, in a wide stretch of country surrounded by mountains, in a broad, bare, rather long, upward slope, like the roof of a tent on an immense scale, stands an enormous frozen procession that has halted here for a moment, a ceremonial parade, as it were, of vast stone figures that leads for two miles or so towards the nearest tomb; that of the Emperor Yung Lo. Famous statesmen of antique times in China, their names familiar as proverbs to the people of two thousand years, lions, camels, unicorns and elephants, stand or kneel, arranged in pairs, nobly spaced, so as to leave a wide and stately road between them. To convey an idea of the proportion of the whole scene, the elephants are thirteen feet high and fourteen feet long, and are each carved out of a single block. These guardians, mythical or real, exist, equally, being portrayed with that singular power of the Chinese sculptors and potters, who found at all epochs a convention to give an appearance of verisimilitude to beings imagined, grotesque, diabolic or angelic, just as much as to animals or men seen every day: thus a horse or dog appears no less or more real than a dragon or phoenix. I visited the tombs on an April morning, equivalent to a May morning in England, and the wide slope of the approach seemed to echo the shape of the shallow blue dome of the sky; and as I walked past these immense men and beasts under the tender but matter-of-fact light of a fine spring day, my footsteps unsounding in the grey sand, it was easy to feel that they were more real than the stranger who regarded them. They swelled for a moment everlasting with an immense actuality. The silence of the tomb here prevailed also outside it: only the lark's song broke in occasionally, spurting down from the blue and slightly misty heights.

The first monument we come to is perhaps also the finest — the tomb of the Emperor Yung Lo,[1] who rebuilt so much of Peking, and made it the capital. In front of his temple is a large stone tablet with, incised on it, the posthumous name of the great Emperor. All these tombs were works of art, but, nevertheless, the great funeral approach of figures that leads to them is even more impressive than the tombs themselves : a cluster of comfortable, worldly temples, wonderfully proportioned, and placed in a cage of fluttering spring leaves woven with sunlight. They were dignified, grand, but dedicated to mundane power and material possessions, which figure here in the death-chamber as largely as in those of ancient Egypt. But as seen on that fragrant day of spring flowers, they had something almost happy about them, and the very silence in their lofty halls is less memorable than that which reigns fitfully in the beehive tombs of Agamemnon and the Atridae, found — in that greatest of all stories of discovery — by Schliemann,[2] who, led thereto, in defiance of all academic opinion, solely by his own commonsense and his belief in the accuracy of Homer's descriptions, first found the tombs, opened them, saw for a moment the bodies of the legendary dead, and then, as he gazed, beheld them in an instant crumble, till only the gold masks they were wearing remained.[3] What can the silence of that moment have

[1] He died in 1424.

[2] Heinrich Schliemann (1822–1890), *Mycenae*, 1877.

[3] Now in the Museum at Athens.

been ? . . . But now, for the door is open, insects drift in from browsing on their fragrant pastures of flower petals on the hill-top outside, and bring in with them, as they flicker like gold pollen through the darkness, the very sound of the sunshine, while at times, too, is heard the deep, Cassandra-like voice of the stream that runs through the rocky gully far below, under the broken walls of the palace with the Lion-Gate where this race of princes lived. . . . Yet the silence is in a sense inviolate and inviolable, so that these sounds seem to leave it intact : nevertheless, silence itself in its highest form must yield in intensity to the hush of holiness. . . . Only once have I encountered it.

The country on the confines of Algeria and Morocco is mountainous in character, almost European, but rather shapeless : of beautiful colour, blue — the colour of the air and of the lupins and irises that grow there in such profusion —, and dark green and white : vegetation, clouds and sky, architecture, all share these same hues ; but in March it can be rather cold, and it was with relief, therefore, that we descended, late one afternoon, into the first obviously African plain we had seen, golden and dusty. There we were to spend the night in an outlying Moroccan town, nameless and featureless, like a maze built in mud baked by the sun. The long secretive streets and alleys ran always between walls of mud, and led nowhere, least of all out of the maze, the doors in the walls seemed never to open, yet the town was full of noise, of children, dogs, copper pots being hammered, and men hawking their wares in distant quarters, and at this hour, just before sunset, when we went for a walk, the glint of the African sun, now almost lateral, lay, like gilt metal too heavy to be borne, on the tops of the disintegrating walls. At last we found ourselves on the outskirts of the town, or so we thought, still in the maze of angular alleys, that grew longer and straighter until they turned at right angles, yet as we went further from the centre, the noise seemed to grow, to intensify, and become more varied ; shouts, songs, cries of pedlars, dogs barking, donkeys braying, children screaming and laughing ; indeed, though we had hardly met one person since we came out, it was a miniature uproar, rising from everywhere round, and very evenly distributed. . . . Of a sudden, all sound stopped, and in its place fell an instant of pure and entranced silence — silence as exciting as any sound could be. Instinctively I looked round, and there, at the end of a long lane, waiting before a door in the wall, stood the cause of it, a tall, robed figure, wearing a green turban which just caught the light of the sun. Two retainers or disciples waited behind at a reverential distance. Even though we were not near him, it was possible to feel the power emanating from him. This sense of utter peace, though it only endured for a few seconds, seemed to contain all eternity : then sound began again, the vulgar, crowded noises of life in a small town in North Africa.

I do not attempt to explain that sudden radiance of stillness, but in our hearts we knew that we had encountered that which can only be induced by the presence of a great teacher, saint or prophet. . . . It was not, for example, the holy innocence which I described in a previous chapter, of Fra Gregorio, nor that which can still be felt in the bright-winged pictures of Fra Angelico, but a great and active spiritual quality, and I came across it only twice, the second time in lesser degree, but again in Morocco. . . . Turning a corner of a street in Morocco, I saw three rabbis talking together in their black robes, reminding me of the drawing of the *Three Doctors of Divinity* by Rowlandson, now in my possession, and the *Three Lawyers* by Daumier (which must derive from it), and I stopped to watch them as unobtrusively as I could. In this living group before me, the middle figure soon put such sardonic thoughts to flight, since he belonged to a rare type, which, though one had never before encountered it in the flesh, was easy to identify: a biblical warrior-prophet, tall, robust, with flaming red hair and beard, and some knife-like sharpness of spirit that illuminated him. . . . Of the holy innocence to which I alluded, I came across another instance on a visit to Djerba, an oasis in the sea off the coast of Tunisia, and often said to be the island of the Lotus-Eaters. In this strange place exists a colony of Jews which is supposed to have settled here before the Captivity. I visited the synagogue, and the adjoining school: a large, plain room, in which a young black-bearded rabbi was sitting cross-legged on the floor, expounding the Talmud to about fifty children, who, cross-legged too, sat round him in a circle. All were intent: he, on what he was teaching, they, on what was being taught. The scene was poignantly traditional. It belonged to the Palestine of the Bible, both in the holy innocence and absorption of the rabbi, and in the rapt attention of the dark-eyed children. It could be felt that the teacher was handing over to their care something of immense and age-old importance, which they in their turn were bound to transmit to the next generation, and that, whatever their shortcomings, whatever their petty vulgarities or the hard bargains they might drive, they would be worthy of this trust, and accept, as the Jewish race had always accepted, their destiny.

The sound of bells breaks in again, and it is useless to talk further of silence or of sacred things. We are plainly back in Southern Europe by the tone, but for all the furious, fractious jangling and intensity of syncopation, there is no rattle of saints' bones in the sound this time : it is mundane and secular, rings only to proclaim that the morning is over, that it is sad blatant noon, with the promise of the day gone.

CHAPTER VIII

THE ELEMENT, WATER

THIS morning water was the governing element. Water poured from the sky, tattooed down from eaves and gutters, dripped and tapped on every surface, on pavement and pillar and step, and drummed on the glossy leaves of the orange-trees. The usual gentle lapping of the sea had increased its volume of sound until it seemed a modified thunder, at times appearing to emulate the breakers of the north, though here the appearance of fury was really obtained by other means, by rainbows, flushed and angry and promising no peace, no cessation of the rain, and by water-spouts that could be perceived dropping from the sky and spinning like witches on their broomsticks along the horizon. These last must occur, too, over British waters, but can never be seen, no doubt, through the spume of the waves ; whereas here the distance remains clear in stormy weather, so that every gyration can be followed. Indeed, an esthetic advantage which the Mediterranean

possesses over all other regions is that, though every new climatic development can be depended on to make its own effect, and though there is no single variation that does not adequately present itself or make its own dramatic effect, yet a sense of proportion always prevails. But, for all that, the very clouds over the sea are more portentous, more interesting in their shape and in the grape-bloom colour they assume, than elsewhere. Fantastic towers and crags and castles trailing into mist, mountain ranges and torn, chaotic images form and then dissolve in the immense battlefield of the sky. Even the rain is never boring, never carries the same feeling of desolation that belongs so essentially to the celebrated English drizzle.

Mediterranean and North Sea certainly differ greatly in their rages, nevertheless when the rhythm of these southern waves had conquered my mind, it swept it back many years, to the winter seas of the Yorkshire coast ; where, at Scarborough, for five or six days at a time, the pounding of the breakers would prevail over all other sounds as they battered the rocks at the base of the cliffs, undermining them, and then gradually devouring the shore, first covering it with a film of salt spray. This thunderous reiteration, together with the trumpet blasts of the wind, crushed down all other sounds, so that in the streets above, neat and prosperous and sheltered, men had to shout to each other to make themselves heard. Even far out on the moors, the lips would still be salt, and the occasional stunted and stripped winter trees, their branches lifted up, away from the sea, as if in terror, would appear to have been frozen or petrified in full flight and in the very act of escaping. As a small boy I would walk for hours on the sands, alternately fascinated and repelled by the insensate display of force, that ominous and tragic blind force that no work of man could hinder. Indeed, though I was then very young, I had already had time to watch walls erected against the sea ; flimsy barriers only to be dashed back almost at once into broken stones by these waves, the foam of which was never white, pure white, as it is in the Mediterranean, but the grey and yellow white of a seagull's wings. Nature itself could not withstand these attacks, and as I followed the culmination of each set of breakers, dependent on some inexplicable movement infinitely remote from this periphery where the battle between land and sea actually took place, it seemed to me that there was a very inappropriate quality about the few beachcombers who always appeared here during storms. Lost souls, clothed in rags, these men searched the gleaming sands minutely at low tide, gently raking for loot, their eyes intent only on what could be found, a tin of sardines from a wrecked ship or some pitiful piece of summer jewellery, light and trivial, dislodged from its hiding-place by the tremendous labour of the waves. Their ears apparently transmitted to their brains no echo of the deep-throated menace so near them, and they remained undistracted by the bitter screaming of the sea-gulls. . . . Certainly this loud bellowing of seas and winter wind presented an ill-proportioned drama of its own, but these long storms alternated here with periods of empty and imbecile calm; whereas the drama of the Mediterranean begins and ends with each sunrise and sunset.

In spite of all the efforts of man to harness it, water remains untamed as fire itself — yet it is perhaps the element of which he has made most use for his own pleasure, whereas fire offers us little else but fireworks — though I write this in no derogatory sense, for these sprays and bouquets and single flowers of flame that blossom and fade so swiftly on the night sky are not to be spurned, nor the fitful lightnings of summer woodlands and lakes, showing for the moment the same illumination that is to be seen occasionally in the pictures of Giorgione and his followers. I have also been fortunate to behold from far off the dome and façade of St. Peter's in Rome, flickering under the light of thousands of candles — candles are always used there for this decorative purpose in preference to electric light — until its whole vast bulk seemed to live and breathe within a quivering coat of fire. . . . Sometimes, too, in distant countries, fire and water have been employed together for pleasant purposes, as in China: for Tun Lich'en [1] records that on the Fifteenth Day of the Seventh Month, known as Chung Yüan, which always occurred at the time of the full moon, the boys of the Peking streets from twilight onwards would light lanterns made of lotus leaves 'in the deep hollow of which they stick a candle, so that it makes a beautiful glow through the green leaf', and go through the streets singing

> Lotus-leaf candles ! Lotus-leaf candles !
> Today you are lighted. Tomorrow thrown away !

[1] *Annual Customs and Festivals in Peking*, by Tun Lich'en. Translated and annotated by Derk Bodde.

Tun Lich'en also adds that they made ropes of glutinous incense from green artemisia plants, and lighted them so that they gleamed like 'the innumerable dots of moving fireflies', while ingenious merchants fashioned similarly, out of coloured paper, lanterns in the form of lotus blossom, lotus leaves, flower baskets, herons and egrets, calling them all lotus-flower lanterns. Many people went later to the Second Sluice on the Grand Canal (Yun Ho) for recreation, and some walked on stilts or dressed up as lions 'to do lion-dances', while during the evening lanterns were lighted along the Canal, this being called '*the Setting Out of River Lanterns*'. Hundreds of small candles fastened to floats were set adrift on the waters, to guide the spirits of those who had been drowned, while men, women and children walked along the banks carrying their lotus-leaf lanterns. These customs prevailed in Tun Lich'en's own day — he wrote *circa* 1900 — and had been handed down, he states, from the time of the Yüan and Ming dynasties. . . . But such amphibian treats as these today are rare, and water supplies us with a thousand pleasures to the three or four offered by fire.

Even apart from the fact that a man is in the summer able to bathe in seas, lakes and pools, and in the winter to skate, he can admire fountains, water lawns and parterres, runnels, jets, cascades, torrents and cataracts. Consider for a moment the various joys of fountains alone: the gigantic plumes of Versailles, tossed aloft and swirling on a flutter of summer wind in their green world; the innumerable and diverse voices of the waters of the Villa d'Este, in the whole of

Europe the most fantastic and fascinating display of taming water, far more to be esteemed than any harnessing of falls for commerce, its triumphal terrace of jets, each looping like a whip in the clear but sombre air beneath the shade of cypress and ilex, the gurglings of the runnels on the flights of steps, which in its turn recalls the full-throated murmur of Spanish gardens, such as La Granja, or the Generalife at Granada, or the splashing of the two rapid streams that leap down through the woods on the Alhambra hill to the city below. . . . Nevertheless, in spite of such delights as these, water, like fire, is never to be trusted. You cannot play with it.

In this connection I recall an unfortunate personal experience. . . . For various reasons, I was, some twenty years ago, obliged to construct a dam in the woods near Renishaw. To pay for this, I had to borrow money from my bankers. When the dam was completed, it proved, sure enough, to have cost more than the estimate I had put forward. Accordingly, I paid a visit to the bank, and explained the circumstances : that my great-grandfather had been compelled to build a similar dam, which had collapsed a century later, and that now I had been forced to construct it again. Thus, though it had proved expensive, it could be regarded as expenditure that only occurred once in a hundred years, and it was now finished and doing its job. . . . I said all this — and the same evening an almost tropical rainstorm poured down the steep Derbyshire hillsides and utterly demolished the new dam. With it went roaring down the valley the living contents and wooden roofs of hen-houses and pigsties, so that not only was it necessary for me to build the dam again at once, instead of someone else having to do it in a century's time, but, in addition, I faced actions for damages by irate owners who blamed me for thus floating their roofs, poultry and livestock.

Water, then, it will be recognised, can be treacherous in its rages, destroying mountain roads and those in valleys. Moreover, it is always — like so much else — most in supply where least in demand. In the places that rain would benefit, such as southern Spain and Italy and the great sandy tracts of Africa and Mexico, it is rare and has to be cupped and treasured in a thousand ingenious ways, while on the other hand the men and women who dwell beneath the walls of a dam or by a waterfall live in perpetual pluvial terror. Their whole world, their lives and deaths are governed by rainfall of an inch, so that the rain we hear drumming down may, for some, signify despondency and death, for others, pleasures and prosperity. Moreover those, apparently, who know best how to make use of this element live, as do the Arabs and Moors, in waterless districts. The oases, for example, are marvels of nature and artifice in conjunction.

Aquatic civilisations, like those of Venice or Montezuma's Mexico City, have always been rare : but such a culture also was that of ancient Cambodia : which, though so tropical in character, was essentially a land of water. Its people — or, rather, the King and the governing class — wove these two elements to their own ends, for, as I have more fully elaborated elsewhere, the wealth that created the golden temples of Angkor, the walled pleasances, the shrines and wide water basins, the ruins of which cover so many square miles, much of it still in the dank virid grip of the jungle, clamped together by the roots of trees or the serpentine coils of its rank vegetation, derived from the sale of kingfishers' wings to the Chinese market; because throughout the huge territories of that vast country, every bride in good circumstances was obliged by force of convention to wear a tiara head-dress made of those vivid blue and green feathers. But kingfishers, in order to prosper and multiply, had to be provided with fish; so that all these formal settings and presentations of water, natural or artificial, with great flights of stone steps, and balustrades, and lines of sculptured gods and nagas with many heads, can be seen to have had a basic commercial purpose, as well as a ceremonial and religious use. And the kingfishers of Cambodia, though many of their former haunts are now dry, or have been devoured by the irresistible green tide of the jungle, have outlived the civilisation that battened on them. The men who designed and built and used these lakes and pools and streams are dead, their names forgotten — no-one today is certain to what race the Khmers belonged or what sudden doom overtook them — but the birds, glittering in their liveries of blue and green, and with, under these two colours, a glint of gold, remain the perfect examples of their kind, and are still very numerous.

In China, on the other hand, it was the decorative rather than the commercial aspect that appealed to the

Emperor, his court and the Mandarins. Lakes were made, like looking-glasses, to reflect ; to double the artfully disposed trees, the islands, the sites of which were most carefully calculated to afford the best views, as much from their own shores as from the mainland of the park, or from the bridges. Pei-Hai, or North Sea Lake, in Peking was one of the most celebrated, strange, and in its own fantastic way, idyllic pieces of ornamental water. It was first excavated and filled for an Emperor of the twelfth century A.D., so tradition holds rather vaguely : and Marco Polo leaves an enthusiastic account of it as it was in the reign of Kubla Khan, who used the park for hunting, and enlarged and improved the lake. The great Emperor made, too, an island and raised on it an artificial hill : the same on which, four centuries later, the White Pagoda was built to celebrate a visit of the Dalai Lama to the capital. That famous builder, the Emperor Yung Lo, who largely reconstructed Peking, ordered the lake to be dug out again. The numerous gigantic carp which still swam in its waters until recently had been placed there, tradition maintained, by the Emperor K'ung Hsi. The Empress Dowager particularly enjoyed floating on these waters, and, indeed, defying changes of dynasty, from the reign of Kubla Khan to that of the last, listless Manchu Emperor, Pei-Hai continued to be a centre of court life and diversion. In the spring of each year, weary dynasts and their families would seek peace, embarking on vast painted barges to observe the burgeoning of shrubs and trees on the shores and islands, which in North China is so fierce in its manifestations, raging like a green fever: and in July and August they would be rowed to the lotus beds, to examine those flowers for which Pei-Hai is famous: while even in the brisk but bitter winter the lake would serve the purposes of pleasure, for, under the Manchu House, men of the Eight Banners would give expert displays of skipping, skating and jumping on the ice, for the benefit of the Emperor who would watch the performance from the Tower of Felicitous Skies, or from some lower pavilion on the shore. Before the exhibition took place, the surface of the ice would be literally ironed-out, for men would be detailed to remove all lumps and smooth all inequalities with hot irons. It may be surmised that the most expert of those who were selected would have come from Manchuria and Mongolia, to whom moving on ice would be as natural as walking on grass to others: for the Eight Banners — the old personal and professional army of the Manchu Emperors — consisted of troops from those two dominions, as well as of Chinese, these last being recruited from those whose ancestors, natives of North China, had joined the invading force and had espoused the cause of the alien Manchus in their long contest with the last Ming Emperors: in short, from the descendants of a successful Fifth Column.

Pei-Hai was first opened to the public after the Revolution, in 1921, and soon sadly deteriorated. Even though by 1934, when I saw it, it had clearly suffered, yet the lake was still there, its banks were still embossed with great temples, full of an antique gloom and majesty, and garnished with lighter pavilions, painted and trellised, and jutting out over the limpid water, and blithe and elegant albeit in decay. The shores were still decorated with plantations and clumps of cypresses and of those cedars known as *smoke-trees*, because to Chinese eyes the grey or blue-green fronds or needles suggest the image of wood smoke lying in layers upon the motionless air : the buildings still bore resounding and imaginative titles, such as *Porch for Washing Orchids* — surely almost as much a work of supererogation as that of painting the lily —, *Joyful Sun Hall*, the *Lute Studio*, and *Saving Time Hall*. But now it is rumoured — I do not know with what truth, for an iron curtain engenders rumours just as surely as it kills facts — that the temples have been allowed to fall down and that the Communist Government have cut all the trees, regarded by them strictly as utilitarian timber, drained the lake, to use its bed for growing food, and divided the Emperor K'ung Hsi's fat carp among the poor.

The northern continuation of Pei-Hai is called the Lake of the Ten Temples (Shih Ch'a Hai), and Tun Lich'en [1] writes of it, 'although other places also have lotoses, no one goes to them for enjoyment. . . . At the time when flowers are blossoming, the scenery along the North Bank Section is most lovely. The green willows droop their streamers, women appear with bright coloured costumes and brilliant cosmetics, and the flowers shine in people's faces, now concealed and now indistinctly apparent, until one knows not whether it is the people who are people, or the flowers which are flowers.' . . . More modern, but scarcely less beauti-

[1] See footnote on page 169.

ful, is the great lake in the grounds of the New Summer Palace. Though a piece of ornamental water had been here for centuries, the Empress Dowager had it designed anew ; and to her it owes its present shape and planting. After the fashion of many tyrants in times past, she was an impassioned lover of nature, of trees and birds and flowers in particular, and in the summer months she would often be rowed in the imperial barge to inspect the lotuses here, as well as at Pei-Hai. She also liked to picnic on the marble boat which lies so heavily on the lightest of waters : a vessel she created with the money obtained from the taxes levied on her subjects on the pretext that ships must be built in order to vanquish the enemy at the time of the Chinese-Japanese War.

Inseparably connected with Chinese lakes are the enchanting bridges which are such a feature of the vistas to be obtained — indeed sometimes so cunningly planned are these arms of water that you feel they have been placed there to show off a bridge, rather than the reverse. Most exquisite of the several types employed in the Chinese system of landscape gardening is that known as the Camel's Back Bridge. Of comparatively recent invention, an excellent example of it is to be seen at the lake in the grounds of I Ho Yüan, the Summer Palace, where it was erected during the long years of the Dowager. The span of such a bridge, as it leaps elegantly into the air, almost completes a circle : certainly at the least it circumscribes three-quarters of one, and offers a curious pattern, a kind of figure 8, when doubled by its reflection. . . . In Peking itself the bridge most celebrated for its beauty is the triple-titled marble bridge which crosses the neck of the North and Middle Lakes in Pei-Hai. The ordinary and modern name for it was Imperial Canal Bridge, but it was also referred to by its original name of *Golden Sea Bridge* as well as by its official style of *Bridge of the Golden Sea Turtle and Jade Butterfly* : all these appellations are written on the arches that lead, one at each end, to the bridge — though, no doubt, by now, if it survives, these will have been erased to make way for a fourth more materialist and correctly Marxian. It is in truth a superb and impressive bridge, of graceful line, and of a light golden colour, with nine arches to support it and intricately though boldly carved balustrades. Chinese poets have continually extolled it in verse, and the lines that the Emperor Ch'ien Lung wrote for it are inscribed on its pillars. . . . But the most renowned of bridges, not in the city, but in the whole neighbourhood, is the Lu Kou Ch'iao or Reed Ditch Bridge, famous to foreigners under the designation of Marco Polo Bridge. This structure, which crosses the Muddy River some seven miles west of the capital, is magnificent, even in its decay. It took five years, from 1189 to 1194, to build, and thousands of men were during that time engaged in working on it.

Marco Polo, who crossed it a century later, after describing its position, writes : '. . . Over this river there is a very fine stone bridge, so fine indeed, that it has very few equals. . . . The fashion of it is this : It is 300 paces in length and it must have a good eight paces in width, for ten mounted men can ride across it abreast.

It has 24 arches and as many water-mills, and is all of a very fine marble, well built and firmly founded. Along the top of the bridge, there is on either side a parapet of marble slabs and columns made in this way : At the beginning of the bridge there is a marble column, and under it a marble lion, so that the column stands upon the lion's loins, whilst on the top of the column there is a second lion, both being of great size and beautifully executed sculpture. At a distance of a pace from this column there is another precisely the same, also with its two lions, and the space between them is closed with slabs of grey marble to prevent people from falling over into the water. And thus the columns run from space to space along either side of the bridge, so that altogether it is a beautiful object.'

Though it now lacks half its arches, these having been washed away in a flood in 1890, and never replaced, it is recognisable to this day from Marco Polo's description. The fact that the bridge has had to be rebuilt on more than one occasion and frequently repaired during the course of the past five centuries may well explain such discrepancies as exist between Marco Polo's account of it and its present appearance — for instance, he credits it with twenty-four arches, whereas now there are only eleven. But in connection with this bridge, counting seems dangerous ; because though the lions carved on the balustrade and pillars are reputed to number two hundred and eighty, it was expressly stated in the reign of the Ming Emperor Chia Ch'ing, when the bridge was repaired, that the quantity of lions was beyond reckoning, while it was related locally that several persons had gone off their heads in the attempt to compile an accurate census of them. . . . Beautiful bridges must have existed in the Venice which Marco Polo had left, yet plainly he was amazed at the size and quality of the Lu Kou Ch'iao ; but then all the bridges in Venice were constructed for human beings, not for horse-drawn traffic : as, indeed, were then the majority of bridges in Europe. From this epoch dates the Devil's Bridge, near the road from La Cava to Vietri on the Salernitan coast. It is a single arch and of stone, and on it there is only room for a single traveller to cross : the appropriate figure to find on it would be, one would imagine, rather than the Devil, a medieval magician in a cloak, and with a steeple hat, who mumbles spells as he gazes into the stream beneath. To the seventeenth century belongs the elegant but discreet bridge, in dark stone, spanning the river at the entrance to the park at Chatsworth — not the least charming feature of that fine domain, and one that is the pattern of many of its period, which have elsewhere been swept away. . . . But as well as having been fortunate enough to see this bridge I have just described, I have been privileged to see some of the most stylised and impressive bridges of today, the aerial and magical elongation of the George Washington Bridge over the Hudson River outside New York, the mathematical complexity of the Triborough Bridge that connects Long Island with New York, and that marvellous feat of engineering, and supreme example of modern architecture, the Golden Gate Bridge of San Francisco. . . . But bridges are to be accounted works

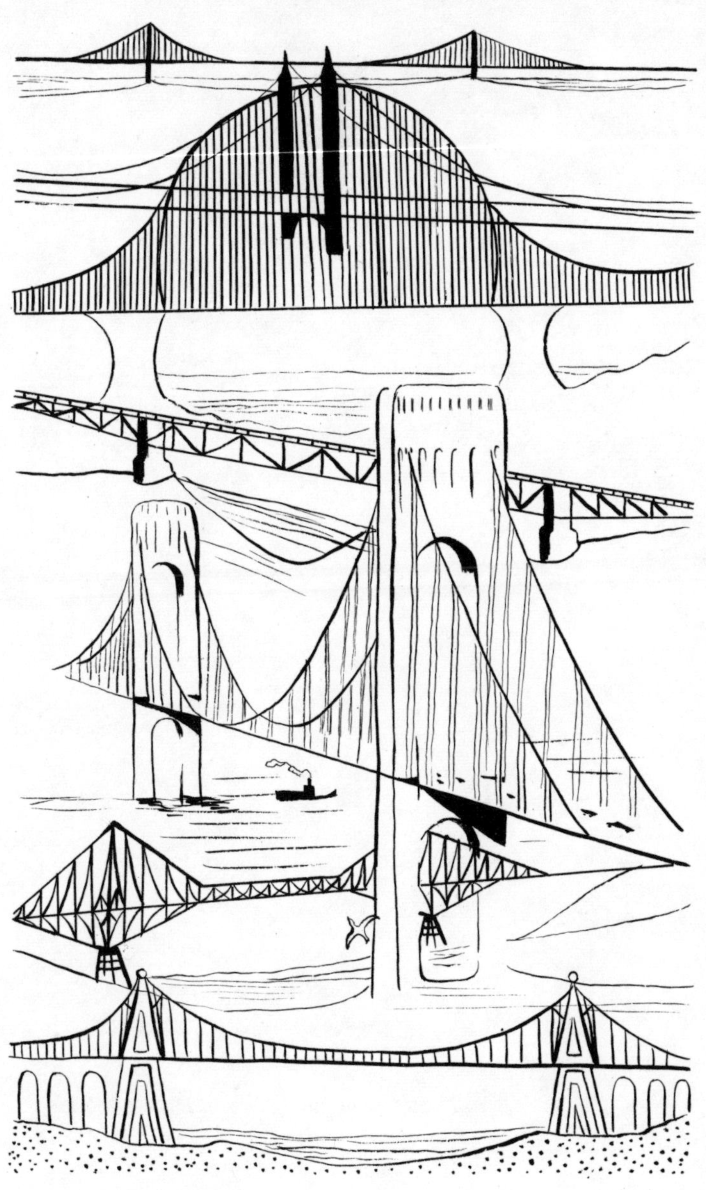

of artifice, as well as being often works of art, and we must return to nature.

Of natural contrasts as opposed to contrived, I take the Fountain of Cyane near Syracuse, and the Niagara Falls (and what a fine and suitable name is that for a gigantic watery display, with the very sound of water drumming and falling and foaming and roaring in the strange lilt of its syllables !) . . . All one April morning we spent, Marion Dorn, Ted Kauffer, Adrian Stokes and I, being rowed up a small stream by a boatman who, in appearance, had strayed into the modern world from the *Odyssey*. Every now and then he would clutch a small crab at the edge of the bank, put it into his mouth and crunch it up, saying, 'Vair goot'. To try to dissuade him from it was hopeless, only added zest to his appetite, but fortunately as we got further away, the crabs grew fewer. Our view was bounded by the banks of the stream, and here, though — or perhaps because — the mediums, earth, air and water, were unaltered and inalterable, the influence of ancient times prevailed, and it was often difficult to recollect that we were not in Greece. The only obvious change in our limited landscape were the great clumps of papyrus, with their long, green-fringed heads, which grew on the banks as you approached the spring, and had been introduced from Lower Egypt by the Saracens at the end of the ninth century. On the surface of the water, time ceased to have any existence, and the hours sped by until we reached the Fountain, with its incomparable depths of clear water, smooth and limpid, but with unexpected tones of blue and brown in it — the very colour of a mermaid's tail. Here tradition maintained that the Nymph Cyane had undergone metamorphosis for opposing Pluto when he was abducting Proserpine, and it would not require much imagination to perceive, at the bottom of the glassy but rather smoky water, the Nymph taking on her form again. Everything about this Fountain is classical and appropriate. The first object we saw when we climbed out of the boat on to dry land was the bleached skull of a bull, looking as if it had just set the pattern for the decoration of an altar to the gods. Every tree, every plant, possessed proportion and therefore significance. It was impossible to think here of storms or disasters, just as, obversely, it would be difficult to think of anything else in connection with Niagara Falls but stress and cataclysm.

I have always loved waterfalls : their spray, spume and fret are to me a continual pleasure, as are all the steps in the gradation between waterfall and fountain. I love those peculiar to the middle slopes of mountains, where from grottoes lined with maidenhair fern the water tumbles into a pool below in great streaks and slabs, with the sound of the rushing of a comet ; I love, though I fear, the rapids in rivers ; I love the rustic, small torrents, where the water foams, and the artificial falls, with water thin, smooth and transparent as sheets of glass, of formal gardens ; I love all cataracts and cascades and the rainbows caught in their spray, and swirling snow water falling into, and forming, green lakes. It was, therefore, with joy that I accepted the invitation of three ladies of Buffalo to take me to see Niagara.

Buffalo itself is a magnified Main Street, leading into idyllic suburbs planted with double avenues of trees. I recall that in the morning, when I arrived at the hotel after an all-night journey, the bell-hop who took me up to my room on the seventeenth storey had at once, directly we entered, turned on the radio. A dismal sound of early-morning crooning came through.

'Please turn that gadget off,' I asked him.

'Then you don't like music!' he commented.

'Then I do like music,' I corrected him.

Later, I had a press conference, attended a large luncheon, and lectured immediately afterwards, so that by the time we started for the Falls I was tired. Nevertheless, the idea of Niagara had supported me all through the day, its pleasures and trials. Directly the lecture and tea were over, we started, and first we crossed the river and drove along the Canadian side — for the beauty of which, with its parkland planting, I had been as little prepared as for the desolation of the American approach.

Many have considered Niagara overpraised : I am not one of them. . . . Often I had wondered about it and the sound it must make, but I had never adequately anticipated the majesty of its thunders, nor the instantaneity with which you encounter them. Nor had I visualised beforehand the lovely colour of it, the glorious shifting greens of snow and weed. Nevertheless, the first sound of this great waterfall was even more impressive than the first sight of it. At one moment the noises of the day are as usual : and the next you can hear nothing but the myriad tongues of the water, roaring variously and mounting crescendo to a climax. The progression and diminution both seem to be without reason, to acknowledge no law. No man could talk and make himself heard. You are in a world struck dumb, but you feel an added energy: the sound and its vibrations fill the body with the same power that comes from the roughest seas breaking upon rocks. The waters leaped and tumbled and snarled like lions, and the breath of them lay on the air for a moment, so that it was as if you were going to be privileged to watch the formation of a cloud. Where the green water ceased, it wore the pelt of a polar bear, white and yellow. The roar of Niagara is the Delphian voice of the great spaces of North America.

Few people were about at this hour, for November dusk was drawing near: but I saw a solitary Redskin watching the rhythm of the rushing and foaming of the Falls with an extraordinary intentness, as if hypnotised by their movement. He looked dejected and desolate, I thought: albeit he may have been paid to stand there, to add to the effect, in the same way that in the latter part of the eighteenth century the owners of Stowe and of other great landscape gardens chartered ancient bearded villagers to pose as anchorites in artificial caves. But such hermits were obliged, as part of their job, to wear appropriate anchoretic tatters, and were this Indian under contract to the municipality, or whatever the local governing body there may be, he would, I apprehend, be similarly expected to sport his full costume and war-paint. As it was, a dingy store suit encased his body, and he had lost his feathers, and, instead, wore a Tyrolean hat on his head. But what, I wondered, was taking place *inside* it, as he dreamed there : what occupied his mind : what stories of past tribal grandeurs, or what visions of catastrophes to come to the Pale-Faces ? Or was he asking himself how it was that thousands of miles of water had failed to keep them out — had indeed brought them here ? He may, looking at rocks and buildings, have wondered whether fortifications — a wall, for instance, since walls are always the last resort of those whose fate is sealed — would have excluded more efficiently the canting hordes.

CHAPTER IX

WALLS

Even as a small boy walking on the top of the neat, squat Roman walls of York, I realised that they could never keep out the east wind, let alone an enemy of more corporeal entity. They seemed to me not only ugly, but useless, and though I was always assured anxiously by the presiding governess or tutor that on these thick stone fortifications 'two chariots could drive abreast', I could never think why they should want to! Consequently I was surprised to find out, not so many years after, that the walls of Lucca, built a millennium and a half later, though plainly obsolete as a defence, presented — quite apart from the avenues of flowering horse-chestnut which grow on them — a quiet beauty of their own. . . . Earlier in this book, I wrote of the doomed idealism of towers, of their bird-like soaring to escape earth's dangers, and of Babel and its fall, which offered so strange an allegoric parallel to the League of Nations and the war that followed its establishment and

dissolution : but far more devoid of hope, because of its absolute and blind materialism, is the reliance on walls. And it is singular that after so many instances could have served as warning to us, the idea of them as a means of defence should have revived in our lifetime with the construction of the Maginot Line. At least the Great Wall of China enclosed a whole vast territory, almost a continent for size, in one unbroken sweep : whereas the Maginot Line was inconsistent — and everyone professionally interested in modern warfare, if no-one else, was aware of it — in that it admitted gaps in its circuit, as if made specially so that the enemy could enter by them. . . . Yet who knows but that this now notorious and classical failure in the art of resistance may, at some unspecified date in the future, acquire that quality of accidental beauty, such as the walls of Lucca, and many other essays in defence, have come by — our own Roman Wall, for example ? No walls, I apprehend, even when they are strong and well manned, can ever stop, or have ever stopped, an enemy : time and attack wear them down. Moreover, there are other methods of capture which can be practised. There is always that of the Trojan Horse or Fifth Column to be tried, or the musical approach, as that to the walls of Jericho — though I should be doubtful of a similar spell working in so unspiritual an age. (Nevertheless I noticed yesterday in an Italian newspaper that the walls of Jericho have been uncovered, and prove to be seven in number ; which affords us a numerical problem, reminiscent of *The Three Bears* : did Joshua blow seven times before each wall collapsed

— which makes forty-nine blasts in all, if my arithmetic can be trusted —, or just once for each of them ?) But nearly all these great barriers of stone, if they be high enough, and sufficiently on the grand scale, are in the course of years converted into objects almost of natural beauty. To gain that fortuitous quality, however, they must first learn to be contemporary, to cease, obviously, to be of any use for the purpose for which they were designed, and attain — and this alone seems easy in any age — to the status of ruins.

I feel rather hesitant of launching on my theme, the beauty of walls, since I remember well an old, very bad painter, wearing somewhat the air of a brigand who had given up his work for a job in the Civil Service, and always when I met him, and would enquire what he was painting, I would inevitably receive the same reply, which used both to amuse and enrage me, 'Masses of Masonry' : (*Masses* rhyming with *classes*). But that is what I am writing about now, and the processes of travelling hither and thither in search of them. I have been fortunate in what I have seen. I have examined not only the walls of cities, but of whole countries : the lofty, golden sheath of Constantinople, the gigantic and now apparently purposeless walls of the Palace, large as a city, of Meknes, in Morocco, the gothic framing of Aigues-Mortes (which we have so often seen before in illuminated missals), and of Carcassonne and Villeneuve-lès-Avignon, the crumbling walls, so exquisite in colour, whether built of rosy brick or of the same dark stone that the Etruscans used, of many Tuscan towns (and it often seems there, indeed, as if the smaller the place, the larger its walls—those of Florence, what remains of them, are insignificant in scale, for instance, when compared with those of Certaldo, Castelfiorentino or San Miniato-al-Tedesco), the stout, rose-pink defensive walls of the Alhambra, crowning a hill — walls that are seldom mentioned, for they are outmatched by the delicate folly of their interior, the pillars and honeycomb ceilings, and marble-paved garden courts of box and water, yet surely among the most beautiful, in the contrast of strength to fragility that they offer. The walls of Mycene, perhaps the most remarkable in the world, are paralleled, or even caricatured, by those of certain industrial buildings of the eighteen-forties in the North of England, and during the claustrophobic course of the 1939–45 war I could at Renishaw sometimes obtain the nostalgic illusion of travel by going for a walk along the old canal bank, with the ruins of its cyclopean keeps and fortresses looming through the steam rising from the water (for the water, pumped out from the factories, is warm, and seems, like all else, itself to be decaying). Nor must I omit from my incomplete catalogue the walls of the Forbidden City in Peking, for they, tilted or aslant at so ancient an angle, count as of the first rank. Moreover, they constitute the representatives in the modern world of those that encircled Nineveh or Babylon : a type infinitely old, and governed by very strict tradition in their building. Above all, I must record that I have been privileged to see the most famous defence in the world, the Great Wall of China.

In order to visit it, we determined to leave Peking in

late May, in some ways the most enticing of all months in that city, and to break our journey home at Shan-Hai-Kuan, a town on the frontier of China and Manchuria, where the Great Wall sweeps over the mountains down to the sea. . . . The journey, though at all times long and tiring, at this particular moment offered its own unique discomforts, more mental than physical: because the brigands who flourished in the then amiable anarchy of North China had lately perfected a new technique, modern and ingenious, and the track on which we were going was their favourite choice for its operations. . . . They — let us postulate twenty or more respectable-looking men, young or middle-aged, and dressed in their best clothes — would make their way separately to the Peking railway-station, and would be careful to betray no knowledge of the existence of their comrades in the enterprise. Each of them would purchase a first-class ticket at the booking-office to different places along the line. They would then take seats in judiciously selected positions, spread about. To the other passengers and to the railway officials they seemed just simple, order-loving Chinese gentlemen scattered over the length of the train — but directly it passed some particular landmark, which had been agreed upon beforehand as the signal for united action, these sheep turned suddenly into a pack of wolves, drew revolvers, overpowered and trussed the guards and ticket-collectors, and took what money and valuables they could find on the passengers. Any traveller whom they suspected of being a rich man, they carried off with them and held for ransom. These robbers, in order to make their get-away, pulled the communication cord. . . . It was an accomplished, streamlined performance: but fortunately we were spared it, and arrived without incident at Shan-Hai-Kuan.

As we descended from the train, the first feature of the landscape that caught the eye was the Great Wall of China, climbing up mountains and streaming down them in a steady progression of stone and brick, ending here, where it touches the waters of the Gulf of Chihli, its dramatic and unrivalled encirclement. Indeed the Great Wall incorporates at this spot the lesser system which protected the town — and also the enemy within it: for Shan-Hai-Kuan was already in Japanese occupation. We stayed in the house of a hospitable and argumentative Irishman who lived there, and whose chief ambition in life was to improve the relations existing between Great Britain and the Japanese. He held on this, as on other matters, his own opinion, and towards his purpose had caused to be engraved on his visiting card, on one side, his name, *Mr. R. T. Foble*, with, disposed artistically round it, a verse of the British National Anthem with a commensurate length of music, on the other the Japanese version of his style, *Foble San*, with similarly set out round it a stanza of the Japanese National Anthem with an equivalent run of the sounds that accompanied it. As yet, I observed, his method had met with as little success as, militarily, had the Great Wall of China; since the Japanese controlled everything and dominated the Chinese citizens, thereby demonstrating once again the futility of walls, the strength of which can be so easily turned to use against their defenders. Nevertheless, abortive as this great monument of military and engineering skill has so often proved itself, no-one could wish — except, as we shall see, on humanitarian grounds — that it had never been erected. A single glance at the famous barrier revealed a little of its scale and splendour, and when later we mounted it at the place where it first joined the town walls, it was possible to follow the course of it over hill and valley as far as the eye could see. The colour of the nearer landscape, as of the majestic mountains beyond, was sombre, brown and grey and olive-green, though we were already in the last week of May, for Shan-Hai-Kuan is far north, and spring comes there tardily. Clouds swathed the mountain-tops, clung to eminences lower down, and even in places hid and, as it were, absorbed stretches of the Great Wall.

The colossal and the intensely strange or monstrous, especially with the passage of time, contribute to any structure their extrinsic qualities of beauty : because wonder and esthetic appreciation as emotions are closely akin. Thus the Seven Wonders of the world seemed always beautiful to those beholding them, and similarly, when we look at the Great Wall, the mind is influenced by some knowledge of its history and extent. To evaluate its qualities of greatness, no less than for a just comprehension of the failure it represents, it is necessary to recall a few facts, facts so odd and proportions so vast that they might easily be deemed fables. . . . The conception and the building of the Great Wall is due to Ch'in Shih Huang ; it was begun in 221 B.C., and took twenty years to complete. Its height varied from twenty to thirty feet, its width from twenty feet at the base to fifteen at the level of the upper platforms, and towers broke the regularity of it at intervals of every three hundred and sixty Chinese feet, so that its defenders could telegraph information by means of smoke signals along the sweep of seventeen hundred miles from Shan-Hai-Kuan to Ch'ia-Yü-Kuan in Kansu, where it approached that remote and unexplored country on the confines of Tibet. Moreover, though the main front covers the distance stated above, this gigantic structure loops and bends and twists and turns in on itself so frequently that in its full extent it is computed to stretch two thousand five hundred miles, or, by a comparison more familiar to us, as far as from London to Leningrad. No fewer than a million men were engaged in the task of making it, and it was largely built by forced labour : for, in addition to the three hundred thousand troops whom Ch'in Shih Huang ordered to be employed on it, every criminal throughout the extent of China was obliged to lend a doubtless unwilling hand, and, in addition — since the Emperor, resembling in this trait other, later tyrants, was a confirmed book-burner —, many scholars, students and men of letters, were seized and compelled to work on the Great Wall. The fabric of it was composed of earth, very closely pressed and rammed down, faced on both sides by brick, except at the base, where stone is used instead. These materials are bound together by a particularly hard and enduring mortar of a peculiarly flashing swan's-wing white; which men no longer know how to make. So many persons died while engaged in the making of the wall that their bodies were just casually thrown into the earth that filled the middle of it or into the embankment on which it stood, and in consequence the Chinese people invented a proverb: 'The Wall is the longest cemetery in the world'. . . . When such facts as these are called to mind, the Great Wall can be seen to constitute the most perfect and the most impressive memorial both to perseverance and to the frequent futility of logic: the Great Wall *should* have worked, it should have kept out Mongols, Manchus, and the Foreign Devils with their ghosts' eyes and smell of mutton (of which the Chinese complain), but never once did it fulfil this purpose. Howbeit, this matchless barrier — or parts of it — found a use, although one that had never been intended: for Chinese doctors maintained that its glittering white mortar possessed valuable therapeutic properties. Unlike most Chinese medicines, which rely as much on quantity as quality, since it is held that volume is an effective psychological factor, impressing the mind no less than the palate of the patient, they must, one assumes, have prescribed this cement in small doses — or perhaps in the same way that those undergoing a cure at, let us say, Bath or Vichy or Marienbad consume a strictly measured-out quantity of the water of the spring at the source itself, so those who needed so fortifying a remedy as this might be recommended to gnaw a cubic inch or two of the Great Wall on the spot.

Next after this prime instance of failure as a defence, the most notoriously unsuccessful of walls — unless, carried away by local patriotism, we decide to grant precedence to that sad, stunted stone quarry, the remaining portion of our own Roman Wall — is the barrier which once encircled Constantinople and so often betrayed its defenders. It is a long time since I visited that great city — how long I do not recall, though I recollect that one of the early Labour Governments was in power in England, for I stayed with Sir George Clerk, that highly stylised and charming Ambassador, and one morning he sent for me and announced, 'The Government have asked me to look after Mr. and Mrs. Sidney Webb : they are coming to lunch today, and if you make one of your jokes it may cost me my job. Please keep that in mind.' The meal passed off, happily, without incident, and after it was over I walked as far as the walls of the city, and marvelled at their beauty. Even in their present condition the marble or fine stone that is the material of them has through the passage of the centuries assumed a tone of rich, dark amber, while the actual construction of them is so closely knitted that it is scarcely possible to discern the dividing lines : the whole mass might, it seems, have been cut from one block. Yet time after time they let into the capital of the world bandit armies, including those of the Crusaders, when an objectionable octogenarian Doge of Venice, Andrea Dandolo, was the first to scale the wall. These waves of invasion were preliminary to the great collapse : they weakened the city, sapped its strength, destroyed its prestige among the barbarians, and so prepared the way for the eventual capture of the city by the Turks, and the translation of its name from the Christian Constantinople to the Mussulman Stamboul. The terror of the inhabitants at the time of the final siege must have been unparalleled, because the Turks had spent seventy years or more mopping up the fragments of the Byzantine Empire, and solidifying it into a domain of their own, and during that period tales had poured into the ancient capital, with the refugees from the surrounding territories, always emphasising the brutality and savagery of the Ottoman armies.

Now nothing was left to the people of the great city, except their walls, their faith, and a few superstitions. Thousands of men, women and children, people of every kind and class, sought shelter under the immense shallow dome of Santa Sophia, not so much to pray as because a well-known prophecy foretold that so long as the two pillars outside the cathedral remained standing, it would never fall to the infidel : (there one of the pillars still rears its full height to this hour : the other is a broken stump). All day, all night, they waited, crowded together so that they could scarcely move, listening to the fierce songs and cries of the besieging armies, and to the furious rolling of their famous kettle-drums — a fury filled with a mumbo-jumbo hatred of Christ. . . . After a passage of time which seemed without end, the infidel at last broke through the walls, and the Sultan led his men direct to the most celebrated church in Christendom, and rode, it was said, straight up to the altar on his horse, slashing the crowd out of his way with his scimitar. Most of the older refugees were butchered where they stood, in front of their children, and the younger men and women were taken as slaves. . . . Since the mosaics were uncovered, I have not seen the famous building, but certainly in the days when it was a mosque it seemed as if the shadow of that appalling massacre still tainted the air — more especially was it to be felt in the very wide, empty galleries which at certain times appeared to harbour great hosts of the unseen. . . . Still, as my father commented to me, in some similar connection, 'There are quite enough horrors today without digging up those of the past' ; let us therefore only reiterate that the beauty of the remaining walls, such as those attached to the Golden Gate, though they so often betrayed the capital they were built to protect, is memorable. Not only, moreover, are they beautiful, but in the city which now is full of mosques that look like bloated spiders, they stand out, though intended for warfare, as most clearly the work of civilised men, and not of a barbarian race of *nouveaux riches* — and this remark leads us across the Mediterranean to Morocco.

There, at Meknes, a vast palace was constructed to the order of the black Sultan of Morocco, Mulai, who aspired for the hand of one of Louis XIV's daughters, and with that matrimonial purpose in view entered into negotiations with the Sun King, as well as preparing for her this huge and intricate building, now in ruins. When whole in all its splendour, it must have seemed like a very much glorified mud palace designed by one of the Bibienas. The very conception of it manifests a vulgar, megalomaniacal magnificence — but a magnificence all the same. These towering cliffs of *pisé*, now unroofed, honey-coloured and slowly mouldering away in the intense heat and leonine light of North Africa, are no less beautiful than the Roman cities of the desert : which, I think, together with whispers of Versailles, must have fired the Sultan's ambition : but whereas the Roman cities were almost indestructible, surviving fire, pillage, iconoclasm, and all the various forms of violence caused by envy, the long corridors of the Sultan's palace have, on the other hand, already become open to the winds, so that they are now roads, edged with a natural border of asphodel. Within the cool shadow of these walls, which have crumbled as rapidly as those of an exhibition building, you can walk for a long way, while many of the great halls have become square meadows of blue lupins and iris : these, and even the granaries — which still retain their vaulting and the immense square blocks of masonry that serve as pillars — and ostrich farms were all planned on the same prodigious scale. Yet we are not aware in what style the palace was lived in, or for how long, or what was the nature of the doom, swift or lingering, that overtook it. We do know, however, that the same Sultan who created it also raised the Black Guard (which gives to all English-speaking peoples a synonym for 'a scoundrelly, foul-mouthed person'), and quartered it here to protect him. The number of clansmen, servants, retainers and slaves who worked here must have been innumerable. Even today we do not know the purpose of some of the gigantic square rooms. . . .

Only the storks, who are the sole permanent inhabitants of the ruined palace, entertain no doubts about the matter. You will see aloft, upon the flat, broad tops of the walls, a multitude of nests, colossal constructions of twigs, each one with an enormous bird — which here looks, in proportion, to be a wren — sitting on it. . . . They *know* : the walls were built for them to nest on. But then they assume equally that the bastioned and buttressed walls of the Moroccan cities, Fez and Marrakesh, were similarly put up for their convenience. . . . On the ramps and walls of Montegufoni, though in their season they abound in wallflowers, snapdragon — or lion's mouth as is the direct Italian translation of its name — and the beautiful passion-flower-like blossom of the wild caper, the fruit of which in English kitchens was formerly indissolubly wedded to boiled mutton — no storks nest. It is, I suppose, too far to the north, or else Italian sportsmen have found in these big birds a target which they cannot miss and have in the end extinguished them. Indeed, that bird life of other smaller kinds continues there is to me a recurring astonishment : because in Italy impassioned sportsmen invade the country districts from the neighbouring towns every Sunday, to shoot at any bird, however rare, inedible or harmless, however diminutive. How is it, then, that they continue to sing each year, especially the chanting centuries of nightingales which call attention, too, to their continuing existence by singing all day as well as all night ? Their will to survive must be very strong, and their habits crafty, or they would be no longer able to fill with their roulades the groves of cypress. . . . But the walls of Montegufoni have housed visitors rarer than storks, and have been set as background for most singular scenes, personal no less than national, modern no less than ancient, not the least curious being the most unusual conversation I shall now describe for you, partly to balance that other complete and solid discursion, *The Man in the Front Seat*, and partly because I would like this morning to talk to the reader again rather than write for him, and so take advantage of the new flexibility of subject-matter which the description of this book, on its title-page, affords. We can lie once more in the sun, and under the rhythm of lapping tides I will tell of one of the last episodes in the long and very personal relationship that existed between my father and myself. This story, or interlude, relates to the conservatory civilisation of the 'seventies, but it belongs more to the drawing-room world of Du Maurier than to the fascinating life of pleasure shown by Tissot on his canvases.

CHAPTER X

MAKING A BOLT FOR IT

In 1937 my mother died in a nursing-home in London on the 12th of July, and in August my father left England for Switzerland, and thence, after a month's visit, returned to Montegufoni. For the long stay he proposed to make there he had provided himself with some companions — acquaintances, it must be admitted, more than buddies — and others we had found for him, in order that he should not be lonely — or, to be precise, not more lonely than the complete suit of armour he had grown for himself in the past half-century, and in which he was now ever encased impenetrably, the vizor down, so that he revealed his face only a little less seldom than his hand ; no more, then, than this very individual steely envelopment rendered inevitable. In addition, I had told him that I would join him in Italy whenever he wished, but I became aware in talking to him that he was not really eager for me to do so, because he liked to be in a position of absolute command, with nobody to gainsay him, and since I, too, was accustomed to having my own way, this encroached on his prerogative. However, during the course of a few weeks he came to cherish a certain sense of grievance, most carefully nurtured by various of his acquaintances, at his children not being round him, and towards the end of November, some two months after his return to Italy, telegrams were suddenly shot at me from all sides with such vigour and poignance that they inevitably recalled the multitude of arrows that pierced the writhing body of St. Sebastian. This barbed shower revealed behind the shafts a formidable power of organisation. They sped from people young and old, men and women, worldly and unworldly, Italian and English, prelates and laymen, but all united to tell me that my father was very ill and that it had now become my duty, however disagreeable, to be at his side. I at once took the train for Florence.

On arrival at the Castello I found arranged for my benefit a tableau, a death-bed scene like one of those that occur in the paintings of the Italian Primitive Masters. My father lay in a four-poster — baroque in style, I must confess, rather than gothic — receiving fruit, fresh eggs, game and sympathy — but not flowers. These last he rejected outright because they were prone to give him hay-fever. . . . As I entered the room, the figures relaxed and the tableau broke up. My father proceeded to dismiss the guests with a little ceremonial flutter of the hand, and went on to tell me at once of his serious illness, although there were no outward signs of it in his physical appearance. I therefore asked him to be allowed to talk to his doctor, Giglioli. He gave me permission, and accordingly I bumped in to Florence in the large, heavy motor-car — known locally as the Ark and described at some length elsewhere — to interview this sympathetic and most intelligent Italian doctor. When I asked him if my father was very ill, he replied :

'The disease which Sir George assumes he has developed is a matter of X-ray plates and not of faith alone. He is an old man of seventy-seven years of age, and of course if he gets a cold it may always turn to pneumonia : but probably he will outlive me and be with us for another twenty years.' (My father did in fact survive his doctor by some five.)

On my return from the city I found the invalid still in bed, and looking intensely depressed. As I opened the door of his room, he enquired in a drooping voice,

'How long does the doctor give me ?'

'About twenty years,' I replied.

At this, he suddenly jumped out of bed with an agility that would have done credit to a man half his age, and said : 'I must dress now.' That night he came down to dinner.

The long journey and change of climate had afflicted me with a bad attack of lumbago, and the next morning I had breakfast in bed, and was therefore rather late in making my appearance. First, from a small room above the Cardinal's Garden, protected from the wind, and full of late November sunlight, of roses and stocks and of drowsy butterflies in the last florid stage before their hibernation, I had observed my father holding court in a deck-chair — or rather in the kind of long wicker chair that he liked because he could put his feet up and thus rest the heart, and of which one was always reserved for him in any garden that he owned. He reclined on these hard openwork planes of wicker, at the top of a flight of steps commanding the view: the valley of vines, and nearer, climbing the Castle hill in steep terraces, the long tank-like stone beds full of blue plumbago, leading up in turn to the surrounding box parterre, in which were growing the flowers he had chosen for it in pale, pastel colours. . . . Round him were grouped the courtiers. . . . There was a man with more false teeth in one mouth than I had ever previously seen gathered together, and rather ill-balanced they were, too, so that his conversation was an act of perpetual conjuring. There was Signor Bracciaforte, smiling as always, full of childish benevolence, easily moved to tears or laughter. There was a young girl, a student of history, her figure slightly foreshortened by fate and a-clink with the old paste jewellery with which my father delighted to hang it. Her eyes, I noticed, seemed to be perpetually full of tears and she had a sweet smile of sympathy showing from a head hung rather on one side. There was another girl, a cousin of ours, and then there was my friend Francis Bamford who had kindly offered to accompany my father to Italy and to look after him. (To him my father had in the past year uttered some of his more sudden, startling and Delphic warnings and aphorisms, such as 'Never be Kind to a Dowager', and 'One can see in my grandchildren how Nature is trying to reproduce *Me* !')

When I got downstairs — with some difficulty — and appeared in the garden under that cloud of awkwardness that always overshadows the late-comer, I said 'Good morning, Father'. He greeted me in return and then gave a significant, rather ominous glance at those round him from under eyelids that seemed to work sideways rather than up and down; a signal which the court knew from experience was calculated to convey dismissal. Watching in silence till his guests were out of earshot, he remarked to me in a voice of unusual dignity and importance:

'Osbert, I wish to speak to you alone.'

I replied rather carelessly:

'Then I'll get a chair and sit by you. How delicious it is out here, Father! This is the first sun I have seen for months.'

To my surprise, for he usually liked to warm himself in the winter sunshine, he answered:

'No, I would prefer to speak to you in the Gothic Library.'

He proceeded to lead the way to a small, cold, high room on the north side of the house. On the faking of it he had for some years been engaged, spending on the process a very considerable sum of money. It was, of course, a library without books — I say, of course, for it could always be noticed that, though he loved books and lived surrounded by them, none the less in any room which he called a library no single volume was ever to be found. At Scarborough, similarly, his library had been bookless, though each of his several sitting-rooms even had books piled up all over the floor. But this library was, its very appearance proclaimed, a State Apartment, to be used solely for giving audiences and making special pronouncements. No book had ever been brought into it or was ever likely to be, and people, it was plain, seldom entered it. Indeed, it proved difficult to do so. First you had to find your way down some break-neck steps set at odd angles at the bottom of a spiral staircase, and then to get yourself through a doorway forbiddingly narrow, like a coffin. When finally you reached the room, it had a recess lined with cypress-wood cupboards. Too shallow to hold books, they were crowned with a flat, gothic fretting as cornice, and their panels were edged with a margin of leaves, rabbits and human figures cut in very flat relief, expertly carved. The detail of the presses, lightly touched with colour, and of the vaulted ceiling, disproportionately high, had, if I am not mistaken, been derived from one of the nine canvases by Carpaccio, depicting the life of St. Ursula, to be seen in San Giorgio degli Schiavoni in Venice. The cupboards had below them, attached to their base, seats that resembled medieval instruments of torture; although, as if in mockery, they were thinly padded in places with flat cushions, like stone pancakes, covered in blue and silver velvet (since used by German troops for the polishing of their boots). Herein and hereon we sat, the two of us facing each other, for the cupboards took up three sides of a square. We bore our discomfort manfully, pretending not to notice it. I can see my father now, as he sat there, very upright, with the sun through the barred window catching the gold glint of his red but greying beard. He was wearing a grey suit and one hand rested on a cushion. In his manner could be perceived, by one familiar with his ways, both a certain air of tension and a wish to surprise. Thus I was prepared for something portentous — and sure enough it came.

He gave a slight bow and said:

'I thought I ought to inform you, Osbert, that Mrs. FitzDudley Gudgeon wishes to marry me.'

This unusual announcement winded me. I had seen Mrs. FitzDudley Gudgeon. She was a widow with no background but a past, and a past of peculiarly unpleasant character, who had for half a century and more trailed behind her a long train of unsavoury financial transactions merging into love affairs, and vice versa. . . . She had contrived to cultivate my father's society for some years. Once at a concert at the Queen's Hall she had come cringing up to me, in the interval, and had said, 'I know your father' — to which I had replied, 'Yes. Better than I do, I believe.' But most clearly I remember the first occasion on which I had seen her. It was at a party, and I recall it vividly because a friend of mine, much older than myself, who had been standing by my side, had turned to me as she entered the room, and had said:

'Here comes the wickedest woman in Europe.'

This had naturally focussed my attention on the neatly dressed, discreet-looking, grey-haired woman who entered. What he said might be true: but hers was, I found out, an unaudacious, flat, mousy, money-grubbing kind of wickedness without any endowment of wit or wits, and lacking in the fun that sometimes attends and makes lively the company of sinners. It demanded a guaranteed sound return, and constituted a real four-per-cent-preference-share brand of evil.

Naturally, I had noticed my father's unusual choice of words. So now I asked him:

'Do *you* wish to marry *her*?'

He replied: 'I am not certain, but she has written to me to say that she would like to come here for a long stay.'

'Well,' I enquired, 'what will you do if she insists on marrying you, and you don't want to?'

'Make a bolt for it, I suppose, as I had to once before. . . .'

Recollecting previous conversations with my father, I seized immediately the implications of this gallant reply: because, when I was younger and he had been fond of warning me of the dangers of everyday life, he had often related to me how, when just down from Christ Church, he had arrived to stay in a famous country-house for a ball. The two daughters of his hostess would be great heiresses; but unfortunately, though he liked them, and they, so he claimed, entertained feelings deeper than friendship for him, yet my father disapproved of both the young ladies: for he considered that they were over fond of pleasure, and feared, moreover, that they might like to spend money too freely. Another motive influenced him even more profoundly. As I have related before, he held very strict views on eugenics, and their noses too nearly resembled his own in shape (so he had told me), and this, if he had married either of them, might have tended to accentuate the aquiline profiles of his offspring, and so have deprived his children of the classical mould of feature for which he hoped, and which indeed he was determined to secure for them. . . . It was difficult to follow precisely what happened. Howbeit, so far as I could make out, on his entering the hall a footman had as usual taken the heavy leather portmanteau with which a man then always travelled — when, to his surprise, he had discovered that the heiress who was his particular friend was waiting for him there as well. Her presence at once convinced him that the young lady expected him immediately to propose to her ; indeed, beyond the hall lay a vista of rooms, and at the end of it the conservatory door could be seen open in classic invitation. He had felt it imperative, if his children were to avoid nasal catastrophe, to act at once. Therefore, hastily snatching back his luggage from the footman's arms, he had pelted back down the drive and through the park without offering to anyone a word of explanation or apology, either at the time or subsequently. . . . This — though I may have gathered some of the details incorrectly — I could have no doubt was the first time he had been obliged to 'make a bolt for it'. . . . But that was nearly sixty years ago, and at the moment I was concerned with stopping the threatened alliance. To take the most obvious of present difficulties first, plainly he would not be able to run so fast at his present age, while Mrs. FitzDudley Gudgeon was quite capable of running after and catching him ! The best way, I concluded, of preventing the marriage was to find for him a rival attraction to Mrs. FitzDudley Gudgeon, because obviously he felt a need for feminine sympathy and of presenting himself in a new light and as a centre of interest. What could be done ? Fortunately my mind lighted on Mrs. Rippon : a woman of character and humour and formerly a celebrated beauty ; a pirate, but kind and audacious, and of quite a different sort. . . . He liked her, and her husband was rumoured to be dying. Accordingly I improvised.

'Well, I must admit I always saw a different future for you,' I remarked.

He said : 'What do you mean ?'

I replied : 'After Colonel Rippon's death, I thought Ethel Rippon would marry you.'

At this he looked very pleased with himself, and I realised that I had defeated Mrs. FitzDudley Gudgeon's scheme once and for all.

. . . . . .

There is little more to add, except that after my father's death, when I returned to Montegufoni at the end of the war, I found among his papers all the correspondence that had passed between him and Mrs. FitzDudley Gudgeon — for he kept and filed copies of letters he wrote, as well as preserving those he received. Just as the letters quoted in the Bardell *v.* Pickwick Trial were said by Serjeant Buzfuz to have been written in code, so that an order for cutlets and tomatoes, 'Chops and Tomata sauce. Yours, Pickwick', conveyed the declaration 'I love you', so these unusual *billets-doux* were couched in the current technical terms of the English and European, but especially of the American and Canadian Exchanges. It was easily to be deduced, the tenderness Mrs. FitzDudley Gudgeon's requests for information about Abitibi shares and the prospects of Brazilian Traction spelt ardent and everlasting devotion for my father and the respect she cherished for his wisdom — still more for his wealth: while his affectionate response to these demonstrations took the form of such phrases as, 'I hear Beralts may pay a bonus' or 'I advise you to stick to Chinese Customs 1882'. Moreover, alas, I am bound to conclude that the counsel he gave her in his final communication, to avoid further 'flutters' and to invest 'all her loose money' in Consols, constituted both a reproof and a call to order, equivalent in that language of love which they had evolved for themselves to the words, 'Let us part on terms of friendship; I wish to be let alone, and have no intention of marrying you'. After that, there came no more letters.

. . . . . .

While, reader, we have been talking — or, more correctly, while I have been talking — the sun has gone in and it is time now to bathe and then climb the steps of the hotel once more.

CHAPTER XI

THE ELEMENT, FIRE

AT Amalfi the sun, directly it appeared, evoked a startling reverberation from rock, wall and sea. The whole world would seem on fire, as cloud after cloud would catch the flame. But this conflagration of nebulae would only endure for a few minutes, and while the colours of the sky faded in intensity my thoughts concerned themselves with a great benefactor of the human race — Prometheus ; to whom we should surely give praise every time we light a fire on a cold day or eat cooked food. . . . What, I wondered, was the reality beyond the fable : who, the person behind the legendary Titan ; how did fire begin ? Was it with a feather plucked from the wing of the Phoenix, as some used to say, or perhaps from a piece of crystal, stalactite or stalagmite, that, broken off and thrown on the ground, accidentally concentrated the rays of the sun, so that outside the cave a few twigs began first to smoke, and then to flare up ? . . . The problem is as mysterious as that of the manner in which men, even more primitive and ignorant than are we, found specifics for illnesses : who, for example, discovered that an extract made from an autumn flower which resembles a crocus would dispel an attack of gout, or that a drug distilled from the bark of a tree, cinchona, native to Central and South America, would be efficacious in cases of malaria ? — because the medicine-men and the missionaries could not possibly experiment with every kind of herb, bush and tree, or they must in the course of this process have certainly poisoned themselves or some of their patients. These great intuitional or empiric healers remain not only unhonoured and unsung, but even nameless. Statues are not usually erected to such heroic pioneers : only the gigantic form of Prometheus tied to his rock reflects some dim memory continuing to stir in the mind of early man, and served to carry his fame by way of legend into the modern world. Even he, however, is portrayed discouragingly — it may be because ignorance really *was* bliss and men were afraid of stepping further across the border that divided them from animals — with an eagle tearing at his liver. What was the identity of the real Prometheus who stole the flame from a pagan heaven ? — though had he been content to wait, it would have been easier for him to pluck fire from the Christian hell. Perhaps he took it, not so much to help humanity, as because fire exercises over some men an almost irresistible attraction : so that certain people in other respects sane have to be detained for long periods to prevent them from setting fire to their own houses, no less than to those of others. It may be that even immortals — or demi-mortals — are not immune from this craving.

Perhaps, then, Prometheus was, in the American phrase, a fire-bug, and Zeus, to ensure the safety of the world, felt obliged to have the incendiary Titan fastened securely to a rock. Once only have I seen fire-bugs, but they plainly belonged to their own separate race of mankind, a tribe set apart — anywhere one would recognise similar beings. In this instance, they consisted of an aunt and nephew; the woman of middle age, the boy seventeen or eighteen years old. About them clung a louring dullness which perhaps only the glint and liveliness of fire could dispel, and in the evidence before the court it was related that the aunt, who had not seen her nephew for some months, sent for him and said, 'It's time again!' and at this esoteric message he had accordingly lit a rick. The flames soon spread, and a young farmer described how, riding homeward after market, he saw great walls of fire where his house had stood. Nevertheless, some pyromaniacs must be more light-hearted, for as I was writing these words I saw reported in the paper the following statement given by a fifteen-year-old girl in Wolverhampton Juvenile Court who had burnt down a whole block of buildings: 'I was lying in bed at home, when the idea came to me that it would be rather nice to burn the whole of the school down'. And now I find a short notice of a somewhat similar nature in *Time*: 'In Peoria, firemen became suspicious when their unofficial mascot, a fourteen-year-old boy,

always arrived at fires before they did, got him to admit that he had started five blazes because he liked "to watch the fire engines go"'. Perhaps these instances are only exaggerations of the pleasure that normal children take in fire, for they are the only beings who dare to play regularly with this element; but though I say this, it must be admitted that fireworks — which present the same relationship to fire that kittens bear to tigers — appear to fascinate equally human beings of every race and age, because they are among the most beautiful, if transient, of man's inventions and for us symbolise, no less than do pealing bells, the ever rarer occasions of joy and triumph. But to see fireworks at their best it is necessary to be on the top of a mountain and then they become dangerous, and I have described elsewhere how I was privileged to look out of a window at the top of a sheer cliff and watch the rockets spread and expand their bouquets below the balcony.

Fireworks are one of the sole features of carnival of which there can never be enough; paper caps are easy to come by, especially dunce's caps, but fireworks are sparse. Then we must consider, too, for a moment bonfires. The most beautiful I know are those to be seen lighting the dusk of the Tuscan autumn on every hillside after the vintage, stacks composed of the prunings of the vines. They have a peculiar fragrance and an atmosphere of ancient pagan religions still clings to them. No sooner has the sun declined, arming itself for its night's journey in full splendour — for the sunsets of October and November in Italy are unmatched elsewhere in any season — than you see these fires breaking out on the slopes, and long after their brave flames have died, in clear weather their fiery cores continue to glow from the ground. In England, too, the gardeners' autumn fires can be admired, though they are more scarce than they used to be, for the gardens where professionals are employed steadily decline in number. But who that has smelt it can ever forget the scent of burning autumn leaves and the harsh smell of damp twigs and branches? Usually they make their fires not far from a tree, so that it retains the scar caused by burning for many long years: (it is almost impossible to persuade gardeners of the strength of a fire and the extent to which it can damage living organisms). But bonfires, as they point to the autumn skies their darkening wings that resemble those of angels in a picture by El Greco, in whose canvases bursts of light explode through smoky feathers, or as their tongues roar out suddenly at some unknown provocation of wind on dry leaves and resinous wood, from a vague smoulder to a general surge of fire, can serve other purposes. They may be equally an instrument of triumph and of rejoicing or flame up sometimes as a caution. . . . The sound of flames, the sudden roar, is always frightening, as are the sounds made by human beings to warn their fellows of the danger. Even as I read these words that I have written in Hollywood, I hear engines rush past and a general wailing begin, so that I know that somewhere in Los Angeles a fire has broken out, though the pillars of flame are invisible as yet and only these mechanical sounds of fury and agonised warning announce the existence of danger in the neighbourhood. But a human voice shouting 'Fire! Fire!', though it refers to the most creative as well as to the most destructive of the elements, is even more appalling. It is the cry to which there is no answer. Moreover, against the real terrors of fire no cry can be heard: for when this element combines with earth it sets even this most static of the elements rolling and roaring down the steep slopes of volcanoes, advancing inexorably over the countryside. Nothing is heard except the bellow of the angry mountain and the hissing of the lava snakes as they proceed. Of the great elemental sounds, the terrestrial are the most alarming: the slowness of volcanic advance is even more frightening than the rush of a huge wave, the shudder and rattle of an earthquake or its prenatal warning, caused by a shift of weight below, worse than the crash of an avalanche. . . We have wandered away, following the track of fire, and must return to the wonders of sunrise.

This spectacle is best to be seen, I think, from the deck of a ship or from an island terrace — divided from it by water, you can watch with complete detachment. At last like a bird of fire the sun rises from its nest — but suddenly the display reduces itself and for the first time, as it seems each day, the ordinary world is revealed in terms of ordinary light, though equipped with the special and tender luminosity of the early morning. Thus, in the Mediterranean, should you climb on deck a few minutes after the sunrise, when all its Homeric rhetoric is spent, at a moment when your small ship is sailing through a cluster of Ionian isles or those of the Dodecanese, that interval in its silence and lack of exaggeration is as moving as the earlier display of aerial pomps that has just finished. You see a traditional world of which you hold, far back, some memory, either inherited, or acquired, and then apparently forgotten, from reading. The cubes of the houses, flat-roofed, are painted in colours classically modest, grey, white,[1] blues, blacks, and occasionally a floury terra-cotta, under a sky that also offers the same realistic freshness of the early morning. How greatly does this small world, with its humanised landscape and well-ordered beauty, contrast with even the northern shores of Africa, which, though they may pertain to the Mediterranean, exhibit a formal and a feral shape.

Nevertheless, Africa, behind its curtain of fire and forest, remains the most mysterious and the most interesting of the four continents. Fire is, as I maintain, the element to which Africa is dedicated. The sun is its strength and weakness, and has even imposed on the red-blooded races that inhabit it that sable skin of different tones and degrees of black and brown which affords them protection from its own rays, that, like Siva the Reaper, both create and destroy. In the forests of this great smouldering continent, as, too, in Central America, there is an amazing and immediate response to the sunrise, the answer of sound to light, the instantaneous hum and whir of insects praising their maker, a hymn of gratitude for their blessings — among which are to be counted the white men who traverse these regions, a recognised delicacy for mos-

[1] Yes, I know that white is not really a colour.

quitoes — while at the same time the flowering trees expand into their full beauty, the flamboyant tree outlining itself in fire, and the jacaranda, its top branches covered, as it were, with a blue rain fallen from the heavens. Even the houses in the oases, built of mud baked in the sun, belong to the governing element, though they are colourless, squat and crowded ; so depressing that on being shown round an oasis I remarked to the friend accompanying me, 'It is just like the slums'. On hearing this, the Arab guide, who was in charge of us, and who spoke French but no English, beamed with pleasure and said proudly, as if a compliment had been paid to his native place : 'Oui, tout le monde dit ça ! C'est tout à fait comme les "*slooms*"'.

In those regions the sun because of its power seems as the day goes on to take all light out of the sky, and to banish every variety of colour from the landscape. A prospect of glittering delusive lakes and actually existing endless dry tents of sand, ribbed by the last winds that passed, soon palls. The pretended sheets of water look tantalisingly cool with their calm, mirror-like surfaces, but as they remain always the same distance from the traveller, who, until their final disappearance, never gets any nearer to them however far he goes, disappointment soon dispels their fascination. Nevertheless, in some way, the very sight of them is healing, and not until the motor breaks down — which in the desert it does frequently — and you are exposed without any protection to the full heat of the day on a tract of sand, do you begin to recognise the African sun's savagery. Yet there are refuges from it: the broad oases with their giant vegetation, but of a darker green than one would have expected; fig-trees three times as large as any in Southern Europe, enormous flowering apricots and peaches, and neatly drawn lines of prosperous vegetables. . . . Then, beyond Marrakesh rise the snow-capped ranges of the Atlas Mountains to temper the heat with their white planes that catch every colour of sky and earth. And as you mount towards them, you pass through forests of blue cedars. There the aromatic ground is covered with scores of different kinds of wild flowers in their season, from peony to cyclamen.

CHAPTER XII

FLOWERS AND ISLANDS

In the spring the blossoms of North Africa surpass those of Sicily or Greece, which must be among the most plentiful and diverse in the world; though in England a patriotic superstition maintains that our island is richer in wild flowers than any other — but how far is this from being the truth! New varieties are no doubt still to be discovered in North Africa, and perhaps nearer in the south of Italy, even today so unknown, and so different a country from the north. The truth is that the climate only changes between Rome and Naples. (It is after that boundary has been passed that Italian travellers first begin to complain of summer heats and to pine for the sparse and withered pleasures of winter or of the mountain-top. Yet they really must enjoy the temperature, or perhaps they merely like to grumble at it, for in such weather passengers flock to the stations and sit in railway carriages drawn up as if to obtain the full force of the sun, there puffing and fanning themselves with a vigour that plainly makes them hotter still. They also, I think, revel in dust and in bumps in the roads, as, equally, they are enchanted by any kind of speed or noise.) . . . But south of this line, I was saying, the most unusual wild flowers are to be found and in the month of March, by the sides of the railway lines that pass through Puglia or Basilicata, you will see tall but sturdy yellow tulips, with big petals, growing in the fields of wheat as poppies do in England. Round Syracuse, from December to March, you will find many varieties of iris springing even from the flat grey rocks above the sea. There you find the snakeshead, a little green iris, with its cushions of sepia velvet, and several sorts of blue iris, the kinds in flower gradually growing bigger as the spring days grow warmer. Even at Montegufoni, though the Tuscan landscape is comparatively so rich and cultivated, and though it lies so much north of the boundary I have propounded, there is a regular progression of flowers from the beginning of March to the end of May. First in early March comes the fanfare of sugar-stick tulips, small flowers with pointed petals striped in pink and white : then later in the month follows the grand floral exhibition when certain fields are full of large tulips, in colour between a red and a terracotta, flowers which I have seen in exhibitions of the Royal Horticultural Society labelled *Florentine Tulips*. Alas, people pass by, stop their motors, get out, tear up and carry back great bunches for themselves or else steal them to sell in the markets in Florence ; but until their glory is discovered these meadows are a magnificent sight. Then a week later comes a tall-stalked, small-flowered yellow tulip, which grows like a weed in the fields — a peculiar tulip which has the effect at a distance, owing to the proportion of blossom to stalk, of a rather lanky lily. Then soon the wood on the hill opposite is full of the very fragrant small-flowered *planta genista*, in England only to be seen for sale in florists', its blossom very yellow, so that patches of light seem to fall everywhere in the glades, while underneath each shrub there flower in profusion clumps of blue *lithospermum*, the equivalent of the English bluebell in colour and in number. And after this show is finished, there ensue weekly displays of orchises of many kinds, and of cyclamen, narcissus and daffodil, a large purple anemone, and violets, of dog-rose and honeysuckle, until the whole exhibition winds up with fields full of love-in-a-mist and of tall and slender magenta gladioli, the last flowers to appear before the vegetation is dried up by the summer heats. Meanwhile, the higher brown and barren slopes — the counterpart of an English or Scottish moor —, sheltered in places by stone pine and cypress, are covered with great bushes of white cistus and pink, large papery flowers with respectively yellow and black centres. But for the rest of the summer there are few flowers, and in the autumn interest centres, rather, round the diverse clumps of fungus in a hundred different mouldy varieties, speckled brown like sparrows or blue and red, and the local children, who seem to have inherited great knowledge in the matter, instead of going to school, wander in the groves and boskets gathering the edible kinds, and bringing them back home in the evening in large knotted handkerchiefs.

. . . . . .

In Corfu, a beautiful sunrise does not necessarily announce a fine day, any more than it would in England : but, as if in compensation, there bad weather is more beautiful than elsewhere. In that island I once spent a long winter, and for ten days of it thunder sounded continuously : it seemed every day that the great range of Albanian mountains across the Straits had grown nearer ; they loomed dark and fleshy as a hippopotamus. . . . Certainly Corfu presents its sinister as well as its idyllic aspect : but it also offers a wonderful beauty and an interest all its own, because it is an island and yet its life has been shaped by both eastern and western influences. And it still — I speak of the breathing-space between the two wars — shows them.

The town, though of a mixed nature, is full of character. Its shops, for example, are similar to those to be seen in Turkey, arranged in groups according to their trade, and open to the air. Outside the butcher's stall hang the carcases of wild boar, and there are mounds of snipe and woodcock from the Albanian wilderness opposite. Then again, a long arcade, somewhat similar to the rue de Rivoli only smaller in scale, which was built when the island was occupied by the French in the time of Napoleon, stands within stone-throwing distance of a noble Regency edifice in grey Maltese stone, plainly influenced in its style by the architect Nash. This palace was formerly the official residence of the English Governor or, more strictly, of the Lord High

Commissioner, Sir Thomas Maitland. Now it is a museum containing many Greek fragments, and a large and remarkable archaic statue. It also contains a portrait of King George IV by Sir Thomas Lawrence — or from his studio — as well as housing a somewhat inconsequent collection of Chinese and Japanese objects. A bronze statue of Sir Frederick Adam, who succeeded Sir Thomas Maitland and ruled the island from 1823 to 1832, stands outside. A mile or two beyond the town is to be seen another building under the influence of Nash, which belongs to the Greek Royal Family, Monrepos. Its grounds are imaginatively dotted with small Greek theatres and with fragments of pillars and statues. The visitor ought also to inspect the former Parliament House, in which Mr. Gladstone once spoke. It was constructed by the British and is now the English church.

To understand the face of Corfu today, it is necessary to recall its history. Though in early times it enjoyed frequent periods of independence, from 1386 to 1797 the island was under Venice. The forts are Venetian, with fine plaques of the Lion of St. Mark let into the wall. There is displayed also the bust of a Venetian Admiral in armour, crowned with the familiar and characteristic round, brimless hat, broader at the top than at the bottom, and flourishing a baton. From 1815 to 1863, together with the other Ionian Islands, Corfu came under the protection of England, who, in the end, gave it back to Greece — our influence still remains : in the country outside the city of Corfu, among the giant olive-trees, the boys still play cricket, a horrid legacy of the English occupation. During their sojourn here the English also established a university, and Lord North's son, the Earl of Guilford — referred to in a contemporary memoir as 'that ramshackle fellow' — was made Chancellor and always wore his robes of office even when at home.

Another of the sights of the district is the Achilleion, a villa built in 1890–1891 by Raffaele Carito for the Empress Elizabeth of Austria. After her assassination at Geneva in 1898 it remained empty for some years, but eventually, in 1908, the German Emperor William II bought it. Though — or perhaps still more because — it is wonderfully situated, it offers an unrivalled example of the worst Graeco-German taste, but it cannot spoil the landscape.

In the world there is little to match the well-ordered quality of beauty to be found in the Italian landscape and townscape of every latitude. But Corfu does, possibly, challenge comparison with it. The island, besides showing so many exotic influences, offers its own stylised beauty, both in natural scenery and in architecture. There are several exquisite small Byzantine churches of uncertain date, whitewashed outside and presenting somehow a marine aspect — they are not, plainly, mainland churches: but their interiors, with their traditional, intricately carved screens of gilded wood, at once proclaim descent from an ancient and rich civilisation. There also exist in the island several convents of Greek Orthodox monks — that at Palaeokastrizza being the best known, the most dramatic in its position and in the view from its terrace; where with the Prior's consent you may have luncheon. The aerial prospect it offers seems at first one of three-dimensional contours like those on a model map, but looking down more directly from your perch, an abrupt and rocky fall leads the eye to an expanse of marbled sea far below. On the way there — for Palaeokastrizza overlooks the west coast at the other end of the island, and ranks therefore as a comparatively long drive — you will be sure to see — at any rate in the days some twenty years ago of which I write — the people of each village wearing their own variation of the island costume. It was fine to watch the peasant women with their superb and erect carriage swinging along the country roads — or, as for that, striding through the streets of the city itself — wearing billowing skirts, either striped in bright colours or snow white, short embroidered jackets and elaborate necklaces of pure gold, often heirlooms which they were in their turn to take as dowries to their husbands. Frequently their garb resembled, in skirt, jacket and in the elaborate horned white head-dress which crowned it, that of the Ugly Duchess in Quentin Matsys's celebrated portrait.

On the occasion of our first visit to Palaeokastrizza, the hotel concierge arranged, in the interests of economy, for us to share a hired motor with two old Scots, retired business men, I should say, from Edinburgh, who always went away together each year for a holiday. Though it was just after Christmas and the weather was hot and sunny as June can sometimes be in England, the two old gentlemen were clad or, rather, smothered from head to foot in substantial brown tweeds and wore on the top of their heads what looked like ritual caps, flat as pancakes. In spite of their long years of friendship, they continued to address each other as 'Mr. Tarn' and 'Mr. Tavish'. On the road they burbled ceaselessly of the League of Nations which in their retirement constituted their prevailing interest, and they seemed to notice nothing of the country through which they passed, until at last, getting out of the motor to see a lake and a view of a mountain behind it, they were silent for a moment and then observed together, with the identical Scottish inflection in their speech, and as if trained to use the same expression and produce it at the same rate of iteration, 'It puts a mon in mind very much of Loch Lomond!'

The *Nomarch* of Corfu, who occupied a position similar to that of Governor, was also staying in the same hotel as we were. He was a man of great charm, and belonged to a patriotic and distinguished Greek family, many of whose members served the state. Moreover, he was very hospitable, though, since he also possessed tact, he was careful never to interrupt our work. Of the most amiable and unassuming nature, yet the moment he donned uniform, or even wore a frock-coat and top-hat to tour the island for the Government, he would assume dignity like a robe. Despite his sense of humour and love of enjoyment, there existed, too, this temporarily almost pompous side to him, which made him, no doubt, the perfect holder — as he proved himself to be — of his office. I recall many delightful meals and excursions in his company — not the least amusing to look back on being a luncheon party he gave at a garden restaurant on the road to Monrepos, although on this occasion his dignity again entered in and lent atmosphere to an otherwise farcical occasion. The guests were the Captain of a British battleship — the Mediterranean fleet was at anchor below —, the daughter of the Admiral of the Fleet, a Greek lady, a younger naval officer and ourselves. First of all we drank ouzo, and ate botargo, a kind of local caviare, a roe salted, pressed and enclosed in wax, and when consumed, cut in thin slices with its casing first removed, then we were given lamb cutlets grilled over a charcoal fire and drank the white resinous wine of the island, an acquired taste, but when you became accustomed to it dry and elating as the air of mountains on a fine summer's day. The table was set in the shade of two fir-trees, the weather was glorious, we talked and everything went with a swing, until suddenly the climate of the gathering abruptly changed, and a turbid dullness swept down on us like a fog — as sometimes occurs without reason. Usually it soon evaporates again : but not so in this instance. The *Nomarch* retired into the shroud of his Greek dignity and each person began to follow his own line of thought aloud, without reference to that of the others, as in a play by Chekhov. At last the Captain, a man of character whose hobby, unusual in his profession, was to collect books of poetry, looked round in a determined way. This rather frightened me, for he had a ribald side to him, and no-one ever knew what he would say next. Evidently he was resolved to enjoy himself, for he remarked to me in a low tone, 'I'm going to break up this freeze'. Then he said suddenly, in the louder voice of general conversation, 'D'you know the story of the two babu clerks? On their way to work they met in a Calcutta street. One said to the other, "How's your wife this morning?" His friend replied, "She's in bed with erysipelas": to which the first remarked, "Let me see — that's the new clerk at Ralli Brothers, isn't it?"' . . . This old story, belonging no doubt to the rollicking days of the *Winning Post* and the *Pink 'Un*, could not have been worse received. The Greek lady, who had fortunately failed to understand it, said 'Pliz?' three times, and wanted it to be repeated and its points carefully explained to her. The *Nomarch*, however, arrayed himself in his national dignity and observed judicially, 'Yes, you are right, it is a Greek word'. Meanwhile the poor young naval officer had fallen into convulsions, which earned him black looks from his superior officer — though the latter had perpetrated the story — and the rest was silence under the shadow of the fir-trees; a silence broken only by the clattering of dishes in the wooden shack behind us, which served as kitchen.

In the hotel in which we were staying some fifteen or sixteen other persons were resident. Most of them were immemorable, and some immemorial: but among them were a remarkably fantastic aunt and niece who were English-speaking. The aunt was very old, active and lively, while the niece — whose pet name was, appropriately, Loopy — contrived to introduce into her conversation, which was copious though somewhat undirected, a character all its own, that can only be rendered on the written page by comparing it to the effect of the old-fashioned long 's' in letters and journals of the eighteenth and nineteenth centuries, when it was frequently mistaken for an 'f' with unusual results. Thus, for example, she would say 'fun' for 'sun', and often some such slight variation would be startling in the different significance it imparted to her sentences. Among the guests, too, I recall, was a Greek whose Christian name was Louis — and who, as he was only asked to luncheon or dinner in order to make the number fourteen, instead of thirteen, was always known as Louis XIV. The rest of the guests, I apprehend, were staying in the hotel, as we were, because it was cheap.

Certainly the cost of accommodation, though this was old-fashioned and by no means luxurious, was low: a large bedroom could be obtained, and unusually good food — including a great quantity of woodcock, snipe, venison and wild boar — at a charge of approximately 4s. 6d. a day. Moreover, it was a good place to work in, since there were not too many, but just sufficient, distractions. Indeed writing was only made difficult by a wood fire that always smoked — in the month of January it can be cold in Corfu — and by the hotel servant, who stood outside my room and indulged a cough. I forget his name — all the waiters and porters bore such famous appellations as Achilles, Dionysus or Spiridion —, but he was a robust, middle-aged man, plainly very healthy, with a remarkably long moustache, very Turkish in style. He took pride in his cough, which was, he obviously considered, distinguished and a mark of personality — actually, it was disgusting and plainly artificial. Whenever I was at work he would stand for hours outside the door and gasp, wheeze and bark at regular intervals. Fortunately I had brought with me, for I had arrived with a cold, a bottle filled with the thick treacle-like cure which found favour at the time. It tasted of cinnamon, tar and cloves, like the mulligatawny soup served relentlessly by British Railways, and was a peculiarly repulsive concoction. One day, irritated beyond measure by the cough, I called him into the room, measured out remorselessly two tablespoonfuls of this medicine, and made him drink it before my eyes. I also told him that if he coughed once more he would be given another dose of the same mixture. In this instance the treatment proved to be magically efficacious. When he had recovered his power of speech, he thanked me and said he was cured. During the remaining three months I stayed there, he never coughed again in my hearing.

How different from the paradise of Corfu is Cyprus: an island which always disappoints me, even in the legendary promise of its own name and of that of the city of Famagusta, of which the sound is so strangely lovely, though when you visit it you find it to be an undistinguished Cotswold village which has been whitewashed. I must admit, though, the beauty of its floral displays, especially of two, one when the fields are full of *anemone fulgens*, bright scarlet with charcoal-dusted centres — the other, on the borders of the streams flowing from the mountains, which in February are a mist of light pink, tawny and beige tamarisk in flower. Another delight in Cyprus is to watch the parties of Turkish men and women and children, escorting down to the port of Ktima a fellow-religionist due to embark on his pilgrimage to Mecca: and what a feast of sherbet and sticky, gelatinous Turkish sweets would follow on his departure! Sometimes it would take place at an open-air café, sometimes on a mound in the open air near by. Turbaned men and veiled women would sit there, side by side, overlooking the shore, munching their heavily powdered and glutinous lollipops. Below them, only a few yards away, lay the beach of Paphos where Aphrodite was born from a wave, in somewhat the same way that Victorian children were told babies were found in cabbages. On that Paphian shore are still to be discerned remains of the two temples which were subsequently built there, broken pieces of porphyry and basalt and of rare marbles. There, too, at the sea's edge we picked up one handle of an encrusted stone amphora, in itself a perfect work of art, resembling the volute from the capital of an Ionian pilaster, but turned by long habitation in the sea to an ammonite or some other kindred fossil. . . . So that while it is true that Cyprus combines everything that is hateful in the Orient and the Occident, there are, it will be seen, compensations: but the most beautiful part of Cyprus and the most interesting architecturally is Bel Paese, with its French-Gothic Abbey bounded by the sea. The importance of this magnificent monument is not to be denied. . . . It was in Cyprus, too, — in Nicosia — that I last saw golden sovereigns being given in exchange in the bazaar by an old man, pale and bald, but bulky and with a thin beard. He sat in the market with his bag of golden pounds, sometimes taking out a handful and examining them. In looks he very much resembled the late Sir Basil Zaharoff. This unfortunately extinct form of exchange was then regularly to be encountered in the island, as Maria Theresa thalers are still to this day legal tender in Abyssinia — but that curious extinct object, the sovereign-case, was already nowhere to be met with ; it consisted of a little circular holder, usually made of silver, with a spring concealed in it, so that when you opened the case and pressed down the sovereign, there was room for it and it could not fall out, since only a steady pressure could release the coins beneath.

If Cyprus can in no way, either in architecture or landscape, ever rival Corfu or Italy, yet it would be unfair to deny that Broussa in Asia Minor challenges comparison with them. Motoring to Broussa from the sea, early in the month of May, you pass through an exquisite Italian landscape, the lines of newly leafed poplars with their glittering golden discs distilling odours of balsam into the already redolent air of the spring. And Broussa itself, when you come to it, proves to be a small city of neat, strict and relevant beauty. However, you are soon disabused of the comparison as you first perceive the minarets and mosques. They are architectural works of delicacy and imagination, more in the style of Persia than of Turkey, and they contain wonderful tiles of blue and green. On a lower scale, Broussa further resembles an Italian city in that its neighbourhood produces a delicate white wine, delicious to drink on the spot but which will not travel. Of an orange-yellow colour, it is made — since Mohammedans are forbidden to drink fermented liquor — by an agricultural colony of Jews long settled here. . . . From Broussa we motored one afternoon to the Bithynian Mount Olympus. Though it was late spring, the snow still lay on the upper slopes. Indeed, as we regarded it, one snow-field began to melt under the rays of the hot sun, to reveal at its edges huge patches of blue scilla in full flower. I had often heard of blossoms coming out in this manner, but had never before been fortunate enough to witness it, and to me it seemed a miracle that this exquisite flower should have reached its full beauty beneath these heavy and cold white quiltings — but there they stood, blue and fragile, straightening themselves a little as the snow vanished and the weight of it was withdrawn, their petals sparkling with innumerable diamantine drops.

CHAPTER XIII

THE ELEMENT, EARTH

TODAY, even here, where the rays of the sun can extricate so much colour from objects which have always appeared dun or neutral, is a dark day: dark throughout in its nature. Earth is plainly the element on which it must depend, and this morning, when I threw open the shutters, the scent of it was almost too strong to be believed, and the configuration of the ground seemed for once to be of greater importance than the flocculent perspectives of the sky. It is March now, and everywhere the damp, brown soil throws out new green shoots, and the moist, mossy branches of almond and peach bear their spangled blossoms, paler or more rosy, and holding within them what light there is, so that posed against the earth, they show transparent and virginal: for the sky is sullen with breaking spring, while the mountains across the sea are so near you could touch them. And when you go out, the stone walls that constitute the terrace frame-

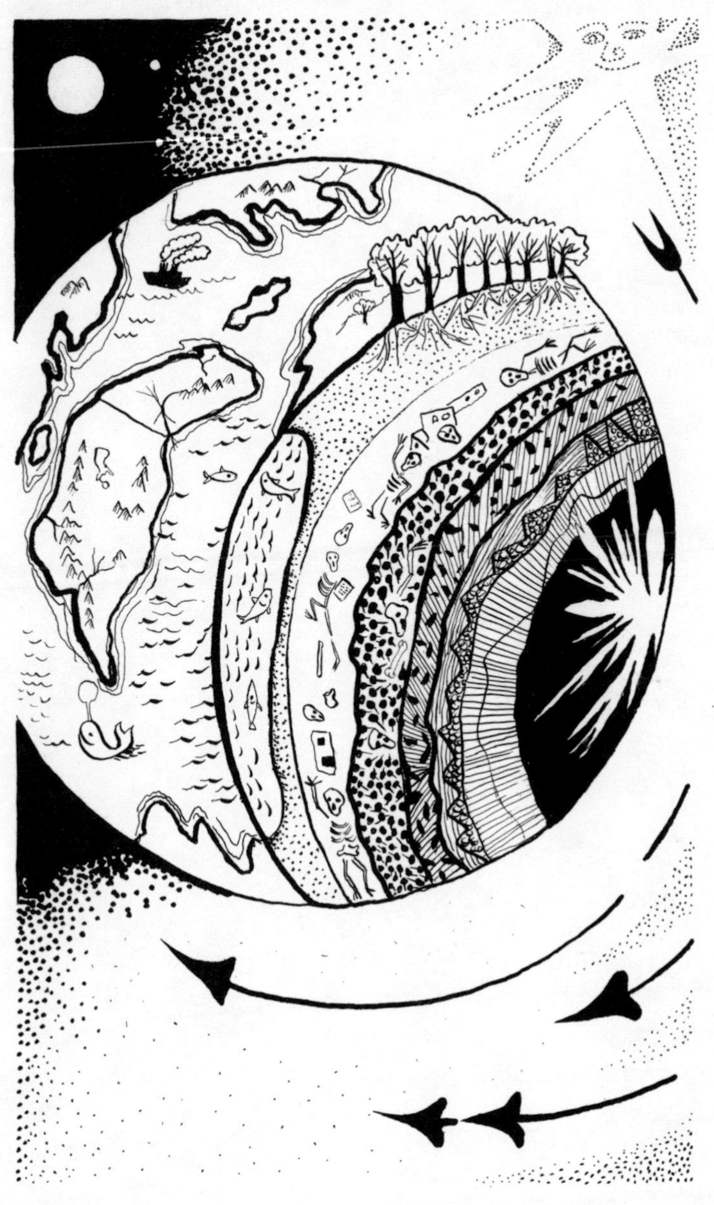

work of this landscape and enclose the brown soil, neatly raked, in rhomboids and rectangles, fitting at various angles and levels into the abrupt descent of the rocky face of the limestone formation, and showing against the sea today in every tone of ultramarine, emerald and cobalt, complete the similarity of the scene to that of Breughel's *Fall of Icarus*. But that I can easily understand, because if a man wished to attempt to fly with no mechanical aid except wings fastened to his shoulders, what better, purer transparency of air could he find than here, on a cliff poised dizzily above the sea; where could the body be lighter, the soul more easily detached?

This surely, I thought, as I secured the shutters, is one of the most beautiful places in which to wake; in my experience, too, only rivalled in strangeness, and in a much more sensational vein, by the town of Antigua in Guatemala. There I had lived, working on a book on Cambodia and China, from January to April 1939, when I returned to England. The reason I chose to go there was that after the Munich Crisis I found the mounting war tension in Europe suffocating, and I felt that I must go far away and obtain a draught of fresh air, before war, so claustrophobic in its character, should break out in the autumn. And in Guatemala, nothing then very much interested the inhabitants that took place outside the country. One was bounded in view but free. Never did one hear about politics, except from a few Europeans who ran *fincas* here. One English lady, who was growing coffee on a mountain slope near by, came to stay in the hotel for a few days, and treated me continuously to her views; which were, of course, that the British should make war at once, everywhere and without any weapons. She did not know my name, and I refrained from disclosing an identity of any kind. I pretended, in order to cut short her lectures on foreign policy and strategy, a complete ignorance and moronic lack of curiosity: until at last she could bear it no longer, and said to me suddenly with scorching scorn: 'Have you *never* heard of the *New Statesman and Nation*?' Never, I assured her, never, in the whole course of my life, and after this reply I was, as I wanted to be, ostracised. . . . But at this time few foreigners visited Antigua. The hotel in which we stayed — a converted eighteenth-century palace, beautiful and original in its architecture, and run by a delightful Italian family — was rather small in capacity, though its rooms were big: so that, after dinner, we would often find ourselves alone in a magnificent drawing-room, over sixty feet long, and with seven windows. You reached this room from a wide open-air gallery, with a balcony which looked down on a particularly fantastic and stylised courtyard, full of cool green plants, tree-ferns and the sound of water. I recall that the Italian proprietress, proud of the fact that her sister — or was it sister-in-law? — was a well-known prima donna at the Metropolitan Opera House in New York, would twice a day — once in the early morning and once at dusk — dart into the *patio*, to sing with a certain air of defiance, although in the orthodox Italian manner, a few bars of *La Bohème* or of *Madam Butterfly*, as if in support of the family and as an act of allegiance to her own country. Sometimes after dinner she would come to the drawing-room and talk to us of her family, and of the prima donna particularly. We would sit very formally on very upright chairs and make conversation in nineteenth-century style : inappropriate enough, for the room retained its pristine character. On the walls still hung portraits of the men and women of the family which had built the house, clad in the elegant finery of their period : the women in pannier skirts, and with dark and sombre eyes, while the white wigs of the men opposed themselves strangely to the sallow, iconic visages and Aztec profiles. The furniture, too, was of its time : tortoiseshell cabinets, gilded console tables and painted chairs. I should add about the hotel that, though the food was of the usual Central American standard, the bread was the best I have ever eaten, the coffee the best I have ever drunk (both are specialities of the country) : and also, perhaps, that two or three slight earthquake shocks occurred nearly every day during luncheon ; until in memory they became part of the meal.

The climate demanded no glass for the windows, and so the first light would creep in with a certain damp freshness of earth cooled after great heat : then, soon the sun would rise, and I would get up and go to my working-room, a disused kitchen built in the local kitchen idiom, very fine and pretty, with four niches at the four corners and a lantern dome. Moreover, being at the back of the palace, it possessed its own terrace, with an unmatched view of the two vast volcanoes, Agua and Fuego. The main tone of the enormous landscape at this dry season, and by this early morning light, was not green, but a singular and pervasive tone of purple, an angry but august tint. In the foreground stretched an expanse of coffee fields, cut out of the jungle, here reduced to reasonable limits: though even from where I stood I could hear the collective hum of the insects as the sun touched the green roof of the trees. Everything in Guatemala, though beautiful, was fantastic and exaggerated, not seldom in a delightful way.

Let us first, for contrast, regard again the exquisite beauty of nature, and of man acting in unison with it, and return to Amalfi for a moment. What is peculiar to these regions of the old Neapolitan kingdom are the different plateaux and terrace-lands, each of which offers a system, almost a domain, of its own, so that you have a new and individual airscape wherever you may climb to, and meet a sirocco, heavy with the fragrance of lemon blossom or violets, at every level, and might, if you were Icarus, start on your aerial journey from any single one of these exposed platforms. Balanced against the sky, as it seems, and almost directly above our heads, so far do the supporting cliffs jut out into the air, stands the village-city of Ravello, said to have contained once a population of over fifty thousand, and thirteen churches, but now supporting a community of about fifteen hundred souls, living largely on the cultivation of vines. . . . After you have seen the cathedral, and the surviving churches and palaces, it is the chestnut wood, behind and above the town, in the higher scoops between the hill-tops that I would like you to visit today: for though the limestone cliffs and crags below, with their flying buttresses of rocks and their caverns and grottoes, are as extravagant as any landscape you can find in Europe, and though these glades, it is true, have a strong and haunted character, yet it is one infinitely reasonable. Here above a stream, which makes its own voice heard, is a damp paradise of moss, fallen leaves, chestnut husks — the visual equivalent in another medium of sea-urchins or hedgehogs — and bare branches lacing the sky. It is the very essence of Europe. From such a spot as this first grew the fine fables of Greece, and all that was reasonable in the ancient and modern worlds, based on a rich soil, an equable climate, and a good water supply: these things make a sane life possible, and one of outward beauty, though very closely bound to the earth; an existence rhythmic in its moods and phases, unexaggerated, but always with overtones of the spirit — though these never demanded more of a man than he could give. Whereas, in Central America, to which we now return, everything is fantastical, grotesque or capricious, the penalties in disease, for example, beyond payment, the beauties extravagant, the squalors incredible. Everything is tinged with the unexpected and the unpredictable.

Certainly an incident that occurred the first time we left the boat to spend a night on Central American soil was marked by this same vein of the exceptional. We were on our way to Barranquilla, where the famous Hotel del Prado offers in combination to the traveller the joys of a tropical Ritz and of an exalted American roadhouse. Puerto Colombia, where we landed about noon, is a small port, boasting a colossal stone quay out of all proportion to the harbour or to the business it does ; a material expression, I apprehend, of some deep-rooted inferiority complex at work in the subconscious mind or the group soul of the Town Council. We started down the pier, followed by two porters with some of the luggage : but I was carrying in my arms, to make quite sure that it was not left behind, a portable gout-cradle. I suppose some readers may consider it an odd object to travel with : but then they can never have suffered the torments of gout. It is, indeed, very useful during an attack. It consists of a folding triptych of light metal designed, when open, to keep the weight of the bedclothes off the victim's feet. Wrapped up, as it was, in brown paper, it must on this occasion have a little resembled in its appearance a box-kite of unusual shape, no less than in the ease with which it finally and so bravely took the air. It was a day, you would have said, of leaden heat, untempered for months by any wind : but a sudden Atlantic gust blew down on us as we walked the seemingly interminable stone quay that led to the town, and snatched the apparatus from my grasp. Up aloft it flew, to the delight of the porters, and of those nondescript, anonymous scarecrows who haunt such equatorial ports. They thought, I apprehend, that I was trying out some new toy. It first ascended quite high in the air, then, after a hesitation, skidded sideways and dived down to the sea — where quickly there followed a gigantic snap, as the strong jaws of a shark snatched at, and secured, the enticing morsel. . . . Could any story be more far-fetched : what can the shark, writhing and threshing in its death agony, have made of this new penalty for greed ? — or perhaps it could 'take it', and may still be swimming round the port, with that light but intricate framework of aluminium in its belly. . . .

Two days later, we joined the boat again, to land at Puerto Barrios, on our way to Guatemala City : we arrived there to find the only train of the day had already left for the capital, and in consequence had to stay in this little place until the next morning. Just as, at Ravello, everything is made pure by the mountain air, and tends to become clean and spotless, so everything here is tainted and putrid. The hotel, a wooden structure resembling a meat-safe, had in some distant past been painted white, but had now turned a contaminated yellow, and the few Europeans who lived in this small and accursed port had undergone a similar transmogrification. The natives were Carib, neither Indian nor the descendants of negro slaves, — and who has ever had a good word to say for the Carib! Only the landscape extended a delusive but none the less alluring beauty : groups of palm-trees on islands, both near and distant, spun into the far horizon, misty with blue and gold : this was the dreaded Mosquito Coast, notorious for many diseases, including, until a few years ago, Yellow Jack.

All the small ports of Central America resemble one another : each contains a population deplorable both physically and mentally, living in the shell of a city too big for it ; a few mouldering palaces, evil in their pretension and in their hobbledehoy squatness, and many churches, some of them now converted into workshops or cinemas. Even Cartagena, a great and famous city, for long the Spanish capital of the Indies, has somewhat the same ramshackle and defiled aspect, though the situation of it is magnificent and it has several buildings of some worth. But the beauty that is to be found there is chiefly that of strangeness : for the city has several unexpected features, such as that the long white streets, with their fine iron balconies and grilles, are usually empty ; except for Arabs and Armenians, who roam about in their own dress, with an air at once practical and melancholy, trying to sell such things as carpets to the secretive and recalcitrant householders. As you survey the scene, those stone streets devoid of life except for these, or for Turks and Egyptians, you might be back in the souks of Africa or in the bazaars of an oriental country, but lacking their vitality or colour. Often the only agreeable spot in a South American port is the Public Garden. . . . A few days previously, our boat had called at Puerto Limón, a port similar to this. We landed in the morning, in equatorial heat — 90 degrees in the shade — with several hours to spend, and nothing to see : so we went to the Public Garden, and as a result enjoyed one of the pleasantest encounters with Natural History that have ever fallen to my lot. . . . At the side was a plantation of palm and other trees. Suddenly my attention was caught by an almost imperceptible movement in the greenery, the eye only being attracted to it because there was evident in it a certain lethargic continuity and rhythm. After I had watched for a considerable time, I perceived what had caused this impression : a sloth was moving through the branches, in search, I suppose, of food, at the pace of a film shown in slow motion : he was near enough for us to see his round, sad face, and the formation of his long claws. For two hours at least we watched this exhibition of snail's-pace technique — in its way as fascinating as the rhythmic swing of monkeys from branch to branch and tree to tree — with unabated interest.

Now at Puerto Barrios, we turned our steps hopefully, therefore, to the Public Garden, trusting that we should enjoy a similar treat, or, perhaps, at least find some tropical tree in blossom that was hitherto unknown to us. On the contrary, it was arid, dusty and unrewarding, except for some fountains and seats made of cement and embodying themes of decoration used by the Aztecs — though the people here could not even pretend to be descended from that mysterious race. The Carib Town Council must have ordered them, I think, after a casual but over-enthusiastic reading of D. H. Lawrence's *The Plumed Serpent* in translation. All at once, in the Garden, instinct warned me to go back to the hotel. . . . Later I learned that had we stayed in the Garden another ten minutes, we should almost certainly have been bitten by the mosquitoes, whose evening dance was about to begin, and should inevitably have contracted the deadly form of malaria which they there transmit. The rest of the evening I spent in the hotel, writing an article on passports for the *News Chronicle*, while outside the cover of metal gauze which filled the windows and kept off the diverse hordes of insects, the vultures posted themselves on the bare branches of a tree that had been struck by lightning, and outlined thus against a very barbarous sunset, in its tone and colour resembling Rembrandt's *Butcher's Shop*, signalled from time to time the good news of another prospective corpse to their brothers in the tainted ether above.

The train for Guatemala City left at nine the next morning and took the usual ten hours to reach it : but the journey was worth what had seemed the eternity spent in the hotel. In a comfortable, old-fashioned Pullman car, while the engine screamed and hooted incessantly — I suppose to frighten wild beasts off the line — we rumbled and shook our way along a raised track laid through the deep jungle, and were able to peer down its green but torrid clerestories, where, if we could have seen them, the iguanas were doubtless munching the tree-tops. No doubt this green maze was full of fears and fevers, of ticks and serpents and vampire-bats : but to the passengers in the train it offered a transcendent spectacle of gigantic flowering trees — often at the very side of the track — blossoming in white or scarlet or blue or yellow : magnolias, flamboyant and coral trees, jacarandas and countless others unknown to me. Somewhere, too, in its northern depths, the jungle hides Copán, with its stone gods and terraces. . . . I hope the beauty and strangeness of the scene took the minds of all the passengers off their journey — or at least off the causes for it, because while some, like ourselves, were tourists, others were Jewish emigrants from Hitler's Germany ; docile and respectable, they had been turned out of their homes and deprived of their fortunes.

About noon we reached a clearing, with a large and businesslike station in it, very well run. This was the junction for Salvador, and here, unexpectedly, we were given an excellent luncheon. . . . Soon after, the train continued its journey, and we began gradually to climb the five-thousand-foot ascent from the coast jungle to the capital. Guatemala City stands on a plateau, which receives no rain during what in Europe would be the winter months ; the land at this season is therefore dry and dusty but the air is clear and crystalline. . . . It is not, though, of Guatemala City that I want to write today : though there are several things about it that are unforgettable. I shall always remember its Sunday mornings, when the streets are empty save for dark, discreetly dressed maids, carrying huge bunches of orchids from one house to another ; these bouquets have just been bought at the market, and are being taken as a gift, with a letter of good wishes, from a mistress to some friend — this is a recognised custom on a Sunday morning. Nor shall I fail to recall the unusualness of the statues in the Public Garden — statues that might have been designed by Tissot — nor the orchid farm which I visited outside the town, nor the owner of it, who collected rare books printed in Central America in the early days of its colonisation, and who a little resembled a charming and learned tortoise. (In his nursery I spent a whole morning choosing plants which flourished at Renishaw for several years, until killed eventually by a gardener whom we had nicknamed the Death Ray, since he had only to direct a single glance at any growing thing for it immediately to wither.) Nor ever will fade from my memory my surprise and indignation when a friendly Englishman came up to me and asked if I were a 'greenhorn': a description which no experienced traveller likes to have thrust upon him, however kindly the intention. . . . But, indeed, before Guatemala City was destroyed by earthquakes in 1917 and 1918, it must have been peculiarly fascinating and unusual in its beauty, as the rare old buildings that survive still testify: such palaces as that of the Archbishop, with its wonderful doors studded with designs in nails, arranged in great bosses and whorls, as was the fashion throughout this country: though these particular doors are perhaps the finest example of this style.

No, it is not of Guatemala City that I want to write, but of Antigua, that most typical and delightful of Guatemalan cities. It lies about thirty miles away, on the same lofty plateau. During the six months from the end of October till April, the temperature in the daytime is always in the neighbourhood of 80 degrees Fahrenheit, and at nightfall sinks to about 70. Antigua for some two hundred years was one of the four capitals of the Indies, but a severe earthquake destroyed much of it in 1773. Nevertheless, the shell and part of the contents of the city still remain: and, indeed, now that the scars have long healed, the buildings that were ruined beyond repair have become even more fantastic than they were in their full glory. It was in the main the taller edifices that suffered, governmental palaces and churches : and the façades of many of them still survive, some of them on the outskirts of the jungle, just beyond the city. The churches present fronts of golden stone, intricately carved from top to bottom by Indian workmen under Jesuit supervision. Inside, the pillars and the naves and aisles still stand, but the roofs outside have turned to meadows, and sheep are pastured or goats graze on them : so that the scene presents an artificial parallel to the domains at different planes we have seen above the Amalfitan coast. The most interesting and beautiful of all Antiguan palaces, and one that is still completely intact, is now the University. Consisting of two storeys, as fortunately for the prospect of their survival do so many of the buildings left, it was the creation of an eclectic architect from Seville, who came to Spanish America to work. His aim (and it must be conceded that he here achieved it) had been to evolve an eighteenth-century style, founded on that of Andalusia, but different in that he wished it to show what it would have become if the Moors had not been turned out of Spain. Thus in the large courtyard stands a Lion Fountain, a development of the famous one in the Alhambra, and in the cloister that surrounds the main court are variations of several kinds on the honeycombed ceilings and calligraphic decorative themes so dear to the builders of the Arab world. In all he did, the designer showed himself to be an architect of original and unusual genius.

The Plaza, in the centre of the city, is still the hub of its life. Three sides of it are formed of deeply-arcaded buildings of the mid-seventeenth century, and the fourth by the Cathedral : in the middle is a pleasant garden, umbrageous but flowery, of which I shall later have more to say. At the end of every street can be seen either the jungle or groups of lofty, blue-blossoming jacaranda trees. Beyond, in clearings that are yet still well shaded, are the villages, built of wattle, in which the Indian tribes or communities live : the money they earn is spent on clothes and drink rather than on their openwork houses. Today they are the most elaborately dressed people in the world, and each village exhibits an entirely different variation, though all the styles are founded on Spanish costume of the sixteenth or seventeenth century, and all, equally, tend to make use only of certain colours, of cream, purple, plum-colour and blue. And all day long, but especially in the hour before sunset, the sound of the national instrument, the marimba, comes from these villages lost in the forest. Sometimes you hear several at a time, a clear sound, like the ringing of glass bells, and waltzes and the most enticing tangos trill out in the green groves now rapidly growing cooler. Sometimes in the morning I would try to trace the sounds : but they were most elusive and carried far, so that but seldom could I pin down these debonair and nimble melodies. . . . On the other hand, one morning I went to Santa Maria, an Indian village on the slopes of Agua, and there it was easy to find the music. The village was as usual built out of what looked like hurdles, but had a particularly gay and care-free atmosphere, though the school examinations were in progress. For the occasion the children wore their best white clothes and their stupidest expressions ; but really they were listening to the marimbas, which we could see outside as well as hear. Probably they were being played on purpose to support the young, to show them that other factors existed in the world besides arithmetic, and generally to give them confidence.

Besides the marimba, the other solace of Indian lives is the market. Often they could dispose of their wares or produce much more easily, and at a better price, by private treaty, but in fact they would rather not sell at all than miss their weekly jaunt, the fun of the outing, and of meeting friends on the way there, and of the market itself. On a market day these small, golden men and women, who so nearly resemble Cambodians in their appearance, can be seen from the earliest hours of light, padding with bare feet along the wide earthen tracks at the side of the roads, trotting — for they never walk — and smiling. Indeed, they are a people of easy and frequent laughter, and seem to retain no racial memory of the white man's iniquities towards them, and to lack altogether the surly aspect of the Mexican Indians, and the temperament that fits it. They seem always to enjoy life, and I recall that one day when I went for a walk in the evening, I saw a young Indian father taking his son of three or four with him for a trot. It was obvious that he was teaching his child how to do it, the right rhythm and breathing, and his son followed him, aping his movements ; both of them were in peals of laughter. The women run at the same pace and in the same style as the men : but a wife will usually trot behind her husband at a discreet distance of some twenty or thirty yards. She will be dressed in the costume which is the fashion in the particular rustic community in which her family lives. Often she will be bare-headed, and sometimes, but far from invariably, a plaited rope of coarse black hair hangs down between her shoulders like a pigtail, or more probably she will be carrying, slung round her back, a baby, so that her hands remain free, in the manner that seems common to all Indian mothers in either North or South America.

The chief market in Antigua is held every Friday in the halls and courts of a derelict and shattered monastery. There, in the strange, deep shadows thrown by broken walls, or with the fierce rays of the sunlight piercing the gloom like the shaft of a searchlight, the trim Indians, in their best finery for the day, sit on the ground, selling such things as eggs, fruit, flowers, or flat circular earthenware dishes, of a classical beauty of shape that recall the discs of the Discobolus (these are used in the making of the famous and, I think, very unpleasant national speciality, the *tortillas* composed of maize, wrapped in banana leaves, which, when you open them, look like the food you give to a sick horse, and taste strongly of incense). Besides the bunches of flowers by the sides of the Indians, there is a special flower hall, with vendors at stalls, dealing in vast bunches of tuberoses and Harrisi lilies, and orchids and violets and magnolias and blossoms unknown to me, as well as the wax spires of yuccas, which rank both as flower and vegetable, for their blossom is frequently used as a salad. Then there are the fruits of the tropics, brought here from coast level: passion-flower fruit, tasting of inspired gooseberries with a dash of nectarine juice, custard apples, with their green alligator-skin, and their soft yellow interior, flavoured with turpentine and with pineapple drops, and of a soft creamy density, and guavas, that etherial version of the homely quince, and mangoes. Near by will be such strange creatures as the iguana, the four-foot-long edible lizard the flesh of which resembles that of a chicken in taste and consistency. In the market it always appears trussed from jaw to tail-tip, like a fried whiting on an English breakfast-table; being thus secured in order to prevent the lively reptile from biting a customer or breaking his leg by threshing its tail. In a big open court at the side, beasts and birds are for sale, cattle, pigs, hens and turkeys, while the native farmers who buy and sell them talk and laugh incessantly. But perhaps most singular sight of all is the ruined monastic kitchen, an enormous stone hall, full of arches and canopies for long-extinguished flames. Here today, in the strongest of black darknesses and the brightest bursts of light, the women may kindle in some corner a few dry sticks to cook a meal for husband and children, because it is many hours since they left their home in the forest. In the violent contrast of its chiaroscuro and the flicker of small flames, the figures move mysteriously, and recall Magnasco's pictures of convent kitchens: the light falls over broken walls like weed in a flowing river, and of human beings only the outline and the contours of the face are to be seen.

By evening, most of the Indians have left the town, first visiting a church to say a prayer. In worship they have their own ways as much as in all else. They often scatter rose petals on the floor, and place among them lighted candles. It is also not uncommon to see the men praying aloud, with arms outstretched in the attitude of crucifixion. Then they trot home — many of them to the hills, where, on the way, they stop to make obeisance again to the hidden and secret stone images of the old religion, inherited from their ancestors before the Spanish Conquest : in this way they take no unnecessary risks. . . . A few of the younger men — some of them wearing enormous hats of straw — will wait for the acronychal concert in the Plaza, where, in a stone arcade on the first floor of the building which was formerly the Governor's Palace, two marimbas are being hammered by four men. Though on this mountain plateau of five thousand feet the evenings are naturally cooler than on the coast, yet the conduct of life here is still equatorial. The crowd saunters or sits decorously in the garden ; the girls stop to smell the scent of the frangipani bushes, the yellow and puce flowers starring thick, rather fleshy, branches. The couples listen quietly to tangos and to American jazz and waltzes. There is no dancing. The courting is formal, and little laughter sounds out.

Though of a different and more dour kind, no less strange to an Englishman are the highland cities of which Quezaltenango is the chief. . . . We travelled by motor, and crossed the great mountains by roads that sometimes ascended to as much as twelve or thirteen thousand feet : but we obtained no general view, since we were for the whole of the high journey wrapped in a thick, tepid Scotch mist. It only cleared sufficiently to show us from time to time the precipice upon the very edge of which the right front wheel was balanced, or the enormous branch of some gigantic tree, thrust out towards us on the same level, so that it was easy to examine. At first sight it might have been a special tray of exotic plants, disposed, for some horticultural show of a particular kind, artfully among mosses and lichens : the branch itself could hardly be seen for the mass of these, contrasting in colour, texture and softness, and among them, and out of them, epiphytes and aerophytes sprang like tufts of feathers or single plumes: (very true, these, in the panache of their habit of growth to the old seventeenth-century conception of this particular quarter of the globe), and stove-plants, those expensive, unwanted treasures of the nineteenth-century hot-house, exhibited their horrid, torrid rings of blue and scarlet, having about them the raw, shiny look of flesh decaying.

Before I describe the journey further, or mention the small towns we passed through on our way to Quezaltenango, I must emphasise one or two features, invariable here but uncommon elsewhere, which imparted to them considerable atmosphere. . . . For instance, a former President, avid of Greek culture, had issued an edict that the authorities in every city, big or small, of the Republic of Guatemala should cause to be erected in some prominent place a copy, preferably in plaster, of a Greek temple. This rather whimsical command, which yet flattered civic pride, was generally obeyed, and its effects were prodigious : for while it may remain a question to what extent nations of Western Europe have inherited the ideals of Ancient Greece, it would at any rate be safe to assert that the one region which plainly possessed, and could possess, no link with classical civilisation was the equatorial lands of Central America : which to this day retain and manifest a very strong indigenous character of their own. Thus those white, powdery ghosts of the Acropolis, evoked so inappropriately in this beautiful but monstrous land of cactus and orchid and emerald-green quetzal, add to these cities their own note of fever and almost of hallucination.

The cemeteries also supply an unusual individuality. The smaller towns are poor, their standard of life very low, but outside each of them you always see a square or rectangle of ground enclosed by walls, well built, while over them can be distinguished the clustered tops of towers, domes, cupolas and canopies in stone or the richest marbles, which to a newcomer suggest an abandoned miniature city built for a race of splendour-loving but spendthrift dwarfs. Inside the enclosure, it can be seen how fiercely the various styles, only united by their incongruity and richness, compete with one another. The façades of these little buildings, elaborately sculptured, writhe and turn in the sunlight, which falls without mercy on the neatly dovetailed marble of the roofs, and on the covey of marble angels mourning aloft on their tall columns. Yet, fantastic as are these little cities of the dead, they manifest, in addition to their absurdity, a certain touching beauty. . . . In the villages, too, the dead were loved better than the living.

To summarise, then, you will on any one long day of motoring pass through many small towns : their aspect will greatly differ with their altitude, and with the blood, Indian, mixed, or Spanish, of those who designed and those who built them : but all of them will have somewhere on the outskirts one of these enclosures, a model city for the dead, and in the most populous centre, a public garden, usually decorated with pieces of sculpture that emulate the stone figures erected during the course of the Third Republic in Paris, but are more clumsy and naïve. Near the garden will stand a mouldering plaster phantom of the Parthenon, minute but nevertheless more unexpected here than would be a plaster cast of the skeleton of some long extinct animal. Then you will pass a large church or cathedral, of golden stone, broad-aisled and impressive, the intricate façade of which is certain to display a native sense of design. The figures carved on it, which will be many, are fast in a kind of eternal rigidity of form : as a chrysalis might hold the butterfly to which it will turn, so these stiff and savage bodies in stone yet seem to harbour within them a Christian soul, which one day will be released. However poor the village — for some of these towns are little more — the interior of the church is certain to have a retable, mounting in tiers and, even by Spanish standards, richly gilded.

The stone or marble pavement may be strewn with rose petals, and have burning among them groups of candles. There will be a few houses, a broad earthen track at the side of the road, and the trotting file of smiling Indians, sometimes coaching their children (with whom they always seem to be on the happiest terms) to run in the same fashion. In many of these cities or villages the houses seem sparse and small, compared with church or tomb or temple, but then the majority of those who work here during the daytime live probably in the jungle in airy pavilions of wattle, and you may, if you walk there and are fortunate, see them issue forth clad in the particular finery proper to the district.

Quezaltenango, though its very name, pronounced aloud or even lying flat on the page, raises in the ear the sound of guitars and marimbas, we found to be, when at last, just before sunset, we reached it, a large stone-built city, somewhat stark and uncompromising, full of commonsense, and a little, let us say, resembling Macclesfield or Rugby. It is the second most important town in the whole country, but not even a compulsory doric temple, nor the perpetual mist in which its altitude of over seven thousand feet involves it, could soften the all too real reality of it, or impart to it any visionary character. There are, however, many fascinating places to see from it. The difficulty — for time and money were limited — was to decide which lions to visit. Accordingly, to find this out, I reverted to a simple but effective method of testing the matter, which I had several times in years past employed with success :

first pick out suitable visitors in your hotel, ask them insinuatingly for their advice, enquire particularly what places are *not* worth seeing, and then, when they tell you, drive direct to them. On this occasion, I selected a delightful American couple on their first divorce honeymoon. To the question I put to them, they answered unhesitatingly, 'Avoid the Valley of the Geysers at Zunil — it's not worth while. The geysers may not be working — they weren't the day we were there, and it's a long drive.' . . . Within ten minutes we were in the motor on the way there. Even before we came near to it, we saw wells and little runnels of hot water on the mountain-tops, so that, albeit the climate was cool — this would be at a height of some eight thousand feet —, we would find at the side of the hot-water stream such plants as need a damp warmth ; at one place, for instance, a *bavardia* with a very waxen, salmon-pink cluster of stars.

Suddenly we saw the valley. It resembled a deep hole driven in the high mountains, the geysers were in full action, and consequently the first impression was that one must be approaching a great industrial city, such as Sheffield, that is situated in a valley. The whole of this immense and dark abyss choked and roared with steam. It shot up in jets and spurts and spouts and clouds and ribbons and whorls and spirals of caliginous vapour : a sombre but dynamic world, it seemed, of heat and strife and effort — and it was hard to comprehend that no man was sweating there to stoke the furnaces, which were, it would appear, subterranean and infernal. Moreover, no light pertained to the heat ;

it was a world without light of any sort, a monochromatic world of mildewed grey or furious black, unredeemed by flame. In some curious manner of its own, this view of it enabled the mind to grasp, however fleetingly and in a sense peculiarly evil, the dark powers of nature, and — far-fetched as this may sound — thereafter I was convinced of the nearness of the coming war, and that nothing man could do would prevent or even delay it. (A world struggle is much more likely to be due, I apprehend, to the phenomenon of sunspots, or to the same unknown factors causing them, than to political reasons, or to national virtue or vice : probably under certain influences human beings cannot reason — or let it be put the other way, that perhaps under other influences they *can* reason. The parade of patriotic virtue and of the enemy's wickedness may be, equally, the revolting result of some radiation : but even the scientist will never convince the nations of this fact, for nothing will shake man in his main conviction, that of his own importance.) If this rage of steam and boiling water, so much more impressive than the glow, flames and occasional bellow of a volcano, if this torrent and struggle were native to the earth, what chance of reason was there to be found among its children, either as individuals or gathered together in nations ? And often in later years, during the seemingly interminable course of the war, when I read of some atrocious cruelty, or some victory or disaster, I would, in my mind's eye, behold again for a moment this never-ending struggle of earth's dark powers.

Very different from this sense of activity unaided by man was San Francisco el Alto, which, situated at between ten and twelve thousand feet, claimed to be the highest market in the world — here was a scene full of comic incident, comfortable human chatter and comfortable human curiosity. The market was particularly famous for its horses and pigs, and took place every Friday on a mountain-top. On a fine morning, the height, together with the quality of the air and sunshine, promoted a curious elation. The sun, which never penetrated to the valley we have just seen, here streamed over us with a particular lightness of gold and with a particular delusive transparency. The surrounding ranges were shaped like tents, and the light drenched them and flowed down their sides. The neighbouring mountains were bare save for the light: but the air at this spot — yet, looking round, there seemed to be no reason it should have been chosen in preference to any other of the similar mountain-tops — was full of the talk of Indians and the squealing of small pigs and grunting of big ones. In the enclosure of wattle reserved for the sale of beasts, from which these sounds came, and which looked so flimsy when set up among these vast spaces, the women who entered were few. It was a closed world, masculine but argumentative. No marimba would sound out on these cold but blazing heights. The Indians, here rather tall and austere compared with their smiling and more volatile cousins of the central plateau, whom we have watched running along the broad tracks at the side of the roads, are slower and more dignified in their movements, and their occasional laughter was loud and open, and not so much that surprised, almost Chinese giggle you hear below. Moreover, they are less ostentatious; their clothing reflects a desire for warmth, rather than the dandiacal desire to cut a figure. The men wear black blankets more often than striped, and wide-brimmed circular straw-hats, and they stride about, it is true with a certain swagger, even though many of them were being tugged along at a brisk rate by several little pigs, secured to their fingers by string. Every now and then the small beasts would panic, and would begin to try to run in different directions. Though their Indian masters swore at them, the little pigs, barred with brown and pink, dashing about with passionate squeals, seemed to exercise a humanising effect on their owners, making them laugh as well as curse, as these stately farmers found themselves obliged to pull their charges up and disentangle the strings. Sometimes there would be as many as ten pigs tugging their owner along, all of them young and enterprising, with the air of a translated prince in a fairy story ; the large, hideous sows and boars were tethered safely to pegs, with perhaps a wattle shelter over them.

In the same enclosure were a number of shaggy mountain ponies, some for sale, others belonging to the masters they had carried here. And outside, in a few sheltered corners — and on these draughty uplands they were rare — Indian women were conjuring up fires with twigs and pieces of stick, preparatory to cooking an aromatic meal for their husbands and children : because on these heights markets are rarer than on the plateau, and the distances that have to be travelled are even greater, so, though it was now only ten, they had been obliged to start from their homes, many of them, in the dark hours before the dawn. Vegetables, fruit, blankets — in great number and demand —, and hats, could be bought, as well as horses, cattle and pigs : though these, of course, and the pigs especially, formed the mainstay of the market. Indeed, the rarefied air of the mountain-top was so elastic, and so full of barter, that before long I had joined in the bidding of a group, and soon found myself, for the sum of one dollar, the owner of a fine young pink-and-black porker. The possession of the creature suddenly loomed on my consciousness, and I began to realise what my enthusiasm had hidden from me, that my new acquisition might be — no, would be, must be — an embarrassment. Plainly I had bought well, for it was a sturdy little brute, and was already darting all over the place, dragging me after it, so that I was continually obliged to break through small knots of people, and to shout apologies to them over my shoulder in halting Spanish. And as I sped along, faster on each experimental run — the animal was capricious and liked in the middle of it to alter his direction —, I tried to think what to do. . . . Should I simply let go of the string ? . . . No, that, too, would end badly : he would probably crash through the earthenware set out on the ground, and I should be responsible for the damage. I had nowhere to take him. I could not bring him back to the hotel. Life was complicated enough there already : (for example, in order to have a bath, one had to cross a courtyard in the very cold dawn or dusk of the altitude, and plunge into a stone bath installed in a roughly roofed outhouse that was part of the stables: one could see nothing for the steam, which seemed almost comparable to that in the Valley of the Geysers). The addition of a small but vivacious pig as companion would only tangle up life further, even were my fellow guests to raise no objections. . . . I could not give my new protégé away here in the market, because that would disgrace me in the eyes of the dealers, who would thus become aware that their time and expert knowledge had been wasted on one who was not really an expert on pigs at all. . . . Eventually I contrived to explain my difficulty to the driver of the motor, who at once sold the little monster for me at a profit of a quetzal. . . . As we drove away, and the chatter of the market suddenly dropped to silence, it was easy to feel that you were on an earth but recently created, such was the splendour of the noonday light, and where no other human beings existed as yet: we passed no living creature for miles (there were no birds), and trees even were rare.

The next morning we motored to Panajachel on Lake Atitlán; which strange piece of water scarcely qualifies to come within the bounds of a chapter dedicated to the element, *Earth*, except that the lake, itself blue and clear as a blue eye, was formed within the crater of an extinct volcano, and is surrounded consequently by steep bare cliffs of Guatemalan purple, that tint which, as we have noticed earlier, is here such a usual and favourite colour, both of nature and man.

At this season the banks of the lake are strikingly devoid of vegetation though a few strongly scented tropical shrubs flower with violence round the villages. Of these there are twelve, each of them named after one of the Twelve Apostles, and each boasting its own recognisably different costume. These fancy-dress hamlets can only be reached by boat, since no road joins them together. On arrival at one of them, your first call should be on the headman — though he is, by nine o'clock in the morning, and thereafter for the rest of the day, completely intoxicated on pulque, or some especially potent local variant of it : so drunk that even though his loyal followers have propped him up against a wall in order to receive his guests, he will gradually subside on to the ground during the course of the ensuing rather difficult and one-sided conversation. In no instance, however, did any of the headmen or their retainers manifest at any time the slightest sense of shame about their condition : if they were drunk, they were drunk and proud of it as are the characters who indulge in those snappy but interminable alcoholic dialogues in Hemingway's novels. But inebriated or sober, these Indians wear clothes that form a remarkable and enchanting exhibition of obsolete finery, such, indeed, as can be found in no other quarter of the globe : and in the same connection I must mention that we motored to a village, some fifty miles away, where the Indians still dressed in the clothes which would have been worn on an ordinary day by those who sat for their portraits to Velasquez.

Each day we made an expedition, starting from a

hotel on the banks of the lake : an English hotel, full of hot, strong tea and marmalade, its garden lush and floral as would have been a river pleasance at Maidenhead in the middle years of the reign of King Edward VII. The whole establishment and small domain was a nostalgic but bold experiment in the Thames Valley style : red, low buildings, I seem to see again, with hanging baskets of geraniums and lobelias such as decorate — or used to decorate — the stationary home-houseboats on the reaches between Windsor and Egham, and the garden a dream of Dorothy Perkins roses and sweet-peas, and those soft, fragrant flowers, nameless to me, which flourish in round beds on trim river banks. This petalled plenitude contrasted with the lake, which perhaps emphasised by the clearness of its waters a singular bareness and vacancy, a lack even of fish. Seldom did a boat cross to the villages. You see little cultivation here, and few people — in this very different from Amalfi ; wherefrom at the beginning of this chapter we set out and to which we now return : for that region supports a population with very ancient roots, and one which is scattered over the various plateaux and terraces that form their own worlds, equipped with animals and vegetation according to the temperature and altitude at which the little rustic communities are placed. Here and there the whole side of a mountain will have been carefully terraced and planted with lemon-trees, which are covered for the winter with a framework supporting dried foliage, to keep off frost or snow, though these are light and infrequent. . . . Balanced above our heads, somewhere in the sky, is the city-village of Ravello, and above it, a little behind it, is that wood of chestnut-trees, the glades of which, as they sweep up the mountain sides, become a forest. The mossy earth, damp from a passing cloud, is sprinkled with purple crocus and with violets. Down the broken steps at a rhythmic run come the peasants, carrying a whole felled grove, you would have said, on their heads and shoulders. In the deep gully worn in the limestone, the water freely courses, and you can hear its voice continuously. This scene, such as can only, I think, be found in Greece or Italy, sane and unexaggerated, though extremely fantastic, offers a classical eloquence of its own. Nevertheless, it is situated also, as are Antigua and Atitlán, in volcanic country. The lava streams, now for the moment static, lie at the back of these mountains; some thirty miles away stands Pompeii. And under that small, sophisticated town of pleasure, Vesuvius has doubtless in its time buried town after town, village after village, right back to the furthest and most remote efforts of men to form communities and live in them — for in Europe, or at least in some favoured parts of it, there was always a unique understanding between nature and man. What, similarly, would be uncovered under the splendid and impressive volcanic territories of Guatemala: the enormous skeletons of extinct animals, and then earth, earth, and more earth again?

CHAPTER XIV

THE ISTHMUS

On leaving Lake Atitlán, we stayed some days in Guatemala City, and then motored to Salvador. The road gradually descended from the tableland to sea-level, but soon after it cut into the forest region, it all but disappeared, so that it became necessary to follow the track with your eyes the whole time, in case it should lose itself in pathless jungle. However, we reached the Guatemalan-Salvadorian frontier at noon and without mishap. The two lightly built wooden structures which respectively served the two countries glared at each other across the road — as did their representatives, who wore identical khaki uniforms, the tunics a-glitter with rows of medals, different in kind and only alike in their equatorial sparkle. No other houses were in sight. There was just this clearing, and the two chalets, backed by innumerable square miles of forest. From the hot, dark interior of the Salvadorian house came an occasional flash of colour, and a high chattering and screaming. At last my curiosity overcame me, and since I had been obliged to show all the contents of my suit-cases to the dark-faced customs-officer, and since the frequent showing of his very white teeth seemed to indicate that he possessed an amiable character, I could not see why I should not be allowed in return to examine the interior of his living-room, and accordingly I walked past him, entered the house and looked through the door on the right. The room was full of an unimaginable tropical brilliance : macaws, blue and yellow, and scarlet and yellow, and white and yellow cockatoos, shrieked and talked incessantly, while among them a strong posse of monkeys swung, capered and gibbered happily. On the tables stood several pots of orchids in bloom. The scene had something familiar, and at the same time unfamiliar, about it : perhaps it recalled one of Douanier Rousseau's jungle pictures : birds, animals and men had about them the same stiffness of body, the same reality, sharp in focus but, in spite of its simplicity, plain if strange, that is to be found in the vision of that extraordinary artist. Perhaps, I reflected, the life of a customs-house officer encourages this kind of manner of seeing things ?

In the late afternoon we safely reached San Salvador, the capital of the republic. Of this city, where all is slum, except for a few streets and a square, there is not much to say, except that we had to stay there until we received word of a steamer leaving the port for Panama, whence a few weeks later we were to embark for home. . . . In the daytime there was little for a stranger to do, and wherever you went you found dust and heat and men dressed in rags carrying burdens too heavy for them. In the Plaza, I recall a large Club, where dark, Spanish-looking old gentlemen — but perhaps a shade darker, and certainly more saurian, than in Spain — sat in the windows, very slowly eating enormous ices, and reading the papers. There was a country club, out of sight of the city, and equipped with many electric fans and a golf-course. . . . The hotel at which we stayed was rather comfortable, in spite of its efforts at international-hotel grandeur, but I had a bedroom on the ground floor, with a French window looking on to a side street, and it was curious and disconcerting to hear the prostitutes outside continually trying to get in, and whispering their propositions through the cracks in the woodwork, almost singing them, throughout the hours of darkness. The night would be silent until you heard footsteps approaching, then the turning of the handle of the shuttered window, followed by the pleading, the whining, and finally by the footsteps dragging away.

At last it was announced that an Italian boat was expected at the Salvadorian port on the Pacific coast, *La Libertad*, bound for Panama, and we obtained our passages and motored over to catch it. This process was not so easy as it sounds, for no quay existed, and in order to board the boat each passenger had to step on to a square wooden raft, and sit on a wooden chair nailed to it, while a crane, with an immense creaking and clanking, lowered the platform from the top of a steep cliff through the void down to the sea below.

Shakily poised above the edge of the vast Pacific, this square raft seemed the very citadel of vertigo, as it swung and tilted slightly, first at one angle, then at another. The very best that could happen when it reached the water, you felt, would be that you would find yourself engaged in a kind of one-man Kon-Tiki Expedition : the reality, though it occupied less time, was scarcely less risky : you had to seize the right moment to jump into a waiting rowing-boat, which was rolling up and down, and sideways too, in an alarming manner, (how greatly then you envied the jungle-monkeys their gift of agility!). I steeled myself, jumped — and in time reached the side of the Italian ship, leapt again, and was soon safely installed.

The Italian captain of our small boat, though — or, perhaps, because — he had long been master of a ship, was in a perpetual state of fear, which he never troubled to disguise in any way. He just shook and trembled at the terrors he summoned up for himself, and of which he liked, indeed, in his spare moments to talk to the passengers. A tall, robust man, with a black beard not too neatly trimmed, he looked placid enough, but this unusual sea-dog was afraid of tidal waves, sea-serpents, '*il gran' serpe di mare*', submarine disturbances, sharks, great tropical winds, whirlpools, icebergs, in their place and season, collision with other ships — the Pacific, he seemed to think, was hardly large enough for him to be able to avoid them — fogs, and rocks which suddenly loomed up uncharted from the ocean bed. Even the prospect of the Panama Canal filled him with terror, in spite of the many occasions on which he had safely negotiated its passage without incident : what, he asked himself, would happen if he were to hit one of the walls, or become entangled in the machinery of a lock. . . . The few passengers on board knew his idiosyncrasy, and liked to play on it (for they were aware that he was in reality a good sailor and reliable), and so, when he came to sit with us, somebody would be sure to ask if it was true that an enormous sea monster had been found on the neighbouring coast, after a storm, or what did he think had really occurred on the *Marie Celeste*. Had he any theories on the subject ? He just sat shivering, and gave no answer. . . . The passengers themselves, I reflected, would not be of much help, if we met with difficulties such as he seemed to envisage. The most active, a nonagenarian of unpleasant character, told me that he came to the tropics every winter, because he knew that if he stayed behind in his home in Chicago he would die, from some snow-born accident — from, let us say, slipping on a step and breaking a thigh — and, as well, the tropics did him more good than a Turkish bath. Next year, he added, he fully intended to come to London — for there was at last a good hotel there, the Cumberland — and he would look me up if he had time.

Though the Captain trembled, and could not wait to get home to Genoa and turn his back on the sea for a while, we reached Balboa safely, and stayed in Cristóbal at the large, wooden-framed American hotel for some ten days, until the ship for which we were waiting to take us home should arrive. . . . I had not been prepared to like the Isthmus, but in fact enjoyed every moment of my stay there. Owing to American commonsense and efficiency, this is the one equatorial region where you can dine in the open air at night without fear of being bitten by an anopheles mosquito, and thus contracting malaria. Similarly you can bathe at the beach, beyond the jungle, in complete security. . . . I recall, too, with pleasure that one night I won so much money playing roulette at the best of the small sub-rosa casinos which abound, that the proprietors, when they paid me, tired of seeing their notes in my hands, asked me to leave and never to return, so that I walked away with my winnings ; money I should otherwise indubitably have lost to them in time. . . . The congregation of towns, now, in effect, one city, is fascinating in the contrasts it offers : Balboa, the port, Cristóbal, the international and commercial shopping centre, and Old Panama City, the diplomatic and political capital of the Republic of Panama. Each of these three retains its own very distinct personality. Balboa, with its slums and warehouses, teams with life, squalid but intense : like Colón, the other side of the Isthmus, it is full of the most fantastic and grotesque human types, crosses between Carib and negro and Chinese and Indian, the result of this mixed blood being often very beautiful or very hideous but seldom grey or ordinary, and offering, perhaps, a prototype to the miscegenated races of the future, which will combine many strains of blood, though with a bias in one direction or another. Cristóbal is plainly richer, and with its many polyglot shops recalls that other canal-line town, across the width of the world, Port Said; similarly here, Greeks, Syrians, Chinese, Indians, Turks, Persians and Armenians are all trying to sell you something. Old Panama itself is singularly charming, with a little the air of a Sicilian city, the same combination of palm and prickly pear and stone buildings, and the same kind of situation as Syracuse, for though its streets lack the architectural interest to be found there, both cities are equally surrounded and indented by the sea. The wide plazas have gardens full of trees and flowers, and the narrow streets seem shady and cool in the equatorial heat. Every now and then you come to a large seventeenth-century church. Its boldly carved wooden doors will be thrown back flat against the walls, and looking into the dark, almost cold, interior, your eyes will detect at the end of the aisle a glint of gold shining richly from a *retablo* — and nowhere in the world is gilding richer than in this region. Every street ends in a burst of sunshine and blue sea — for even the smallest alley leads to the Pacific Ocean, and from ancient terraces and fortifications now open to the public you can watch the rollers and listen to the thunder of their rhythm. . . . Aloof, and though only some twelve miles across the Isthmus, belonging to the Atlantic instead of to the Pacific, is Colón, very much in opposition to the lively knot of towns I have just described. A sour, dour town, once a slave port, its squat houses and tall, wasted palm-trees cringe still under the yellow winds from Africa. It exists in a turbid atmosphere of sand blown on a gale, a hot gale. The air, though in violent movement, is as full of grains as a snow-storm is full of snow. You feel battered and tired as you push your way — always, it seems, against the wind — through the empty streets: for everyone who can stays indoors when the waves thunder in this fashion, and the grit hurts your eyes.

Nevertheless, the city was enjoyable to visit, because though in some ways typical, and in some unpleasant, it had a very distinct individuality. And if it lacked human interest, when I returned to my hotel in Cristóbal, I would have a talk to Euphrosyne —, and that was not the least pleasurable part of my sojourn there. . . . The hotel was large, composed of three or four storeys, and we were on the second floor, in that lattice-work and wire-gauze world of the white man in the tropics before air-conditioning was invented. Even the over-doors and the tops of the walls were made of the same sieve-like material, semi-transparent, to let the air in — but as well as letting the air in, it let every syllable one spoke out. The acoustics were perfect. Each separate word was audible next door, and beyond, down the hundred yards or more of broad corridor that divided the two rows of bedrooms or open-air cubicles. Over this twilight territory presided Euphrosyne — pronounced *Ufrōzȳne* — a negress maid of remarkable charm and character. She hailed from Jamaica, and was a home-loving girl of Baptist denomination. Her colour was very dark, much darker than that of the ordinary American negro. She looked, indeed, as if her face had been black-leaded, she wore an English housemaid's print dress, with a bunch of keys at the waist, and her sable, unruly hair was crowned by an old-fashioned cap. She spoke good, clear, slow English, with no accent, except that she could not pronounce, as we do, certain words : thus she said 'd' for 'th', — 'dey', for example, instead of 'they' — which endowed her speech with an air of Old Plantation, while in her laughter, which would suddenly come on her in a burst at her most serious, could be distinguished an African jungle-chuckle. But in spite of the frequency of this delightful sound, she was of an earnest turn of mind, and spent her spare time in writing letters to her mother, whom plainly she adored, in chapel-going, and in hotel — or it may help to define it further, to call it pension — politics. In this art she had developed her own technique : for though infinitely ingenuous and good-natured, she did not easily overlook slights or rudeness, and at times she encountered both. Because of the audibility of everything said in passage and room, she had cultivated a special whisper, deep but penetrating ; kin, I imagine, to crooning. The purpose of it was that obviously she could not shout remarks outside the bedrooms about people who had offended her, but she could, and did, murmur to herself at the end of the passage, and these — as she intended it to be thought — impromptu observations would carry further than if she had spoken them in her ordinary voice. Every word, every vocal inflection could be heard clearly at a hundred yards. Such virtuosity, I used to think, should be given to the public ; put on the air, I used to tell her : and I gathered that, in spite of her shyness, she rather liked the idea of the B.B.C., but nothing, alas, came of my suggestion. Certainly, however, her very individual whisper enabled her to get her own back on denigrators and persecutors.

One day, then, when she saw me leaving my room, she rolled her eyes, smiled ingratiatingly, and waited about, as if she had something to say.

'What is it, Euphrosyne ?' I enquired.

'It's doze two old American women at the end of de passage,' she replied, producing every hushed syllable as might a prima donna, 'dey never tank me for anyting I do. Would you mind, Sah, going back for a moment, and den calling me in to do your rooms ? I'll be in deir rooms, and begin working, for dey want me to do dem soon. Den you'll call, just shout "Euphrosyne!" like dat, and I'll hear, and say to dem, "Hush! Dere's dat English gentleman calling. I must do his room first — for he's a guest. And GUESTS COME BEFORE BOARDERS."'

By what insensitiveness the two ladies contrived to elude her whispers I cannot imagine, but by their loud consternation when all went according to plan, they were plainly unprepared. . . . But though her simple scheming and, still more, the elaborate dark webs she wove, amused me, I rejoiced still more in her ordinary conversation. One day, for example, she said,

'Excuse me, Sah. . . . You're English. . . . Do you come from London ?'

'Yes, Euphrosyne, I do,' I replied. At which answer she tapped her dusky temple several times with her forefinger, rolled her eyes round in an impressive manner, and announced slowly, in a tone of immense significance, as if between us we shared some momentous secret, 'Dat's where Mama says dey've got de brains!'

Often later in that year, and during the next, I would wonder what had led Euphrosyne's mother to this singular conclusion: but, at the time, I was delighted, and tried on many other occasions to persuade her to return to the subject of her home life, or to the Maxims of Mama: but for some reason Euphrosyne was suspicious, and when I did so used to regard me very closely. . . . More readily would she talk of her present difficulties. . . . She really feared, she confided in me, to go out by herself in the street here. No respectable young girl was safe, such was the lubricity of the males in this region. Very different in this respect from Jamaica, and especially from Kingston, where you could walk anywhere with complete confidence. Here — even on her way to chapel on Sunday, dressed in grey alpaca, like a nurse, with her hair straightened out and bundled into a bonnet, and holding a prayer-book in one hand and a parasol in the other (because all the members of her family, she confided to me one day, were prone to get sunburnt very quickly, and she was afraid of her own skin becoming dark): even though she was careful never to answer when she was addressed in the street, and never even to look round, but to gaze with determination straight in front of her: in spite, then, of all these precautions, men would pounce out from doorways as she passed and nip her retreating back ('And my! don't dem pinches hurt!'). Before she realised what she was doing, she would cry out and begin to run. . . . It was an undignified and regrettable position, to a Jamaican it would be unthinkable to behave in such a manner. Nobody there would attempt such a familiarity. It just wasn't done — whereas here, as she'd told Mama in her last letter, no respectable girl could sit down and drink a glass of coca-cola by herself at a cafeteria on her day out without immediately being 'propositioned', as they called it. . . . Poor things, she supposed they couldn't help it. They were hardly better than cannibals.

In Panama the only other coloured person I knew besides Euphrosyne, was Jeff, the chauffeur, whose conduct and bearing entirely belied her generalities. By birth an American Negro, he had almost an imposing appearance: a tall, middle-aged man of rather light-brown skin, with an air of intellect and seriousness. His general knowledge was wide, and he was as respectable and law-abiding, I would have hazarded, as Euphrosyne herself. His powers of comprehension were indeed unusual, and I was continually surprised at the speed and ease with which he caught the meaning of even intentionally rather elusive remarks. His voice and manner were persuasive and we would employ him every day in the late afternoon to take us some miles away to a beach beyond the jungle. On the way clouds of insects *sang* — no, sang is too mild and happy a term to use, just as *roared* would be too warm-blooded, belonging too surely to the animal creation, though at least that word would express the volume of sound; perhaps *chant* is the most indicative —, filled, then, the warm air with their minatory but exultant chanting, foretelling, no doubt, the days, not so far distant in the processes of evolution, when the white man would retire from equatorial regions, when the canal would again return to a series of locked and stagnant pools, reservoirs of tropical fevers, and they, whirring and light of wing, would once again command these tracts. The sound was high but susurrous, as of the exaggerated noise of wind humming and whistling through a tangle of wire, omnipresent, all-pervading and impressive ; it ceased the moment you left the jungle. . . . The beach lay a mile or two beyond the edge of the forest, and swung its crescent of white sand towards the evening sun. Walking along it — and so wide a stretch was never crowded — proved nearly as delightful as bathing, because by the side of the clear, blue water could be found shells of exquisite colour and form, though for the most part rather small ; less grand and less abundant than the mother-of-pearl tents, rococo marquees in miniature, that are to be discovered in Nassau scattered along the less-frequented beaches, or the shells — the finest in the world, without doubt — that lie clustered together along the barbarous and deserted coasts of the Red Sea, near Djibuti : shells of many shapes, some spiked and twisted, but with lips red and rounded as the mouths of negresses, others of classical form and colour, that once served tritons for their trumpets, when, thrusting their bodies up from the sea, and standing waist-high in the warm African waters, they proclaimed the glories and pleasures of Neptune's empire. All those shells sparkled and glittered in the light of

Africa, which invests all objects visible with its own gold armour : but the shells at Panama, where the sun is very different from that of Africa or Asia, more merciful, creating an opulent but opalescent light, shine more rationally, and even lie half-buried among the ashen sand, seem discarded models to illustrate the logic of architecture, blue-prints transposed to carvings in nacre, or when, as sometimes, very ancient-looking, bone-white and dry, they appear to be the designs, tentative albeit perfect in form, of some perished race.

The sights of the Isthmus in reality are not many, apart from the Canal itself : but Jeff induced us to take a long run in the motor, so as to visit a celebrated snake-farm, conducted by an eminent scientist, who had lived there for a generation, tending and pampering the most venomous of serpents, in order to extract their poison and to experiment with it for the purpose of discovering the perfect and fool-proof antidote. To a degree he had already been successful, and people admired his perseverance, applauded his courage, and marvelled that during the twenty or thirty years he had spent in continual contact with his snakes, they had never attacked him. . . . That afternoon, however, I shall always recall, because, when we reached the farm, we were informed that the grounds were shut to the public. An hour before, the scientist had at last been bitten by a snake of the most virulent kind, against whose bane he had as yet never been able to discover a cure, and sadness brooded over the farm, for his life-work was finished, and at this moment he lay dying upstairs. . . . Thus even the use of scientific methods to protect the individual is liable to fail. As barriers against danger they are hardly less fragile and frail than those erected to make cities safe or nations : the Great Wall of China that I have described to you earlier, the Maginot Line or the walls of Constantinople. No antidote has ever in the end caught up with the poison, no defence triumphs finally over attack. No wall has ever yet kept out an enemy, unless you make an exception of the walls of Pompeii with which, strictly, this book begins : but that was only due to the infinity of ashes which covered and buttressed the whole of this town, and in the course of time turned to earth and so excluded everyone whether friend or foe for some seventeen hundred years. Earth, indeed, is the only effective wall, barrier and refuge. It is the strongest of the elements, more enduring in its static depths than the rages of fire or the terrors of water, the sudden uprising of floods or the rush of gigantic and overwhelming waves, less dramatic, perhaps, than the menaces of air, such as tornado and whirlwind. It is, in spite of the flowers with which it decks itself, sombre and sullen, monotonous and engulfing. It is patient and can afford to wait. Out of the earth we came : to it we go back.

THE END

PRINTED BY R. & R. CLARK, LTD., EDINBURGH